Brief Handbook for Writers

JAMES F. HOWELL
and
DEAN MEMERING

Central Michigan University

Prentice-Hall · Englewood Cliffs, New Jersey 07632

Library of Congress Cataloging-in-Publication Data

Howell, James [date]
    Brief handbook for writers.

    Includes index.
        1. English language—Grammar
    2. English language—Rhetoric.   I. Memering,
    Dean [date]   II. Title.
    PE1112.H69   1986   808″.042   85–16755
    ISBN 0–13–082025–3

Development editor: Joyce Perkins
Editorial supervision: Serena Hoffman
Art supervision: Linda Conway
Interior design: Levavi & Levavi
Cover design: Chris Wolf
Manufacturing buyer: Harry Baisley

PRINTED IN THE UNITED STATES OF AMERICA

10 9 8 7 6 5 4 3 2

ISBN 0-13-082025-3 01

PRENTICE-HALL INTERNATIONAL (UK) LIMITED, *London*
PRENTICE-HALL OF AUSTRALIA PTY. LIMITED, *Sydney*
PRENTICE-HALL CANADA INC., *Toronto*
PRENTICE-HALL HISPANOAMERICANA, S.A., *Mexico*
PRENTICE-HALL OF INDIA PRIVATE LIMITED, *New Delhi*
PRENTICE-HALL OF JAPAN, INC., *Tokyo*
PRENTICE-HALL OF SOUTHEAST ASIA PTE. LTD., *Singapore*
EDITORA PRENTICE-HALL DO BRASIL, LTDA., *Rio de Janeiro*
WHITEHALL BOOKS LIMITED, *Wellington, New Zealand*

Contents

GRAMMAR 47

SENTENCE ERRORS 77

Preface

TO THE TEACHER

This handbook gives rules, principles, and guidelines for good writing. Not everything about writing can be reduced to rules, of course, nor is there universal agreement about what is essential in writing. But *Brief Handbook for Writers* presents the best of modern as well as traditional rhetoric, grammar, mechanics, and writing assignments.

Brief Handbook is intended as a reference book for writers and as a text in composition classes, as are many handbooks. However, instead of presenting rules in isolation as if each aspect of writing had nothing to do with the others, we have structured the handbook around the writing process many writers actually use, the process often described in research on composing. The handbook presents writing as a recursive process from prewriting to drafting to revising and proofreading. In this view, writing becomes repeated rewriting, an organic process in which writers review, rethink, re-evaluate, and rework their ideas from simplest beginning notes to polished finished drafts.

Within the process, then, the individual skills contribute to the overall composition. Rules of grammatical usage and punctuation, for example, are not simply criteria of correctness for students to apply mechanically, but are instead guidelines by which to reach an audience with the desired effect, especially in situations demanding formal writing. There can be no such thing as a well-planned composition or a well-constructed paragraph or a well-written sentence or a well-chosen word without the context of situation, purpose, and point of view toward self, subject, and audience. Within such a context, the writing process calls for repeated efforts to find material, to focus ideas, to organize information, and to perfect expression.

Emphasizing revision, this handbook encourages students to view their writing as a developmental process in which they must find their composition through constant revising. During revision, the various elements of writing apply with different emphases, from matters of invention and planning to matters of tone and effect. The pragmatic needs of the writer—finding and organizing material, constructing paragraphs and sentences, choosing effective language, and observing the conventions of standard English—are embedded in the rhetoric of the writing situation. Revision is not often a simple question of right and wrong; it is more often a question of appropriateness and effectiveness. Students must be shown *how* to revise, how to make decisions about writing based on context, on the writing situation, on the effect they wish to have upon readers. Revision, we believe, is the true art of writing, and it applies not as a discrete activity at a particular point in the writing process (after a draft has been written, for example) but throughout the process, from the very beginning until the writer is satisfied with the composition.

TO THE STUDENT

One of the chief characteristics of higher education is its emphasis on writing. At the upper levels you are expected to write informed papers about thermonuclear reactors, the international monetary fund, stress-related anxiety, Shakespearian drama. The ability to write well is an important attribute of the educated person. Technologically advanced societies, moreover, have entered the "Information Age," in which information processing is a primary characteristic of professions and pastimes alike. Because technological societies put such heavy emphasis on language skills, you must become a sophisticated user of language.

Beyond that, writing imposes advanced intellectual processes on the mind. Many people cannot separate themselves from their language. For most "natural" speakers, language just happens—it pours out like water—spontaneously as they think; words and ideas seem the same. But to plan an utterance, to manipulate language, to shape discourse to a desired end—these are the skills of effective writing. Writers learn to anticipate the effects of language on distant readers and the effect on subject matter of being expressed in certain words and certain organizations rather than others. Writers learn subtle nuances of language and effective habits of composing.

Few writers are inspired geniuses who "get" ideas and then copy them down on paper. Few skillful writers compose without prewriting or rewriting. For analytical writing—writing that deals with abstractions, concepts, and values—and for writing about difficult and unfamiliar subject matter, the "inspired genius" theory of writing is downright destructive. Through the act of writing itself—through notetaking and scribbling and false starts and rewriting and rewriting—writers begin to find out what they have to say. Meaning is not floating loose in the air; by struggling with language and ideas, writers make meaning.

Through writing, you have opportunities for extending yourself. Writing allows you to discover thoughts and ideas you didn't know you were capable of. Writing allows you to think about your thoughts; while revising your words, you can see your ideas on the page. You can see when they fail to express your intended meaning. Writers know an important fact: there are discrepancies among *thought* and *language* and *reality*. You may not always comprehend exactly what you see; your ideas about events are your own and seldom the same as someone else's. All writers have their own *versions* of reality, and the words you use may not exactly match your thoughts, your vision of the truth. The effort to reconcile these discrepancies—to bridge the gaps between what you observe, what you think, and what you write—will help you to grow intellectually. The ideas and words already on paper trigger other ideas; writing is thinking on paper. This skill—the ability to manipulate and revise language—gives writing its power.

Writing seems mysterious to many people because they have not seen the hours upon hours of writing and rewriting. The end result looks so logically organized and well worded that it appears magical. But writing is not magic. It is impossible to produce thoughtful writing as if it were a spontaneous oral performance, with no prior planning and no conscious control. It may take only minutes to read a short composition, but it takes hours of work to produce one. The reader does not see the cross-outs and rewrites, the writer struggling; the reader cannot see the writer's greatest skill—revision. For most writers, even the very best, writing is rewriting, rewriting, and more rewriting.

The true art—the craft—of writing is rewriting. It is in the process of working with language that ideas emerge. That is why ghost writers flourish: it is not enough to have a story to tell; a good story must have a skillful telling. How to organize, how to develop, how to add missing information, cut extraneous language, clarify awkward sentences, supply precise and effective words—these are the writer's skills. For this reason, we have emphasized revision throughout *Brief Handbook for Writers*.

HOW TO USE THIS BOOK

The handbook is organized in sections illustrating the writing process, a review of traditional concepts of grammar, sentence errors, sentence structure, punctuation, mechanics, diction, paragraphs, reasoning, and writing assignments. To assist instructors and students in finding specific items to study or review, each major guideline or rule is numbered. There are numerous activities to help students practice the concepts presented. At the end of the book there are two glossaries, one covering grammatical terminology and another covering specific items of usage. The table of contents and the comprehensive index at the end of the book will enable students and teachers to find anything in the book quickly. In addition, the end-papers set out in schematic form the numbering system and revision symbols used throughout the book.

When the handbook is used as the text in a composition class, teachers may wish to proceed in sequence through each section, discussing the concepts and assigning the activities for practice. Many teachers prefer to use the book as a reference guide when evaluating student drafts. When the book is used in this fashion, the numbering system or abbreviated references to items in the book can be used to direct students to the relevant sections. On their own, students can use the handbook at every stage of the writing process. The revision section will lead students through a careful analysis of each assignment, the title of the composition, its beginning, body, and conclusion. It also will help students to monitor the elements of good writing: purpose, tone, and style. Finally, it will support students in mastering the details of the writer's craft: accurate and effective sentences and diction and proofreading for the conventions of academic writing.

ACKNOWLEDGEMENTS

Much difficult work goes into the publication of a new book, and many more hands are involved than those of the authors. While it is not possible to name all the individuals whom we might wish to acknowledge, we cordially applaud the splendid editorial staff at Prentice-Hall, especially Joyce Perkins, whose keen eyes and incisive mind ever assisted the authors in finding their way.

The authors gratefully acknowledge our students, many of whom have provided sample papers, paragraphs, or sentences for the book, and all of whom have helped us over the years understand a little the problems of young people struggling with the written word and the conventions of formal English.

We are pleased to acknowledge the contributions of the several readers who offered feedback at various stages in the production of the book: M. F. Austin, Columbia State Community College; Michael Bailey, Wallace Community College; Linda J. Bowie, Furman University; Vivian Brown, Laredo Junior College; C. R. Embry, Truckee Meadows Community College; Louis Emond, Dean Junior College; Patricia H. Graves, Georgia State University; Mary Middleton Harp, Troy State University; Charlotte Laughlin, Howard Payne University; John W. Martin, Moraine Valley Community College; Carol Niederlander, St. Louis Community College at Forest Park; Joan Patrie, Jamestown Community College; Lowry Pei, Harvard University; David Raabe, University of Nebraska at Omaha; Joseph Yokelson, Bridgewater State College.

Finally, we offer our thanks to Joan and Kathy, for patiently enduring the hours upon hours we devoted to the work of the book and for encouraging us along the way.

James F. Howell
Dean Memering

Brief Handbook for Writers

The Writing Process

plan

1 PLANNING

The planning of an essay includes everything that leads from a writing situation to a working draft. In this section you learn to analyze writing situations, those events or occasions that call for writing. Writing situations are often started by someone other than the writer: students writing for teachers, employees for employers. When someone puts you in a writing situation, first understand what you are being asked for, and then think about what responses will be appropriate to the situation. Make sure you understand the assignment. Are you being asked for your opinion? Are you being asked to defend a thesis? In any writing situation there is a writer (you), a subject, and an audience, each of which must be analyzed as you work toward a rough draft. This section will survey several sources of material for writing and will describe several techniques for exploring that material and arriving at a tentative thesis statement, a brief statement that limits your subject and identifies what your paper is about. In the planning stage you will search for ideas, take notes, make trial outlines. Your writing will be judged on how much and how well you have planned; you must revise your planning notes until a composition begins to take shape.

1a Analyze the assignment.

OPEN-ENDED ASSIGNMENTS

An open-ended assignment suggests a general subject, but does not impose any restrictions on your writing. You may be asked to write about "something related to government," "one of Yeats' poems," "some aspect of Renaissance life," or "something that interests you." When an assignment is given in this open-ended fashion, you must *find* your subject. You are expected to transform the general assignment into a limited, specific topic.

STRUCTURED ASSIGNMENTS

A structured assignment specifies a limited subject to write about but may not suggest what focus you should use. You may be given a specific assignment to write a paper about Shakespeare's animal imagery in *The Tempest* or a report about the Works Project Administration during the Great Depression. You are expected to find your own approach to the subject. The subject is *what* you are writing about, but you must answer the question *What about it?* What *purpose* will your paper serve?

ESSAYS AND REPORTS

An essay requires a thesis statement, an assertion about what the essay will attempt to show (see **2b**), a declaration such as "Hamlet was insane" or "America should return to the gold standard." An essay is an opinion, with evidence to show why the writer holds the opinion. If you believe Hamlet was insane, you should quote evidence of his insanity from the play. It is not necessary to quote authorities who also hold that opinion. You might do some research for your paper, but an essay is not a research paper and should not be a compilation of what other people think.

A report, on the other hand, is a compilation of information; a report is usually not an opinion. Unlike essays, reports normally require quotations and paraphrasing and typically involve documentation—either in-text references or endnotes or footnotes. See sections 46–50, Writing Assignments, for a detailed discussion of reports and other kinds of assigned writing.

1b Determine your writing purpose.

Whether you have been given an open-ended or a structured assignment, you should begin to think about *purpose*. Purpose encompasses your intentions throughout the course of the planning process. At the beginning, you may think your only writing purpose is to finish the assignment. Finishing is certainly a reasonable objective, but as a writing purpose it won't help you structure your composition. Finding a subject that interests you is a more useful first objective. Writing, full of choices as it is, becomes easier as you *plan*   think about and specify goals and purposes. The clearer you are about your objectives, the more successfully you will fulfill them. A writer's purpose cannot be merely "to write about" something. Vague, inexact purposes lead to vague, inexact writing.

In his English class, Todd was given an open-ended assignment: "Write a brief essay on some subject that interests you." Todd has chosen his topic: fraternities. But this is only the general subject; Todd does not plan to write everything about fraternities. He must search for his *point of view*, something specific *about* fraternities.

To complete this assignment, Todd must find some idea about which he can give his opinion. His purpose is to tell readers something about fraternities, but what? and why? Is this an important subject? Will it interest Todd's readers?

Todd's purpose depends in part on who his reader is. If Todd were writing a letter to a friend, he might choose to tell stories about parties and fraternity events. But Todd is writing for a composition class. What can he tell this audience about fraternities that they would find worth hearing? Like Todd, you too must think about your reader to understand what you want to accomplish. You will quickly discover that what you can tell your reader depends on what you *know* about your subject.

1c Explore various sources for finding subject matter.

Once you have a general idea of your topic, you must find material to develop it.

EXPERIENCES

If you are writing an informal essay or opinion paper, you may be able to draw on your own experiences for material. For example, a thesis like "Our schools teach conformity and obedience" might be supported by examples from your own experience with school.

OBSERVATIONS

Sometimes you can develop a topic with material based on your own observations. For a botany report you might be asked to find and describe various examples of flora. In sociology class, you might

be asked to observe human behaviors and write a case study based *plan*
on those observations.

COURSE WORK

The subjects you are studying in school can provide material for compositions. In English classes, you may read a novel, poem, or play, or you may be asked to read a work outside of class. You can use your reading as a source for writing; analyze the theme of a poem; discuss the characters of a novel, and so on. If you are studying American history, you may be able to find an idea for an essay. To write an essay on whether "England forced the American colonies to rebel," you must show evidence from your study of history that supports this idea. Obvious places to find such material are in your textbook, in outside reading, or in class lectures notes. Look carefully for information that will support your essay.

THE LIBRARY

Much academic writing requires students to find material in the library. You are likely to be given assignments involving unfamiliar material. In such cases, finding and studying library materials will let you come to know a new subject well enough to write about it. Using the library for research is a specialized skill of higher education (see Writing Assignments for more about library and research skills).

1d Use various techniques for exploring and analyzing subject matter.

BRAINSTORMING

The easiest way to generate ideas is brainstorming: jotting down ideas in no particular order, "thinking on paper." To brainstorm a subject means to jot down as rough notes everything you can think of related to the subject. The technique works best when it is done rapidly and without making judgments about the validity or relevance of the ideas. Anything and everything should be written down; you must *write*, not merely think, so that later you will have a record of the ideas to review and analyze.

plan

When you have written down everything you can think of, sort your ideas and look for patterns. During this process you will discover that you have more to say about some things than others. This fact can be a clue to you either to drop some ideas or develop them more fully (with research, for example). Whereas in the first step of brainstorming you approach a subject from any and all directions, in the second step you look for the controlling idea you will write about. Step two allows you to *focus* on your thesis question.

Since Todd's assignment calls for a *brief* essay, and he has some first-hand knowledge of fraternities, he tries to brainstorm. As ideas occur to him he jots them down:

BRAINSTORMING NOTES

fraternities (sororities?) frat houses 3 million in
societies   history of
brothers   pins, paddles, rings
                    frats getting popular again

Sigmas   Greeks
snobs, rich kids?   costs of fraternities?

pledging (why?) friends, companions, brotherhood,
                    contacts for business
                    (national organizations)
                    loyalty, commitment.

secret societies
beer, booze, girls — v.s. social relevance/socially useful:
                    blood drives
                    cleanup campaigns

hazing?
        Should hazing be allowed?
        injuries, abuses, etc.

ACTIVITY 1
Try a prewriting of your own. Assume you have an assignment like Todd's: write a brief essay on a familiar subject. Brainstorm to see how many ideas you can jot down.

INFORMAL OUTLINING

Create a rough outline of your major thoughts on a subject to determine whether they are worth pursuing and to see the relationships among them. For example, after brainstorming Todd types an informal outline for himself that begins with a specific question about his subject:

```
INFORMAL OUTLINE
    I. Thesis
       (Do frats do anything worthwhile?)
   II. Examples
       A (They help students get through college.)
       B (They donate services to the community.)
           1 Blood drives
           2 Cleanup campaigns
           3 Money for charity
       C (They train future leaders.)
  III. Conclusion
       (Yes, frats are worthwhile.)
```

Notice what Todd has done. From his brainstorming he has rejected possibilities like the history of fraternities, their cost, their revival. He has attempted to select from his random thoughts a specific point of view, with concrete examples to support it. This outline represents Todd's first attempt to focus his subject, and it, like any other phase of writing might be revised several times.

ACTIVITY 2
Write an informal outline for an essay you will write from your previous brainstorming, or start with a new subject.

plan

FREEWRITING

Todd is still thinking about his subject. Something about his outline looks unsatisfactory to him. Perhaps his stance is too easy, too obvious. Todd tries a "freewriting" or thinking-on-paper technique, shifting his point of view. His outline reflects a positive view of fraternities, but sometimes a better essay can come from an opposing stance, an unpopular point of view. Freewriting is not a "draft" of Todd's paper; it is another effort to find a satisfactory focus on his subject.

FREEWRITING

Does fraternity hazing have a place in our society. Do fraternities kid themselves when they think they aren't doing anything wrong. How can they justify something that has been proven to hurt so many people. Where do we draw the limit. I think that these ceremonies should be monitored by an elected staff of people from each fraternity. These people shouldn't be allowed to drink & should keep an open mind, but not be biased toward the fraternities side . . . their brothers side. With the limit self-imposed by people from the group this would insure as much. . . . Also there should be heavy fines for any individual that on his own or through his instigation causes any mental or physical punishment that might impair a persons health. Something has to be done. This is apparent. Maybe it could be done in steps. Maybe the nationals could set up new forms of initiation. They would have to visit every fraternity & set this up. Too many people have been killed. 55 that I know of.

Probably a lot more. These deaths are so senseless when you think that they never need to occur at all. What kind of things could prove the loyalty & commitment that hazing apparently provides.

ACTIVITY 3

Try a freewriting of your own. Assuming you are trying to find material for a brief essay, as Todd was, write whatever comes into your mind. Write quickly, without trying to guide your ideas, and without regard for spelling or grammar. Freewriting works best as a spontaneous flow of thoughts, even if the thoughts seem to wander.

FOCUSED ANALYSIS

From his first outline to his freewriting, Todd has uncovered two conflicting views of the subject. Todd realizes that his freewriting lacks organization; he is "thinking out loud" on paper rather than following a plan. But this technique has helped him begin to understand his subject. Now he focuses on fraternity hazing.

FOCUSED NOTES

Fraternity Hazing

deaths   proves a commitment
physical abuse   proves loyalty
mental abuse   proves reasons for joining
humiliation   assures secrecy
    bad outweighs the good

I. Fraternity Hazing
  A. What it is
  B. Thesis statement

9

plan

II *Examples*
   A. *The mental abuse*
   B. *Injuries*
   C. *Deaths*
III *Abolishing Hazing*
   — *restate thesis*
   — *go over three points made*
   — *personal opinion*

At last Todd is beginning to find his idea. Though he is aware of positive aspects of fraternities, Todd intends to write about hazing. This rough outline may be enough to get him started in the right direction.

1e Limit the scope of the essay with a thesis statement.

After you have analyzed the writing situation, your material, and your purpose, you can write a thesis statement for your composition. A thesis statement is a clear expression of what you are going to write about; it is a single sentence that states precisely what the composition is about. For example, "The poor should not have to pay taxes."

A thesis statement for an essay has two components. It specifies some topic ("the poor") and makes a limited statement about it ("should not have to pay taxes"). The thesis limits your subject. Think of the many questions or subtopics you might find under any subject in an encyclopedia. A subject like "poverty" is very big and will produce many subtopics: what is poverty? what causes it? how many "poor" people live in America, in Europe, in Asia? what can be done about poverty? how does poverty affect people? is poverty the result of politics? The more questions and ideas the subject yields, the bigger it is. You cannot write everything about poverty in a short paper; you must find a subtopic small enough to deal with. The search for this subtopic is a search for your thesis. A

plan

thesis like "the poor should not have to pay taxes" confines the writer to examining only the reasons why the poor should not pay taxes; other material about the poor that does not relate directly to the thesis will not be included. The more limited a thesis statement, the easier it will be to bring the essay into focus.

Notice that in Todd's brainstorming (pp. 5 – 6) a number of ideas occur to him: fraternities have a long history, fraternities are becoming popular again, fraternities are socially relevant, and so on. He knows he cannot merely summarize all this; he cannot write everything about fraternities in a short paper. Therefore, in his first outline (p. 7) he selects the thesis "fraternities are worthwhile." With this limitation on his subject, he no longer needs to concern himself with matters like history or cost.

Avoid overly broad, ambiguous, intangible concepts. Avoid thesis statements, like the following, that are too broad to cover adequately in a short paper: national defense policies should be revised; automation is changing our society; the English novel takes many forms. "Limiting" the thesis does not necessarily involve the physical size of the subject. A paper about "Chicago" is not necessarily more limited than a paper about "America," even though Chicago is physically smaller than America. A paper about "My Dog" is not necessarily more limited than one about "Domestic Animals." It is not the subject that determines the size of a thesis but the *focus* on the subject. It is not *what* the subject is, but *what about it* that determines size.

Nevertheless, some subjects are so big to begin with that almost no thesis can focus them sufficiently for a short paper. Abstract, philosophical subjects like communism, theology, human motivation, morality, and so forth are very large, general concepts suitable for books and doctoral dissertations. It is very difficult to write anything at all about such huge subjects without a great deal of research. In part this is so because large subjects like these have long, complicated histories. Today there is not one social-economic theory called "communism" but several: communism as Karl Marx understood it, communism as Joseph Stalin understood it, Russian communism, Chinese communism, Polish, Albanian, Cuban, French, and Italian communism. A good thesis for a college composition must be clear and specific. You should avoid ambiguous words and intangible concepts like *justice, ethics, society,* and so forth. Since *plan* these words mean different things to different people, they are not good choices for a thesis. While it is possible to write about such subjects, they are not good choices for short papers. They are not good subjects for most students unless and until the subjects can be made specific and concrete. Note that Todd's first attempt at a thesis contains the idea that fraternities are "worthwhile," but this is a vague concept. What is worthwhile to one person may be worthless to another. Todd decides to continue revising his ideas; he is looking for a more specific, less ambiguous idea (see his freewriting, pp. 8–9).

Avoid self-evident, trivial, or overworked subjects. Since very large and abstract subjects are so difficult to deal with, many students go to the other extreme and select a very simple thesis. Avoid obvious statements: murder is wrong; pollution of the environment should be controlled; smoking may lead to cancer. While such theses may be more workable, they violate the basic purpose of composition. There is no point in telling readers what they already know. There is no point in arguing a question that no one disputes. A thesis must be worthwhile to the reader. You must ask yourself not only "What interests me?" but also "What will be of interest to educated readers?" For that reason you should avoid trivial, immature subjects like "Getting ready for school each morning is hard work" or trite, overworked subjects like "Christmas has become too commercial." Every writing situation has three components—the writer, the subject, and the reader—and a good thesis must take account of each of them. You must revise your thesis until it satisfies you personally, does justice to the subject matter, and is appropriate for your audience.

Todd finally discovers his true thesis, the one he really wants to write about and the one he is confident he can handle in a short paper: "Fraternity hazing should be abolished." This is a good thesis because it satisfies the three components of the writing situation: he is interested in the subject himself, it is a significant subject in our colleges, and it is likely to interest educated readers. Then too, this thesis imposes an obligation on Todd; he is not free to write whatever occurs to him about fraternities. The thesis limits his choices: he must stick to fraternity hazing, and specifically to the idea that hazing should be abolished. The reader will be able to evaluate the paper on how well Todd illustrates his thesis.

1f Evaluate the thesis.

You can evaluate your own thesis on three criteria: (1) Is it specific enough? Does it name an unambiguous subject? (2) Is it limited enough? Is the focus narrow enough for a thorough treatment in a short paper? (3) Is it a worthwhile thesis? Does it satisfy the three components of the writing situation: worthwhile to you personally, appropriately focused for the nature of the subject itself, and appropriate for the intended audience?

GENERAL SUBJECTS	REVISED TO MORE SPECIFIC SUBTOPICS
love	love of country, romantic love, self-love
war	the arms race, the peace movement, the draft
the President	the President's economic policy, personal appeal, leadership qualities

BROAD TOPICS	REVISED TO MORE LIMITED TOPICS
romantic love	teenaged marriages
the arm's race	the star wars weapons
the President's appeal	the President's speech techniques

TRIAL THESES	REVISED TO THE WRITING SITUATION
Teenaged marriages are a bad idea.	Teenagers are not mature enough for marriage.
Star wars weapons will defend us.	Star wars weapons are impractical.
The President is a great communicator.	The President uses humor to show that he means well

ACTIVITY 4

Evaluate each of the following statements. Write your analysis for each one. Which ones might make good thesis statements for short compositions? If you feel any of these is not good, explain why.

plan

1. All college students should learn to operate a computer.
2. We should protect our national resources.
3. There are many advantages to a career in forestry.
4. Mandatory public education violates the citizens' freedom of choice.
5. Friendships are valuable.
6. America is better than Russia.
7. The MX missile is essential to our national defense.
8. Male college students should not wear earrings.
9. Butter pecan is the best ice cream flavor.
10. Dogs are easier to train than cats.

Todd needs a *limited* subject. The overall subject, "fraternities," was too big and too general. Through prewriting Todd has narrowed it to "fraternity hazing." Todd must consider his own position and his readers' position: what is likely to have appeal for his composition class, educated general readers? At last Todd discovers his thesis; he believes that "Hazing should be abolished." He is ready to try a rough draft.

ACTIVITY 5

Make a list of a dozen thesis statements for short compositions you might care to write. If you wish, you may state them as questions. Be prepared to explain why they would be effective and what kind of support they would require.

ACTIVITY 6

Select a thesis statement from Activity 5 and write a brainstorming or a freewriting sheet for it. From these ideas, and others as they occur to you, make an informal outline. Be prepared to explain your choices.

ACTIVITY 7

Prewrite a topic (from Activity 6 above) for a possible composition. Describe your purpose. Jot down notes on the material you will use. Keep writing until you have two or three pages of notes; continue prewriting until you have exhausted your ideas—until you cannot think of anything more to say. Evaluate and revise your thesis statement.

2 DRAFTING

When you have found sufficient information for your paper, you can begin a first draft. As you have seen, it is possible to put together rough outlines and freewriting early in the writing process. However, in the drafting stage, you must become more and more specific about your subject and your approach to it; you must begin to put ideas on paper.

At this stage, writing is tentative and rough. Drafting and then revising is the best route to a successful paper. Your writing will profit from the number of your drafts and the thought and thoroughness you put into reviewing and revising them.

2a Clarify the aim of the composition.

Early in a writing situation it is often easier to decide on your own intentions than on the final purpose of your writing. At the point of the first draft, though, you should be able to describe that overall intention as *informative, argumentative or persuasive*, or *expressive*.

Aims, purposes, motives can be complex, and your own motives may not be entirely clear to you. But through analysis and working with your drafts, the aim of the writing must become clear to you if it is to become clear to your reader. Ask yourself, "What do I want to achieve with this paper?" Is the paper to focus on the information, on the reader, or on you, the writer?

INFORMATIVE

Informative writing reports and explains facts; it is the most widely used form of academic writing. The aim of such writing is to give information to the reader. For example, papers like "The New Tax Proposal," "The President's Human Rights Record," and "The Development of Modern Music" all call for a straightforward presentation of information—as opposed to arguments or opinions.

draft

ARGUMENTATIVE AND PERSUASIVE

Argumentative or persuasive writing seeks to change the reader's mind. If the evidence is strictly objective, presenting only facts and figures, it is called "argumentation." In effect, writers rely upon the evidence by itself to move the mind of a reasonable reader. But if the composition uses emotional arguments and ethical appeals as well as logical ones, readers are likely to call the composition "persuasive." These distinctions are usually too narrow to be of much consequence: readers believe they are "convinced" by appeals to the mind, but "persuaded" by appeals to emotions and morals. The truth is that many compositions of this type are both argumentative and persuasive.

EXPRESSIVE

Expressive writing attempts to show the writer's emotions, to share human experiences. It is most commonly used in nonfiction for autobiographical writing—the writer gives his or her personal experience, expresses feelings, explores ideas from a purely personal point of view.

2b Control the first draft with the thesis statement.

Once you have decided on the aim of your essay, you must apply your thesis statement to that aim. For example, Todd has decided to write an argumentative/persuasive essay that will provide evidence showing why fraternity hazing should be abolished. His thesis statement, then, will control his paper so that everything he writes will help in carrying out his specific aim. As he selects his material, he asks himself if it will contribute to the goal of convincing the reader that hazing should be banned. If it will not, he rejects it. This practice will help Todd write a unified essay that sticks to the one major point he has selected.

Using the thesis statement as a controlling device for his writing will also suggest to Todd what material *ought* to be included. He knows that he needs a definition of hazing, effective examples, and a logical structure showing why the practice should be eliminated. Todd's thesis suggests what kind of information and how much of it he needs (see **1e**). He knows he cannot simply make assertions and *draft* express moral disapproval. Todd's personal opinion of hazing cannot move his readers, who may have different opinions. To *convince* his readers, Todd must illustrate his thesis with specific examples of what is wrong with hazing. His thesis suggests serious action against fraternities, and therefore he will not write much about mere silly pranks, but will write as much as possible about serious dangers in hazing.

2c Select a developmental strategy for the whole composition.

Writers must determine the general strategy for their compositions. It is possible to use several strategies in a composition, but you may find it easier to stick with a single strategy. You must keep in mind that compositions are not written by pattern, and these strategies are not offered as patterns for writing. They are options to help you think about subject matter. (See **43a** for developmental patterns.)

NARRATION

Narrative writing uses chronological order. Stories, of course, usually develop through narration, but this pattern can also be used in many other kinds of writing. Events are listed in a time sequence such as beginning, middle, and end. The chronology need not start at the beginning, so long as the reader can follow the order of events.

A Proposal for a Computer Lab

Since 1975, faculty members have been using computers in their own research and writing. In 1976 two professors published a large textbook they had written entirely on computers. As more professors discovered the benefits of computers, they began to discuss ways in which students, too, might benefit from use of the machines. Then in 1980, a faculty committee wrote a proposal for "A Study of the Benefits to Students of Using Computers for Writing." The study described in that proposal was completed in 1984. The study showed positive results when students used computers. Based on that study

draft

and other research, the following proposal establishes the benefits of a lab in which students would be trained to use computers for writing.

DESCRIPTION

Descriptive writing presents items according to their relationships in space. For example a description of a room can start with the items nearest the observer (the writer) and then move to items farther and farther away. Any pattern of arrangement is possible so long as the reader is given clear signals to follow.

The lab is set up in a horseshoe pattern, with machines along three walls. As students enter the room, they are met by the lab assistant, who sits at a table near the door. To the right of the door is the first wall of computers.

ILLUSTRATION

The most frequently used pattern of development is illustration: writers provide *examples* to support (illustrate) their points. If you write an informal essay about your roommate's bad habits, for example, you would need to illustrate those habits by giving examples.

Students at first encounter many frustrating problems with the computers. For example, after typing in several pages of a composition, some students forget that they must tell the computer to "save" their work. Without the "save" command, all the work is lost when the machine is turned off.

CLASSIFICATION

When dealing with large numbers of things, it is useful to arrange them into groups, to classify them by type. For instance, you might write about "students" by classifying them with some criterion you select such as "reasons for coming to college": those who come to study, those who come to play, those who come because they were forced to, and so on.

Students react in different ways to the computer. Some students are immediately intrigued by the technology. Seeing their work appear on the screen as they type is a novelty for such students. Others feel frustrated and anxious about the strangeness of the commands.

Beeps from the machine, indicating errors, fluster these students.
Still others, those who are excellent typists, prefer to use their type-
writers. Their familiarity and expertise with the typewriter make the
computer seem unnecessary.

DEFINITION

Some academic writing calls upon students to define things.
What is democracy? What is a social order? What is a sonnet? In
the dictionary sense, a definition specifies a group or class (a sonnet
is a poem) and a subgroup or distinguishing characteristic (of fourteen lines). Less formally, you may use other ways to define concepts such as what the word means to you personally, what it means
in actual practice, what it means in comparison to other similar
terms.

Computer assisted instruction uses the computer as if it were a
teacher or a textbook. The computer can help students revise by
asking questions and by showing principles of revision. Some CAI
programs can identify errors and problems in writing and suggest
possible ways to revise them.

COMPARISON

Compositions may use a compare and contrast strategy to show
differences and similarities. You can compare the old with the new,
the human-made with the natural, and so on. In academic writing
you may be called upon to compare two books, two theories, two
historical periods.

Writing with the computer is similar to using a typewriter, but there
are a number of differences. The typewriter and the computer have
similar keyboards. Both machines print on paper. However, revising
on a traditional typewriter means retyping everything; revising on
the computer means typing only the changes.

ANALYSIS (PROCESS)

A process analysis describes the stages of development in actions
or events. An objective description of the steps in designing a house
tells the reader how to do it, how to design a house. If the composition is thought of as a recipe or set of directions for the reader,
then the writer must be very specific, providing the reader with all
the information required to repeat the process.

draft

To start the Apple IIe with a program like Appleworks, a word processing program, requires three steps. First you must insert a start-up disk into the disk drive and then turn on the machine. This prepares the computer to accept a program. Next you must insert the program disk. When the program disk is fully loaded, the machine will ask you for your data disk. Finally, remove the program disk and insert your disk.

ANALYSIS (CAUSAL)

A causal analysis describes a cause and effect sequence of events. You may analyze something physical, such as the causes of an accident, or something less tangible, such as the causes of the Civil War.

Sometimes the computer sends an error message: "Cannot read disk." This error may be caused by a number of mistakes. Often the disk has not been properly formatted; you must start over and tell the computer to format the disk. Sometimes the disk has been put into the wrong drive; remove the disk and put it into the proper drive. Once in a while students accidentally put the disk in backwards or upside down.

ACTIVITY 8
Write a substantial paragraph on some subject you know well. Use one of the standard organizational strategies to guide your thinking.

2d Clarify point of view toward the reader, the subject matter, and yourself as writer.

Point of view is the writer's attitude, a "slant" on the writing situation. Several writers might cover the same subject, for example, but each with a different point of view. Point of view is made up of the writer's attitudes (or "views") toward the reader, toward subject matter, and toward self.

Adopt an appropriate attitude toward the reader. Many problems in writing arise from faulty assumptions about the reader. If you are writing for teachers, you can assume they prefer clear, concise, and accurate language. Readers do not expect to see ungrammatical writing or unproofread papers. You should also be careful about using big words and difficult sentences. Adult readers do not

enjoy papers that sound immature, but that does not mean your
teachers expect heavy writing from you. If you are indifferent, your
readers will see that offensive attitude in your writing.

Maintain an appropriate tone toward the subject matter. You
may be asked to write about unfamiliar subjects. However, it is a
mistake to pretend to know more than you do; writers must study,
collect information, and come to know their subjects well. Attitudes
like sarcasm, cuteness, or indifference are seldom appropriate: they
indicate the writer feels superior to the subject or the reader. On
the other hand, if your attitude is *too* serious, the result will sound
heavy and pretentious.

Express an appropriate attitude toward yourself as writer. You
may not realize that your writing expresses your personality. Readers hear your "voice" in what you write. If you are bored, your
"voice" will sound bored. If you are sarcastic, the sarcasm will come
through the writing (not a good idea). Flippancy, misplaced humor,
condescension, pretentiousness, pomposity, and other unnatural
voices are mistakes. The nonfiction writer needs to sound credible
and trustworthy. Avoid insincerity or other distortions of voice.

2e Construct an outline that shows the organization of the material and support for the thesis.

Outlines can be formal or informal, but either way the outline
will help you to organize your material. The outline separates major
and minor points and shows the reader how they relate to each
other. For example:

```
            The Legal Drinking Age Should Be Lowered
    I. Background to the question
   II. The conventional view: drinking at age 21
        A. Keeping alcohol out of high school
        B. Preventing addiction to alcohol
        C. Reducing alcohol-related accidents and crime
        D. Preserving conventional social values
```

draft

III. The liberal view: lowering the drinking age to 18
    A. Preventing rebellion of minors
    B. Standardizing rights of all citizens
    C. Treating alcohol related problems consistently
        1. Openly identifying nature and extent of
           problems
        2. Providing counselling, treatment for all
           citizens with abuse or addiction problems
    D. Contradicting accident and crime statistics
  IV. Thesis question answered
    A. Summary of main points
    B. Closing statement

The outline provides a standard organizational pattern for otherwise random information. Use of the outline can help you to clarify your thoughts, identify the points you want to make, set up a plan for your paper that the reader will understand. Note that standard parts of an outline like the introduction and conclusion are not labelled as such; use a descriptive heading instead.

The sequence of levels in a standard outline is as follows: roman numerals, capital letters, arabic numerals, lower case letters, arabic numerals in parentheses, lower case letters in parentheses.

```
I.
    A.
        1.
        2.
            a.
            b.
                (1)
                (2)
                    (a)
                    (b)
    B.
        1.
        2.
            a.
            b.
                (1)
                (2)
                    (a)
                    (b)
II.
```

draft

There is no standard procedure for additional levels in this kind of an outline, and it is unlikely that you will need more divisions than this for most outlines. However, if you did decide to add additional levels, you might try using brackets [A], [1], or lower case roman numerals (i, ii, iii) or some other logical extension of the system.

Note that a formal outline uses parallel language: all the points are expressed in similar language. Whether to use full sentences or topical statements is the writer's choice, so long as the outline is consistent (do not mix full sentences with topical statements).

In a formal outline there should be no such thing as a "1" without a "2" or an "a" without a "b" because each level is considered a *division* of the subject; a "division" with only one item in it looks illogical (like "Apples" as the only item under "Fruits"). If you find any one-item categories in your outline, you should revise. The most common solution is to reword the main heading so that the subpoint is absorbed. For example:

```
ILLOGICAL (ONE-ITEM SUBPOINT)

  I. Cause of hypertension
     A. Excess sugar in the diet
 II. Treatments of hypertension

REVISED (SUBPOINT ABSORBED IN MAIN POINT)

  I. Excess sugar in the diet as cause of hypertension
 II. Treatments of hypertension
```

However, often these single-item divisions of an outline are clues to the writer that more research is needed. In the example above, the writer should investigate further to find additional causes of hypertension. Thus the outline can help you understand how well you have researched, and can show you where your paper is weak.

ACTIVITY 9
Prepare a formal outline for an essay of several paragraphs. You may select the topic you used in Activity 1 or some other topic that interests you.

2f Give the composition an effective title.

Every paper should have a title. The title should give readers an idea of your subject and arouse their interest. Often a title can help you find your approach to a subject; however, sometimes the best time to select a title is after you have written the draft, when you are sure of your thesis. In either case, the title should be concise and fit the tone of your paper. A title of "Bombed Out" for a serious paper on the destruction of Dresden during World War II sets the wrong tone, trivializes the topic. Try to avoid vague or inappropriate titles and ones that promise more than they can deliver. "An In-depth View of the Problems of Disarmament" promises a serious discussion of a very big subject and probably cannot be delivered in a short paper. A title like "Problems with the B1 Bomber" promises a more realistically limited paper.

2g Write the first draft.

After making decisions about the overall purpose of your essay, its organization, and your point of view, you may be ready to try a first draft. Thorough work in the prewriting and drafting stages is well worth the time it takes. In fact, at this point some writers may not be ready for a draft, but instead may wish to return to prewriting.

In the first draft, concentrate on getting on paper the general idea and organization of your composition. Since there are going to be revisions anyway, you need not labor too much over the first draft. Avoid crumpling up papers and starting over. Force yourself to go on to the end, even if you have to skip over hard parts.

Working from his informal outline, Todd has analyzed his point of view toward his audience (his composition class), his subject matter, and himself as author. He has produced the following rough draft. Describe his point of view: what is his attitude toward his reader, subject matter, himself? What aim or purpose has he selected? What strategy of development has he used?

Fraternities offer many good services to the community. When blood is needed at the hospital, the fraternity brothers quickly volunteer. And at least once a year several of the fraternities get out to help clean up the town. Through car washes, bottle collecting, and door to door collecting fraternities help to raise money for charity. Yes, there are many good points to a fraternity, but one thing must be changed.

There are over 3 million college men in about 400 fraternities across the country. Through pledging these various fraternities there have been about 55 deaths. An amount that should be zero when you consider there shouldn't be any in the first place.

Injuries are also frequent and sometimes very serious. What promotes a person to pour a toxic chemicle on sombodies skin? This question & others are why fraternity hazing is looked at with such a criticizing eye. Other injuries & poinsoning are also frequent in todays fraternity rituals.

Mental abuse is also an important issue when discussing hazing. Can a person be the same after having relay races with sardines being passed with only the buttocks—what one does the rest follow. One would hardly think so. Many pledges have suffered mentally from pledging & even dropped out of school because of the embarrassment.

Fraternity hazing should be abolished because of the potential harm it creates. Deaths resulting from extravagant pledging rites, injuries due to sloppily done initiation ceremonies, & the possible mental implications from doing things one would never normally do. These things convince me that our fraternity systems must find another way to put pledges through & fill the hazing abolition vacuum.

rev

Using a brainstorming sheet you prepared earlier or a new one, write a rough draft. Assume you are writing for an audience of educated readers, like your composition class. Choose a subject you know well, as Todd did. Try to convince your readers to see the subject as you see it by providing examples, details, and reasons that illustrate your point.

3 REVISING AND EDITING

Revision is the key to effective writing, and your work may be evaluated on the number and kinds of revisions you make. This section presents an overview of the principles and techniques of revision and often refers you to places in this book where you will find additional information.

The writing process is not linear; few writers can move forward from planning to drafting to final copy without circling back to rethink and revise. Although Section 3 concentrates on revisions of drafts, you should understand that preliminary work—notes, freewritings, outlines, thesis statements—too can be revised. At any time, anywhere in the writing process you may need to return to your notes and outlines for additions and clarifications.

Once you have a first draft, you may be tempted to check briefly for spelling and punctuation, type it up and hand it in. Writing is hard work, and you may be reluctant to "do it over"; the temptation to be rid of the paper is strong. But handing in a first draft would be like a furniture maker selecting pieces of fine oak to build a table, then just tacking the pieces together without cutting, shaping, fitting, sanding, staining or polishing them. The result may resemble a table, but it is not finished.

Your ideas may be good, like the oak, but ideas need to be developed, language needs to be polished, and parts of the paper may need to be rearranged, added to, or deleted.

rev

3a Revise the first draft.

A serious writer rarely submits a first draft, no matter how good it might seem. The first draft should attempt to flesh out your outline—capture the organization of the paper and the main points. If it can do more than that, so much the better, but no matter what is accomplished in the first draft, there is still significant work to do.

Once you have this draft down, the real work of shaping and refining can begin. It is here that the art of writing occurs, in the decisions about changes and improvements. You must reconsider the choices you have made, trying to be objective and looking at your paper as someone else would. (Whenever possible, ask a friend to read your work and react critically and honestly.)

Always let a draft "cool off": wait at least a day before rereading it. The cooling off period increases your objective distance and allows you to focus on problems, to see what needs to be changed, added or deleted. Force yourself to read the draft slowly aloud, sentence by sentence, word by word. Assume that at least three types of revision are *always* necessary: (1) you need more information, (2) you need to delete extraneous words, and (3) you need to clarify your sentences.

Most writers develop their own revising procedures, but this section suggests a useful general system. Moving from the general to the more specific elements of your paper, keeping in mind your concern for purpose, tone, and style, look at its beginning, middle, and end.

ACTIVITY 11
Read Todd's first draft (p. 25). What are its strengths and weaknesses? What kinds of revisions would you suggest?

Clarify the aim of your composition. Is your paper intended as informative only, without opinions on your part? Or are you attempting to present an argument, to convince the reader with evidence, or to persuade the reader with ethical and emotional appeals? You may have begun to change your mind about the aim of the composition; or your ideas may have begun to drift from one aim to another, without your realizing it, as you put those ideas into *rev*   words. If your paper has an expressive aim, it will focus on you the writer, your personality, your experiences and ideas. It is possible for a paper to have more than one aim, but you must clarify in your own mind exactly what you are trying to achieve and then revise to make sure your paper supports this aim. **2a.**

Make sure the draft and the thesis statement agree. All information in your paper must conform to the thesis; all matters of evidence, reasoning, and organization must reflect the thesis. A good thesis statement helps to control how much information you need, how to organize it, and when to end a paper. Check each paragraph, each sentence, and every word against the thesis. Ask yourself about each element of your paper, "Does this belong here? Does this illustrate the thesis?" Many "No" answers may mean you need to develop a new thesis statement. **2b, 44, 45.**

Clarify the developmental strategy of the composition. Is the sequence of information or events clear enough for the reader? Hopping around from present to past to future, skipping over important events, and other expressions of faltering organization will confuse most readers. Your writing must present the information and structure the presentation in a clear way. Make sure that not only you but also your readers will be able to see the logic of your strategy.

Ask yourself whether readers will be able to follow your ideas; could they produce a coherent outline from your paper if they wanted to? As you work on your paper, you may discover that you have changed strategies; what started as narrative may have become purely analytical. You must either refocus on your original strategy or go with the new one and revise accordingly. **2c.**

Clarify the point of view. Rethink your audience. Who will read your paper? What will be effective for this audience? Look at each sentence and each word in your draft. Is each item in your paper appropriate to the subject? If your subject is a serious one, does everything in your paper contribute to that effect? What do your words and ideas say about you as the writer? What kind of character does your paper project? Is the voice in the paper one your presumed reader will listen to? **2d.**

Make sure the draft and the outline agree. No matter how you develop your ideas, the reader must be able to see the logic of your organization. If you have made an outline, check to verify that each of its main points has become a major idea in your paper. Do you have enough subpoints under your main points? Can some of the points be reworded, producing new main points or subpoints?

An effective way to check organization is to outline the draft, listing the points that appear in the draft of the paper. Each paragraph should make only one point, and the progression of points must make sense to a reader. Look for ideas that do not seem to fit. Ask yourself, "What point am I making in this paragraph? Why is this point here?" Check this outline of your draft against the outline in your planning notes: do they agree? If they do not, decide why that is so and then revise the outline, the draft, or both, as necessary. **2e, 43.**

Revise for effective paragraphs. Each paragraph in your paper should have a purpose you can both name and relate to the thesis statement and an outline. Moreover, the paragraphs themselves must hang together as well as connect to each other internally. **43a-c.**

Both the first and the last paragraphs of your composition are especially important and may be especially hard to write. The opening paragraph of a paper should accomplish three things: it should lead the reader into the focus of the paper; it should make the reader want to continue reading; and it should set the tone for what is to follow. It is sometimes a good idea to postpone serious work on the opening until after the paper is completed. We have provided some options for beginnings (**43d**); you decide which strategy best fits your purpose, tone, and topic. Check that your introductory paragraph is not one of the problem types (**43d**).

ACTIVITY 12

Practice revising for effective introductions. Assume you are writing a review of a recent film for your school newspaper. Write a rough draft introduction of several sentences, and then revise your introduction. Make a clean copy.

ACTIVITY 13

Revise the introduction you wrote for Activity 2. Assume a different audience, such as a class in film criticism or a citizens' group that opposes the film. Revise the introduction to make it appropriate for this new audience.

29

ACTIVITY 14

Look again at the introduction of Todd's first draft (p. 25). Is it effective? If you think it is not, how would you advise him to change it?

Examine your paragraphs for repetitions; eliminate the excess. To prevent using the same word too often, find effective synonyms or consider combining sentences (p. 37). Also eliminate ideas that are not directly connected to the purpose of the paragraph, even though they may be good ideas by themselves.

ACTIVITY 15

Revise the following paragraph on UFOs for repetitions and irrelevant material. You may add words necessary for transition, but try to reduce the paragraph to its most economical form. Type up the revised version.

There are many explanations of UFO sightings, and beyond these explanations there are reasons to question the legitimacy of so-called evidence of UFO sightings. Hundreds of reports of UFO sightings are discovered to be hoaxes. And most experts agree that ninety to ninety-five percent of the pictures of UFOs and their occupants are double exposures or some other contrived hoax or deception. A double exposure occurs when one picture is taken on top of another, without advancing the film. Of the evidence collected from purported UFO landing sites, none has been identified by experts as being other than ''earthly.''

Use transitions for smooth paragraph movement. Your paper should not jump from point to point but should flow naturally with a sense of connection. A number of transitional devices will help you give signals to the reader (**43b**). Writers must not rely too much on "implied transitions"; do not assume the reader will be able to infer the connection.

Ending the paper can be troublesome: writers may try to do too much or may leave the reader hanging, expecting something more. Ask two questions about the ending: "Will your readers get a sense

rev

of closure when they finish the essay, that there is nothing else coming? And has the paper fulfilled the thesis obligation, done what it said it was going to do?" If these two questions can be answered satisfactorily, your ending will be effective. **43e**

Evaluate the need for changes in organization and purpose. After making changes in your paragraphs, you should again look at your total paper to see how your changes have affected the overall organization. Determine whether changes in paragraphs require changes in your outline.

If you have made additions, deletions, or altered topic sentences, you may have upset the organizational outline. Go back to the outline and make any necessary adjustments, then determine whether you still have a clearly observable pattern of development. If not, rearrange the structure: move paragraphs to create an effective sequence of development. You can check this by making a new outline of the rearranged paragraphs.

Determine, too, whether changes in paragraphs require changes in your thesis. After various revisions, the focus of your paper may have shifted. The thesis may not fit exactly what you now have in the body of your paper. Ask yourself what thesis statement would best suit the revised material; then ask whether the new thesis is what you want to accomplish. You must be willing to go where your revisions are leading you; do not be reluctant to rethink both the thesis and the body of the paper.

ACTIVITY 16

Study the following paragraph. Notice the changes in wording that have been made. Write a brief analysis of the effect of each revision.

When the lights came up, Mick Jagger, Keith Richard, and
Ronnie Wood ~~came out together~~ [lurch onto the stage in a cluster], and Bill Wyman, looking
~~uncourageous~~ [timidly] rather than ~~in an evil way like he didn't care~~ [satanically withdrawn], goes
into his spot in front of his stack. Wood, cigarette ~~held~~ [mounted] at a
~~happy~~ [jaunty] angle, ~~goes~~ [scuttles] over to his amp. Keith Richard ~~rubs his hand~~ [ruffles]
~~in~~ [hitches] his hair and ~~picks~~ up his ~~instrument~~ [guitar]. Jagger--wearing a ~~shiny silver leather jacket~~ ~~coat~~ [1972 offstage wardrobe -- parades]
that looks to be part of David Bowie's ~~old clothes~~ ~~goes~~ [stage with a gait like his pout expanded into an]
around the ~~place with his usually silly~~ movements [entire body style].

rev

When Todd begins to rethink his first draft (p. 25), he finds a number of places to improve. This draft is not bad, but it is very general; there is little *information* in it. When Todd considers his audience, he realizes they probably don't need to be told that hazing abuses are bad; they need facts, examples, illustrations. The paper seems underdeveloped.

Now read Todd's revised first draft.

Fraternity hazing is any action taken that may produce mental or physical discomfort. It can be humiliating and degrading. University officials for a long time have been trying to abolish hazing. *tried to help in deterring their chapters hazing rituals.* Nationals, also, ~~have~~ The problem still exists however, and is in ~~dire~~ *immediate* need of drastic action. I think fraternity hazing should be abolished. ~~Illustrated in the following points.~~ *because of the harm it does its particularly degrading and dangerous nature.* *This is* *examples.*

Fraternities offer many good services to the community. When blood is needed at the hospital, the fraternity brothers quickly volunteer. And at least once a year several of the fraternities get out to help clean up the town. Through car washes, bottle collecting, and door to door collecting fraternities help to raise money for charity. Yes, there are many good points to a fraternity, but one thing must be changed. *Take Out*

There are over 3 million college men in about 400 fraternities across the country. Through pledging these various fraternities there have been about 55 deaths. An amount that should be zero when you consider there shouldn't be any in the first place. *are the cause of* *Highway incident* *One such death involved a pledge that was walking across a highway blindfolded when a car struck and killed him. This death and others could have been prevented with stricter hazing laws.*

Injuries are also frequent and sometimes very serious. What promotes a person to ~~badly burn~~ *STEP* pour a toxic chemicle on ~~somebodies~~ *a pledges* skin? This question & others are why fraternity hazing is looked at with such a criticizing eye. Other injuries *&* ~~poinsoning~~ are also frequent in todays fraternity rituals, *such as: Alcohol poisoning, suffocation, and so on.* ~~Another incident was~~ *One boy from the University of West Virginia was badly burned when lighter fluid ighited his body during an init. rite.*

Mental abuse is also an important issue when discussing hazing. Can a person be the same after having relay races with sardines being passed with only the buttocks--what one does the rest follow. One would hardly think so. Many pledges have suffered mentally from pledging & even dropped out of school bexause of the embarrassment.

Fraternity hazing should be abolished because of the potential harm it ~~creates~~ *can cause*. Deaths resulting from extravagant pledging rites, injuries due to sloppily ~~done~~ *run* initiation

ceromonies, & the possible mental implications from doing things
show the urgency of the situation. The vaccuum hazing abolition
one would never normally do. ~~These things convince me that our~~
would leave must be filled by a more constructive set of guidelines and ensure
~~fraternity systems must find another way to put pledges through &~~
the safety of new inductees and the continuance of our frat system.
~~fill the hazing abolition vacuum.~~

Note that Todd has replaced or revised both the introduction and the conclusion, two hard spots in any composition. He has added examples to illustrate his point, giving the revised writing a much more developed sound. With the new beginning and ending, the reader can see his point clearly. Todd can see that these revisions improve his composition, and he types a second draft incorporating them.

Some students might feel the paper is now ready to hand in. Todd has already put a good deal of work into it, and it is now better than it was. But there is still work to do on this composition. Now that the general structure and substance of the paper have been decided, Todd can turn his attention to matters of clarity and accuracy and the style of his sentences.

ACTIVITY 17

Practice revision. Following is a paragraph excerpted from a story about an accident in which a young girl was killed. If you were trying to improve this first draft, what would you do to it? Use your imagination to supply missing details. After you have revised it, type a clean copy.

We were coming back from the game. My friend and I
were heading back to school. I needed to change my
clothes for the dance. The game had been close, but we
lost. As we were driving back to school the dark road
was dark, naturally. Country roads, of course, do not
have lights. The radio was on loud. Suddenly I see
coming right up behind me, lights. They were coming
right along at a high rate of speed. All of the sudden
this car passes me quickly and goes into a curve. In the
dark I saw a flash of blue paint as it went by. The only
thing was that it never came out of the curve. Here we
had been going along, and suddenly—an accident! The car
was old and went sideways, and the next thing I knew I
saw headlights spinning through the air. It went off the

rev

pavement and into a ditch. The car rolled several times
through the ditch and came to a stop about forty yards
out in a hay field. It turned right side up. I could
imagine what the farmer would say about tire ruts in his
field!

3b Revise the second draft.

Most professional writers work through several drafts, striving
for perfection. All this rewriting makes long and weary work for the
author, but it also holds great promise: each draft should come
closer and closer to realizing the author's objectives.

Monitor style as well as content. It is not easy for writers to
separate *what* they say from *how* they say it; the two things go hand
in hand. However, in revising, it is possible to return to a draft and
change or improve both the *content* (*what* you say, the ideas in your
paper) and the *style* (*how* you express your ideas).

Style is the result of the choices you make in selecting words,
constructing sentences, paragraphs, whole essays. These choices are
an important part of the message that you are trying to convey because style projects personality, attitude, point of view along with
the information. First, decide whether you have maintained the
proper distance with your audience (**2d**). Then look at the words
you have used (**40–42**), the sentence structures you have selected
(**6b, 16–20**), the organizational pattern of your paper (**2c**). Do these
elements fit together? Are they consistent? Does the style suit your
thesis? Note the level of formality word choice creates. Suit word
choice to the topic and to your audience. Using every big word from
the thesaurus when writing about relatively common subjects is seldom appropriate. For example:

> After studying at length the offered documentation relevant to the
> situation concerning community water supplies pollutionwise, one
> could readily come to the conclusion that neither the negative nor
> the positive result could be recommended.

Readers generally are unimpressed by big words and difficult
34 sentences. This is called the "pretentious" style—it pretends to be

rev

more important than it is. No one likes hard-to-read sentences. Any writer can make simple subjects seem complex by using a pretentious style; however, the goal is to present complex subjects simply: "The report on water pollution made no recommendation."

The preferred style for most writing is a "plain style": clear, concise, accurate sentences in a simple, "natural" English. Good style for academic writing is plain English modified for educated readers, meaning that you are required to use the forms of formal writing, use standard grammar, avoid slang, write readable sentences. Use conventional spelling and punctuation. However, none of these requirements justifies dull or colorless writing.

ACTIVITY 18

What is wrong with the style of the following composition? Mark revisions to improve the style. Imagine a person entering a prison as part of a visiting ball team. Is this the way you would describe such an experience? After marking your revisions, prepare a clean copy.

We arrived at the entrance to the prison at about eleven o'clock in the morning. We were required to go through a guarded gate in order to enter. After passing through several security tests we were allowed to proceed into the parking lot. From there we were led into a building which had a small lockerroom, and we were told to keep our valuables in a strongbox which was under constant guard. Before we could proceed to the field, we were searched by two security guards. We were then led to a set of two sliding iron bar doors which led into a large visitor's lobby, where the prisoners are allowed to see their families. This lobby was unattractive. We then proceeded through two more iron doors and were marked with a liquid on our hands for identification. This liquid only shows up under a black light. Finally after a long walk through a corridor we approached the last iron gate, which led into the courtyard.

rev **Revise for accurate and effective sentences.** Paragraphs and whole essays are, like many other things, only as good as what goes into them. In reviewing your paper on the sentence level, consider the most basic things first.

Make your sentences clear. Look for sentences that might be awkward, badly worded, overly complicated, or ambiguous. If in doubt about any sentence, read it aloud slowly, either to yourself or to someone else. Try different variations until you are satisfied that you have expressed yourself as clearly as possible. Every sentence *can* be changed; your job is to decide which changes will have the best effect on the reader. **16–20.**

Make your sentences economical. Economy in writing means saying exactly what you want to say in the fewest words. This is not to suggest that you should write only simple little sentences of five or six words, but rather that you must eliminate unnecessary repetitions, irrelevant information, any words that do not contribute to the effect you are trying to achieve. If it is possible to delete words without losing the meaning you are after, they should be eliminated. **20.**

ACTIVITY 19

Carefully evaluate each sentence in the following paragraph. Revise to make the sentences effective not only in themselves but also in the context of the other sentences in the paragraph.

```
In 1972 the policy of the Israeli people toward
terrorism were put to a severe test. During the Olympic
games in Munich Germany Arab terrorists seized nine
Israeli athletes. And killed two others in the process.
Their demand; two hundred Arab prisoners who are to be
flown and to be released to the Arab capital. The
Israeli government refused to negotiate, instead they
decided by means of planning an ambush in which they
hoped to either kill or capture the Arab commandos, the
group of hostages and their captors were transported to
a nearby airport. In the early morning hours five West
```

German sharpshooters open fire on the hostages contained
in the helicopter and kidnappers. There weren't any
survivors.

rev

Create variety in sentence structure. Are all your sentences structured alike? Writers can fall into a habit of using the same sentence pattern over and over, creating a monotonous rhythm, much like repeating the same beat or chord in music again and again. Too many of your sentences may begin the same way, either by using the same words or by using the same pattern of ideas. Shift some of the sentences around to create different beginnings, different structures. **6, 20.**

Check your sentences for variety in length. Pay particular attention to the number of short, simple sentences. Try combining sentences, or rephrasing if there are too many short ones. **Sentence combining** refers to adding, deleting, replacing, or rearranging words in two or more sentences to produce a single, effective sentence.

SHORT SENTENCES	COMBINED
The officer ordered the man to halt. The man was running down the street. He was carrying a new TV set.	The officer ordered the man running down the street with a new TV set to halt.

As a general rule, short sentences should be reserved for emphasis, to make a point stand out. **20.**

Check your sentences for emphasis. Each of your sentences should be clear, and your most important point should be in a position in the sentence that carries stress. Experiment with your sentences, shift things around, rearrange or embed sentence elements to create the emphasis you desire. After you make any changes, rethink your sentences; check for smoothness and fluency. **20.**

ACTIVITY 20

Using your own sense of language rhythm, revise the following paragraph. Make up details to add information. Revise the sentences for greater variety and emphasis. Make the paragraph sound more realistic and mature.

rev

I told my parents I was going away to college. I was
praying they'd understand. It was hard to tell them. It
was the hardest thing I did in my life. It's not fair to
bring up anything like this so suddenly. They didn't
even know I had applied to out-of-state schools. My
mother thought I was kidding at first. All hell broke
loose later because she realized I was telling the
truth. She was crying and saying things, they didn't
make sense. I tried explaining, I tried to defend myself
against her accusations. She said I didn't love her and
my father. She said I didn't want to help my father in
the shop anymore. I wanted her to understand. I wanted
him to understand too. All our hopes and dreams would
have a greater chance of becoming a reality. But only if
I went to college and learned how to really design
machine tools. They settled down and thought it over.
They decided I might be right.

Revise for accurate and effective word choice. Word choice is
vital in creating your point of view and fulfilling your purpose. Ask
yourself whether your word choice is appropriate: is it suited exactly
to you as a writer and to what you are trying to accomplish with
your reader? A single misused word can put the reader off and cause
you to lose credibility. Even with the most precise language possible, there may be some readers who will not understand you; and
your readers will surely misunderstand if your language is general,
vague, inexact. Your obligation as a writer is to be specific, precise,
and as clear and accurate as possible. (**40–42.**)

Replace general words with specific nouns and verbs. Look at
the nouns you have chosen. Do they fit your purpose? Are they as
descriptive as they need to be? Do they suit your your audience?
For example, can you achieve your effect with a word like *collie,
mongrel, cur, puppy, hound, mutt, stray?* Or is it sufficient to use
the general word, *dog?* Are your verbs exact? Suppose you are describing a politician besieged by reporters after his trial for drug
possession. Does he *talk, yell, speak, rant, bellow, whisper, shout,*

orate, posture, whine? What picture are you trying to create for *rev* your reader? **40–42.**

Replace vague, commonplace language with effective modifiers. Examine your modifiers, the adjectives and adverbs, phrases and clauses. Here too, look for vagueness and ineffective generality. What, for example, do *beautiful* and *pleasant* mean in this sentence?

She was a beautiful woman with a pleasant personality.

You know what you mean, but your audience gets only a general idea and cannot see the woman. Many modifiers are not only vague, they are dull and commonplace. You need fresh, clear, descriptive language to make your writing come alive. **41–42**

Revise for appropriate tone. Tone shows your attitude toward your subject. Is the tone serious, humorous, sarcastic, angry, flippant? Is that tone appropriate? For example, if you are trying to persuade someone to your point of view, using a hostile or sarcastic tone of voice will not work. Tone should be consistent throughout the paper; it should not include two extremes like seriousness and flippancy. A humorous anecdote may sometimes be appropriate in a paper dealing with an important subject, but the writer must not confuse the reader with inconsistent shifts in tone. **(19)**

Revise the title. Check to make sure that your title still reflects your thesis and the tone of your paper. Changes in the content or the style of your paper may call for changes in your title **(2f).**

ACTIVITY 21

Here are Todd's revisions of the second draft. Read the paper carefully. Be prepared to discuss the revisions. What has Todd changed? Are the changes helpful?

```
                    Fraternity Hazing


        Fraternity hazing is any action taken that may produce
mental or physical discomfort.  It can be humiliating or
degrading.  University officials have, for a long time, been
trying to abolish hazing.  Nationals have also tried to help in
```

rev

detering thier chapters ri hazing rituals The problem still
exists however and is in immediate need of drastic action. I
think fraternity hazing should be abolished because of its
particulary degrading and dangerous nature. ~~This is illustrated
in the following points.~~

There are over a million college men in about 400
fraternities across the country. Through pledging these various
fraternities are the cause of about 55 deaths. ~~An amount that
should be zero when you consider there shouldn't be any in the
first place.~~ One such death involved a pledge that was walking
across a highway blindfolded when a car struck and killed him.
This death and others could have been prevented with stricter
hazing laws.

Injuries are also frequent and sometimes very serious. What
promotes a person to pour a toxic chemicle on a pledges skin?
This question, and others are why fraternity hazing is looked at
with such a criticizing eye. One boy, from the university of
West Virginia was badly burned when lighter fluid ignighted his
body during an intiation rite. Other injuries are also frequent
in todays freaternity rituals, such as; Alcohol poisoning,
soffocation, and so on. stabbing wounds

Mental abuse is also an important issue when discussing
fraternity hazing. Can a person be the same after having relay
races with sardines being passed with only the buttocks. One
would hardly think so. Many pledges have suffered mentally from
pledging and even dropped out of school because of the
embarrassment. This must surely end if uor fraternity systems
are to survive.

Fraternity hazing sould be abolished because of the
potential harm it can cause. Deaths resulting from extravagant
pledging rites, injuries due to sloppily run initiation
ceromonies, and the possible mental implications from doing
things one would never normally do show thw urgency of the
situation. The hazing abolition would leave must be filled by a
more constructive set of guidelines and insure the safety of new
inductees and the continuance of our fraternity system.

3c End the revision process.

rev

It is always possible to make one more change, but at some point additional changes may become excessive fiddling with the manuscript. By the time you have revised a second draft and incorporated all your changes into the third draft, you will usually be ready to stop revising. You will not be through working, but if you have looked at your paper in the ways described in 3a and 3b, you should have a well-structured and worthwhile composition nearing completion.

3d Edit the third draft.

By the time you have typed up a third draft, most of the big decisions and structural changes will usually have been made. It is then time to make any minor changes (or major ones, of course, if necessary) to polish your language, to ensure that what you have written flows, makes good sense, is unified in tone and point of view.

Polish your composition. In the third draft, writers narrow their focus to small details. If you should find anything else at this point, any problems in ideas, organization, language, by all means make the changes. But the chief function of the third draft is to *polish* your composition, give it the finished, professional look of a skilled writer.

Revise your sentences for formal grammar. Educated readers do not expect to find grammatical errors in serious writing. Revising your sentences for standard English shows that you understand and respect your audience. There are various options for sentence grammar, but for the most part, you should follow the conventional guidelines. Keep an eye on subject/verb and pronoun/antecedent agreement (**9–10**). The reader must be certain who is doing what in each of your sentences. Correctness of pronoun case (such as the difference between *who* and *whom*) and verb usage (like the difference between *lie* and *lay*) mark the differences between formal and informal writing. Check carefully to catch and correct any fragments, comma splices, or run-on sentences (**7,8**).

rev **Edit for punctuation and mechanics.** Make sure your punctuation is conventional and expresses what you want and that your readers will understand it. If you have any doubts, see "Punctuation." Check for small things like the use of apostrophes, hyphens, underlining, capitalization, abbreviations and numbers, and spelling. Look up the spelling of any word of which you are even slightly unsure or that does not look right. Good writing must also *look* good; spelling errors may cost you not only a grade but credibility with your readers. See Mechanics.

Eventually Todd produces an *edited draft*, the one that is as nearly perfect as he can get it. In addition to the care he has taken to make his draft correct according to the rules and conventions of standard English, Todd has switched his paragraphs around so that the most important point comes last.

Compare this version with Todd's second draft on pp. 32–33. What changes did he make? Did he miss any problems? Compare this version with his rough draft (p. 25). Would you agree Todd has improved his writing?

Fraternity Hazing

Fraternity hazing is any action that may produce mental or physical discomfort. It can be humiliating and degrading. For a long time, university officials have been trying to abolish hazing. Nationals have also tried to deter hazing rituals in their chapters. The problem still exists, however, and is in drastic need of immediate action. Fraternity hazing should be abolished because of its particularly degrading and dangerous nature.

Hazing abuse can be not only physical but mental as well. Can a person be the same after participating in relay races in which sardines are passed using only the buttocks? One would hardly think so. Many initiation rites require pledges to remove part or all of their clothing; some of these rites are vaguely—others clearly—sexual in nature. Numbers of pledges have suffered mentally from such initiation rites. Some have even dropped out of school because of the humiliation, harrassment, and ridicule. This must surely end if our fraternity systems are to survive.

Injuries too are frequent and sometimes very serious. What causes a person to pour a toxic chemical on a pledge's skin? Questions like these are why fraternity hazing is looked at so critically. One young man from West Virginia University was badly burned when lighter fluid ignited his body during an intiation rite. Other injuries, such as alcohol poisoning, suffocation, and stabbing wounds, are also frequent in today's fraternity rituals.

There are over a million college men in about 400 fraternities across the nation. Through the rites of pledging there have been an estimated 55 deaths among these young men. One such death involved a pledge who was walking across a highway blindfolded when a car struck and killed him. This death and others could have been prevented with stricter hazing laws.

Fraternity hazing should be abolished because of the potential harm it can cause. Mental disturbances from doing things against your own moral code; injuries due to sloppily run initiation ceremonies; and deaths resulting from extravagant, bizarre, and cruel pledging rites are urgent reasons for abolition. Instead of hazing we need a more constructive set of guidelines. There is no need for any student to become injured or to die in college. Abolish hazing.

3e Type the clean copy according to format standards.

Before typing your final draft, be sure you understand the format your instructor requires. If a title page is asked for, what information should appear on it? How is that information to be arranged on *rev*   the page? If your paper involved research, how does the instructor want the footnotes and bibliography handled? What quality of paper is acceptable? Is your typewriter ribbon still dark? All these little things reflect the fact that you are a careful writer, aware of your audience.

STANDARD TYPING GUIDELINES

1. Type all papers unless told otherwise. When handwriting is allowed, use neat, legible writing in dark blue or black ink. Give your work a professional appearance.

2. Use standard typing paper of medium weight. Don't use expensive, heavyweight paper, onion-skin paper, or easy-to-erase paper. Type on one side of the paper only.

3. Do not attempt to erase or blot out errors. Learn to use correction liquid or tape to cover errors.

4. Type double-spaced. Double-space everything, even indented quotations and footnotes, but triple space above and below indented quotations. (See "Punctuation.")

5. Use a one-inch margin on all four sides. If your machine has no indicator for the bottom margin, mark your paper with a light pencil dot one inch from the bottom.

6. Title pages are usually not required for short papers. Unless told otherwise, put your name, the date, the assignment, and other information in the upper right-hand corner of the first page. You may single-space this information.

7. Center the title of your paper one inch from the top of the first page. Capitalize the first and last word and all important words in the title. Don't use quotation marks or underlining for your title.

8. To fasten pages together, use a staple. Don't pin, fold, or tear corners to fasten pages together.

9. Number your pages, starting with page two, in the upper right-hand corner. Do not use "p." or "pg." or "page" or any other label.

10. Indent five spaces for each new paragraph (or set a tab for five). Indent handwritten paragraphs at least half an inch.

11. Avoid dividing words at the ends of lines in typed papers. If you run into the margin, take the entire word to the next line.

12. Make last-minute corrections with a pen. You may make penned-in corrections on clean copy, if there aren't too many of them. (More than two per page is too many.)

3f Proofread the clean copy.

rev

The last stage in the writing process is to proofread the copy you will submit. Check spelling, punctuation, and capitalization to be sure that this final copy reflects your editing changes. Typographical mistakes may not seem serious, but they can make your sentences unclear and may convince your audience that you are not treating your subject and your reader with respect.

Look carefully for material that might have been left out, for transposed letters, for all those mistakes that frequently occur during typing. Pay particular attention if you have had someone else do the typing. Read the paper slowly and repeatedly, sentence by sentence, forcing yourself to look at the paper word by word. There is no such thing as a perfect, unalterable composition. Even at the proofreading stage, continue to follow the revisers' rule: if it *can* be changed for the better, it *should* be.

Prepare and hand in your clean copy. Perfection is the goal, but even very skilled writers may miss an error now and then. If you should find a mistake at the last minute, draw one (and only one) line through the error and write the correction neatly above it in ink.

ACTIVITY 22

Write a composition on some subject you know well. Make prewriting notes, outlines, brainstorming sheets, freewritings; show how you arrived at your rough draft.

Write the first draft, leaving space for revisions. Let some time pass before marking this first draft for revisions.

Type up the *revised* first draft. Again, let some time pass before marking this second draft for revisions.

Type up the revised second draft. Let some time pass before editing this draft.

When you are satisfied with your composition, carefully type and proofread the clean copy.

Grammar

gr   Grammar describes what is possible in a language; grammatical concepts may be used to help you judge what is acceptable or not, understandable or not, in your writing. Revise your sentences so that they conform to the grammar of English. Section 4 discusses parts of speech: words and how they function. Section 5 discusses sentence elements: multiword groups and how they function. Section 6 discusses sentence types.

4 PARTS OF SPEECH

A part of speech identifies the function of a word in a sentence. Every word can be classified as a particular "part" of speech, but many words can be used in more than one way, depending on context. For example, *paint* can be a noun: "The *paint* on this wall is faded," but it can also be a verb: "We will *paint* this wall soon." The eight parts of speech are nouns, pronouns, verbs, adjectives, adverbs, conjunctions, prepositions, and interjections.

4a Noun

A noun indicates a person, place, object, or idea: *person, Lee, Chicago, Maple Avenue, tree, justice, heroism.*

A noun test: any word that can be modified by an article *(a, an, the)* is a noun: *a* person, *the* explosion, *an* apple. (This test also works for proper nouns—specific names—if you imagine a sentence such as *"The Jane* I am talking about is the one who drives a taxi" or *"The America* of today is very different from George Washington's America.")

There are six kinds of nouns:

Abstract nouns name ideas, concepts, intangible qualities (things not observable with the senses). Abstract contrasts with *physical* or *concrete: freedom, justice, religion, courage.*

Concrete nouns name physical objects: *ground, house, mountain, tree.*

Collective nouns name groups of things: *family, company, group, organization.*   *gr*

Mass nouns name things measured by volume, quantity, bulk: *corn, coal, wheat.*

Common nouns name general categories and types of things: *dog, girl, house, man.*

Proper nouns name specific persons. places, and things: *Carole, Chicago, Fido, Easter.*

Some nouns (compound nouns) are formed with more than one word: *jack-in-the-box, high school, Fourth of July.*

4b Pronoun

A pronoun is a word that can "stand for," or take the place of, a noun. "John is a good friend; *he* helps *me* work." There are several kinds of pronouns, classified according to use.

Demonstrative pronouns point back or ahead to a noun: *this, that, these, those.*

We are reading a fine novel; *this* is the story of a great whale.
That is what is making all the noise, our new dog.
Apples, bananas, oranges—*these* are what we are serving.
Those are the students to work with, Marie and Anton.

Indefinite pronouns refer to non-specific individuals, persons or things in general: *all, another, any, anybody, anyone, each, either, everybody, everyone, few, many, most, nobody, none, no one, one, several, some, somebody, someone.*

All will be clear as soon as we talk to the President.
Lowering the tax rates will benefit *everyone.*
Somebody has been removing art supplies from the closet.

Intensive pronouns are used for emphasis; they intensify their antecedents. Intensive pronouns always immediately follow their antecedents: *myself, yourself, herself, himself, itself, ourselves, yourselves, themselves.*

The students *themselves* provided the exam questions.
The Queen *herself* inspected the troops.

I *myself* have visited Paris twice.
We *ourselves* will have to do the work.

Interrogative pronouns indicate questions: *who, whom, whose, what, which.*

Who left the window open?
Whose parka bears the initials "JSM"?
Whom can we ask to clean the garage?

Personal pronouns refer to specific persons or things. Personal pronouns have singular and plural forms:

SINGULAR	PLURAL
I, me	we, us
you	you
he, him, she, her, it	they, them

In the following example, the pronoun *they* substitutes for the names *Tracy* and *Theo.*

Tracy and Theo started a small business; *they* soon made a small profit.

The words to which pronouns refer are called *antecedents*. The antecedent of *they* in the example is the nouns, *Tracy* and *Theo.*

Possessive pronouns are personal pronoun forms used to show possession. Possessive pronouns have singular and plural forms:

SINGULAR	PLURAL
my, mine	our, ours
your, yours	your, yours
his, her, hers, its	their, theirs

The computer belongs to Irene; the machine is *hers.*
The kitten chased *its* tail for several minutes.
My brother and I examined *our* family photographs.

Reflexive pronouns are used to show the subject of a clause acting upon itself: *myself, yourself, herself, himself, itself, ourselves, yourselves, themselves.*

I accidentally shot *myself* in the foot.   *gr*
The dog tangled *itself* in the leash.
The Russians prepared *themselves* for the conference.

Relative pronouns are used to begin dependent clauses: *that,
what, which, whichever, who, whoever, whomever, whose.* The relative pronoun is usually the first word of the clause, but it serves
either as the subject or the object of its own clause.

We all applauded the performer *who sang in Swahili.* [The relative
pronoun is subject of its own clause]
The prize goes to *whoever can dance the longest.* [The relative pronoun is subject of a clause, the entire clause acting as object of a
preposition.]
The Senator was a person *whom we could trust.* [The relative pronoun is object of its own clause.]

ACTIVITY 1

Identify the nouns and pronouns in the following sentences. Underline
and label each noun and pronoun. Be prepared to identify the class of
each noun and pronoun.

1. Despite his illness, Mark still wanted to attend our party.
2. The third secretary neglected his duties, so the ambassador decided to have him relieved.
3. I myself wanted to plant roses, but our neighbors suggested tu-
   lips.
4. When you go to the credit office, what will you say about the
   unpaid loan?
5. They wanted to give themselves a treat, so the brothers skipped
   class and went to see *Star Wars III.*
6. The quest for personal freedom often conflicts with society's conventions.
7. Anyone can see which is the correct choice between Carol and
   the former diving champion.
8. This does not fulfill the assignment, but I admire your effort.
9. The army no longer drafts eighteen-year-olds, but they still must
   register.
10. Each of you must decide for herself.

ACTIVITY 2

Using pronouns, revise each of the following sets of short sentences
into a single, effective sentence. You may combine sentences, add
words, change the form of words, delete words, and make other   **51**

gr changes that will produce effective sentences. Avoid using *and, but, or* to connect ideas.

1. A student can do well. Any student can. The student studies hard enough. The student would do well in school.
2. I lost something. It was a dollar. I lost it yesterday. I lost it in the cafeteria. Someone finds the dollar. Whoever it is can keep it.
3. We cause much misery. We do it to ourselves. It is misery we could avoid. We should have a little foresight.

4c Verb

Every complete sentence must contain a verb. Most verbs indicate action: *shoot, cut, run, strike*. A few (parts of the verb *to be*) indicate that something exists: *is, are*. And a few others indicate appearances or a state of being: *appear, look, seem, feel*. Verbs can also be classified by their function in a sentence: *helping* (sometimes called *auxiliary*), used with a main verb to complete its meaning; *linking*, used to state a condition or state of being and also to connect the subject with its complement. Verbs are also classified according to their relationship to each other in clauses: *main*, the verb of the main, or independent, clause; *secondary*, the verb of a dependent clause (see **5i**).

Action verbs identify the actions of their subjects. Action verbs can be classified according to whether their action is transferred to an object (which receives the action) or their action is not aimed at an object.

Transitive verbs are action verbs whose action is aimed at an object.

The pilot *flew* the plane. [The object answers the question "flew what?" *The plane* is the object of the transitive verb *flew*.]
Congress *passed* a new law. [Congress passed what? *A new law* is the object of the transitive verb *passed*.]

Intransitive verbs are action verbs that do not take an object.

Upon hearing the joke, we suddenly *laughed*.
Slowly the door *opened*.

An object must be a noun or some word or words that can act like a noun. Adverbs and prepositions (see **4e,4g**) are not objects.

> The snake *struck* at the mongoose. [The snake struck what? There is no object in this example; *at the mongoose* is not a noun but a prepositional phrase.]

Some verbs can be either transitive or intransitive, depending on context.

> At noon, Lionel *called* his sister. [transitive]
> At noon, Lionel *called*. [intransitive]

Helping verbs are used to form verb phrases that help a verb express tense or mood (see Glossary). Helping verbs include: *to be (am, is, are, was, were, be, being, been), to do (do, did, does); to have (have, has, had);* and *may, might, must; can, could; shall, should; will, would).*

> Jean *is* going.
> The paper *had been* written. [The verb in this example is *written, had* and *been* are helping verbs.]
> Our canary *does* sing sometimes.
> The work *may have been* done by Shakespeare.
> I *can* appreciate your attitude.
> Let it *be* known to everyone.
> *Will* the school accept independent studies?

Linking verbs do not express action; instead they "link" a subject to a condition or state of being. Linking verbs include forms of the verb *to be, (am, is, are, was, were, be, being, been),* and the forms of *appear, become, feel, grow, keep, look, remain, seem, smell, sound, stay, taste.*

> They *were* tired.
> The man *seemed* troubled.
> We all eventually *grow* old.
> At last she *became* President.
> The album *sounds* scratchy.
> Our coffee *tastes* sour.
> He always *remains* calm.

None of the words following the verbs in these examples is an object; the word *President* above, for example, is not an object; only *gr*   action verbs can take objects. See Predicate Adjectives, **5g,** and Predicate Nouns, **5f.** Some verbs can be linking in one context and transitive in another:

> The dog *feels* wet.
> The doctor *feels* your throat for lumps.

Main verbs are the verbs in main or independent clauses (groups of words that could stand alone, like a sentence). **Secondary verbs** are verbs in dependent clauses (groups of words that cannot stand alone). See **5i.**

> MAIN   SECONDARY
> The Cambodians *fled* when Vietnamese soldiers *invaded* their country.
>   SECONDARY   MAIN
> Until the bell *rings,* the students *must work* on their essays.

Note the difference between a verb and a noun. Nouns, like *explosion,* name an action; but verbs, like *explode,* express the action itself. Nouns can always be modified by one of the articles (*an* explosion, *the* explosion), but verbs cannot (*an* explode?).

A verb test: Any verb can take one of the personal pronouns for a subject: *I* command (but not *I* commandment), *it* destroys (but not *it* destruction), *they* alter (but not *they* alteration). However, you must remember three things: (1) Some words can be more than one part of speech—only context will tell you whether *thought* is a verb (*I* thought) or a noun (*a* thought); some verb forms require auxiliary verbs : I *am* running, she *has* swum, it *will be* snowing; (3) some verb forms (participles, gerunds, infinitives) are used as modifiers or nouns (see **5h**):

> The *laughing* child is happy. [Here the verb form is used as a participle, to describe a noun.]
> *Swimming* is good for you. [Here the verb form is used as a gerund, like a noun.]
> *To win* was his only goal. [Here the verb form is used as an infinitive, like a noun.]

Note a difference between helping verbs and linking verbs. Helping verbs form phrases with other verbs; linking verbs form phrases with adjectives or nouns.

HELPING VERB WITH ACTION VERB

Everyone *will see* the solar eclipse at noon.

LINKING VERB WITH NOUN

Clayton *was captain* of the team. [Use the noun test: *a* captain, *the* captain.]

LINKING VERB WITH ADJECTIVE

Viola *seemed interested* in our work. [Use an adjective test—modify adjectives with adverbs: *really* interested, *very* interested.]

ACTIVITY 3

Underline the verbs in the following sentences. Be prepared to explain whether the verb is main or secondary; transitive or intransitive; helping, being, or linking. Some verbs may have two or three classifications, such as main and action or secondary and transitive.

1. The snake slithered across the hot sand to where the old man had collapsed.
2. The barrel careened noisily down the ramp and seemed to be heading for the open door.
3. The left fielder hit the ball sharply into the hole that had opened up between first and second.
4. Jimbo was devastated after wrecking the car for the second time.
5. John was the director, but he did not look the part.
6. Although tax reform appeared necessary, no one was doing anything about it.
7. Boy George led his group triumphantly onto the stage that had just been erected.
8. Jerry fished all day for bluegills, but he came up empty again.
9. The group asked Penny to make a presentation, and she gladly agreed.
10. The square of the hypotenuse is equal to the sum of the squares of the other two sides.

ACTIVITY 4

Revise each of the following sets of short sentences into a single, effective sentence. You may combine sentences, add words, change the form of words, delete words, and make other changes to produce effective sentences. Avoid using *and, but, or* to string ideas together.

1. It slipped out of my fingers. It was my bowling ball. It crashed across the lanes, six of them. It exploded. It went into a dozen fragments. It was like a bomb.

gr

2. Father raced toward the car. He was roaring. It was like a bear. I backed the car. I did it slowly. It backed toward the oak. It was standing at the end of the driveway.
3. Everyone became ill. They were on the swim team. It happened when we learned something. The pool had been contaminated. It was pesticide.

4d Adjective

Adjectives describe, limit, change, or in some other way modify nouns or pronouns: *young* person, *gold* coin, *healthy* one. Adjectives identify *who, which, what kind,* or *how many.* Other types of adjectives: *articles, demonstrative, indefinite, possessive, predicate.*

Articles *(a, an, the)* identify either a definite or an indefinite person, place, or thing:

The bird escaped from its cage. [A definite bird is indicated.]
A bird escaped from its cage. [An indefinite bird, some bird, is indicated.]
An eagle flew over head. [An indefinite eagle, some eagle, is indicated.]

Demonstrative adjectives *(this, that, these, those)* are demonstrative pronouns used like adjectives:

This lesson is very difficult.
That dog is a pointer.

Indefinite adjectives *(all, another, any, anybody, anyone, each, either, everybody, everyone, few, many, most, neither, nobody, no one, one, several, some, somebody, someone)* are indefinite pronouns used like adjectives:

Some books are meant to be read slowly.
Any questions about Milton will be answered tomorrow.
Each event will be introduced by the announcer.
Every racer must examine his or her vehicle carefully.

Possessive adjectives are possessive pronouns used like adjectives:

His trial will be held in Colorado.
Her job pays $50,000 a year.

Predicate adjectives follow linking verbs and modify the subject of the sentence.

The company was *successful.*
The future will be *bright.*
The jeep is *hers.*

Proper adjectives are adjectives formed from proper nouns.

He is *Irish.*
Haiku is a form of *Japanese* poetry.
Lady Macbeth is a *Shakespearian* character.

4e Adverb

Adverbs modify (describe) adjectives, adverbs, and verbs: *very* pretty, *too* quickly, walk *slowly.* Most (but not all) words ending in *-ly* are adverbs. Adverbs indicate time *(now, then, soon)*, place *(here, there)*, manner *(softly, quickly)*, degree *(frequently, often)*, and reason in phrases and clauses *(for his own good, because he wanted to succeed).*

The orchestra *seldom* played rock music.
Lisa closed her book *quietly.*
Our new car *very easily* fit our garage.
The prisoners ate the food *because they had no choice.*
For his health, my uncle ate garlic raw.
We painted the barn *bright* red.
When the lights went out, we were forced to leave.
Pirates buried treasure *where no one could find it.*

Note the difference between an adjective ending in *-ly* and an adverb:

The clowns were *silly.* [*Silly* is a predicate adjective describing *clowns.*]
The clowns behaved *foolishly.* [*Foolishly* is an adverb describing the verb *behaved.*]

gr

ACTIVITY 5

Underline the adjectives and adverbs in each of the following sentences. Be prepared to give the type of each adjective and the function of each adjective and adverb.

1. Marshall gradually became aware of the young lady's presence.
2. Since the inexperienced doctor had never encountered those symptoms, he gratefully accepted the assistance of the older physician.
3. Laboriously he panted up the final hill, not at all convinced he could finish the marathon.
4. Eyes wide and gleaming, Lindsay reached out carefully to touch the pet raccoon.
5. The many grateful refugees eagerly embraced the woman as she walked through the door of the reception hall.
6. There were only seven volunteers for the time-consuming assignment, and they were reluctant.
7. The garish brochure talked glowingly about golden sunshine, white sands, and blue surf.
8. Because she wanted instant success, Leslie took every shortcut, legitimate or not.
9. Here we go again; John's dragging out the family album.
10. Slowly, carefully, Heidi began to put the shattered pieces of the antique vase back together.

ACTIVITY 6

Revise each of the following sets of short sentences into a single, effective sentence using adjectives and adverbs. You may combine sentences, add words, change the form of words, delete words, and make other changes that will produce effective sentences. Avoid using *and, but,* or *to* string ideas together.

1. An eagle flew. It was a great one. It was golden. It went into the area. It was where we had planted something. It was seedlings. They were pine. They were young.
2. The King was dead. Hamlet was the Prince. He no longer felt young. He no longer felt light-hearted. But he felt melancholy. He felt suspicious.
3. The beer bottles erupted. They erupted in geysers. The geysers were foaming. They were homemade brew. It happened suddenly. It happened unexpectedly. It happened with a pop. the pop was loud.

Conjunctions are connective words. They join clauses, phrases, and words. Types of conjunctions: *coordinate, correlative, subordinate*.

Coordinate conjunctions connect items that have equal structures, such as two or more nouns, two or more phrases, or two or more clauses: *and, but, or, nor, so, for, yet.*

> Mike *and* Jim went to the game.
> Mike went, *but* Jim stayed home.
> Your choice is to go to the game *or* to stay home.

Correlative conjunctions are always used in pairs: *both/and, either/or, neither/nor, not only/but also.*

> *Both* the President *and* the Vice-President spoke to the crowd.
> *Either* put up *or* shut up.
> *Neither* a borrower *nor* a lender be.
> *Not only* the cow *but also* her calf had wandered out of the barn.

Subordinate conjunctions connect items that are unequal in structure, such as independent and dependent clauses:

after	before	until
although	if	when
as	since	whenever
as if	though	where
because	unless	wherever
		while

> *Since* you have had experience with computers, you may explain the lesson.
> The law will pass, *if* that is the voters' will.
> The camera failed to work, *although* it had just been repaired.

4g Preposition

Most prepositions are position words: *in, at, on,* and so forth. A few do not indicate position *(during, except),* and some prepositions can also be used as adverbs. What makes these words prepositions *gr*   instead of adverbs is the presence of an object: in the *well*, at the *house*, on the *table*, during the *war*, except the *girls*. The preposition and its object form a prepositional phrase. Common prepositions include:

aboard	before	in regard to	regardless of
about	behind	inside	since
above	below	in spite of	through
according to	beneath	instead of	throughout
across	beside	into	to
after	between	like	toward
against	beyond	near	under
along	but	next to	underneath
amid	by	of	until
among	concerning	off	unto
around	despite	on	up
as	during	on account of	upon
aside from	except	on behalf of	with
as to	for	out of	within
as well as	from	outside	without
at	in	over	
because of	in front of	past	

4h   Interjection

Interjections are exclamatory words and expressions. *Oh! Help!* An interjection need not be punctuated with an exclamation point.

So! Now we've got you.
Alas! my punishment is too cruel.
Ah, now I see what you mean.

ACTIVITY 7

Identify the part of speech of each word in the following sentences:

1. An old man snored noisily in the night.
2. "Ach!" the captain said afterward, "I had a very bad dream, and it frightened me terribly."
3. Long ago in a galaxy beyond the stars an ancient astronaut asked himself, "Do others exist, somewhere?"

4. Neither those who are ever cool nor those whose hot tempers *sent el*
burn with passion shall be our models.
5. Alas, she walked slowly toward the sea and stepped blindly into
its too tender embrace.

ACTIVITY 8

Revise each of the following sets of short sentences into a single, effective sentence. You may combine sentences, add words, change the form of words, delete words, and make other changes to produce effective sentences. Avoid using *and, but, or* to string ideas together.

1. I said ouch. I stumbled back. I went blindly. I went from the doorway. I had managed to give myself a gash. It was bloody. It was across my forehead.
2. We will have to do something. It will be either one or the other. We will have to shovel out some of this junk. It will be in the morning. We will have to move. It will be to an apartment. It will be bigger.
3. The glasses sat in a row. They were on the porch railing. They were tall. They were crystal. They were filled with ice tea. They were where we could see them. They were glistening in the sun. The sun was hot.

ACTIVITY 9

Write a sentence of your own for each of the eight parts of speech. Underline and label the part of speech your sentence illustrates. You may illustrate more than one at a time, if you wish.

---

5 SENTENCE ELEMENTS

A sentence is a group of words containing a subject and a predicate expressing a complete thought. Besides these two major elements, sentences might contain complements, direct objects, indirect objects, predicate nouns, predicate adjectives, phrases, and clauses. One of the criteria upon which your writing will be judged is the quality of your sentences, their clarity and correctness. Complete, well-written sentences are required in formal writing situations. In order to construct better sentences, in order to revise and *sent el*   improve the quality of your sentences, it is important that you understand the elements of your sentences. This section will discuss sentence elements and their functions.

5a Subject

The subject is the *actor* in sentences expressing action; the subject is usually a noun or pronoun (or some other "nominal," a word or words used like a noun). In most sentences, the subject comes first (before the predicate). The *simple subject* is a single word: "The wooden *raft* was floating on the river." The *complete* subject is the simple subject plus all modifiers attached to it: "*The wooden raft* was floating on the river."

SIMPLE SUBJECT
The young *officers* read their orders.
A bright green little *snake* darted among the leaves.
The two old *men* who made the pies received blue ribbons.

COMPLETE SUBJECT
The young officers read their orders.
A bright green little snake darted among the leaves.
The two old men who made the pies received blue ribbons.

The subject of a sentence can be a "nominal," a word or group of words used like a noun.

NOMINAL SUBJECT
Swimming is good for you.
At the beach is where we held the picnic.
Whoever broke the window must pay for it.

The subject of a sentence need not come first.

Alas, *Peter* had spent everything.
In the evenings, *we* watched television.
After the closing of the store, *the clerks* checked their receipts.

Some sentences have an *understood subject:* "Shut the door quietly, please." The sentence means: "[*You*] shut the door quietly, please."

UNDERSTOOD SUBJECT

Answer the phone. [*You* answer the phone.]
Take the kettle off the stove. [*You* take the kettle off the stove.]
Before leaving the house, turn off the lights. [Before leaving the house, *you* turn off the lights.]

5b Predicate

The predicate makes a statement about the subject. The *simple predicate* is the main verb (with its helping verbs): "The wooden raft *was floating* on the river." The *complete predicate* is the main verb and any modifiers or complements attached to it. "The wooden raft *was floating on the river.*"

SIMPLE PREDICATE

We *opened* the door cautiously.
The marines *landed* on the beach at dawn.
Congress *sent* a message to the President.

COMPLETE PREDICATE

We *opened the door cautiously.*
The marines *landed on the beach at dawn.*
Congress *sent a message to the President.*

A sentence can have more than one verb: "The wooden raft *was floating* on the river that *ran* by our house." In such sentences, the simple predicate is the *main* verb: *was floating* is the main verb because it states what the raft was doing; *ran* is a secondary verb in a modifying clause describing the river. The main verb occurs in the part of the sentence that could stand by itself (called an independent clause, **5i**):

SIMPLE PREDICATE	SECONDARY VERB

We *saw* the men who *built* the bridge. [*We saw the men* could stand alone.]
My sister *bought* the car that *cost* the least. [*My sister bought the car* could stand alone.]
The play *closed* after the actor *died.* [*The play closed* could stand alone.]

63

sent el   Both predicates and subjects can be *compound*. Compound. elements are joined by conjunctions.

COMPOUND SUBJECT

Boys, girls, and *adults* were all playing baseball together.
Neither the people on the hill nor *those waiting below* could see the plane circling the woods.

COMPOUND PREDICATE

The little dog *danced* and *did tricks*.
The President *addressed the nation* but *explained very little about his new economic policy.*

ACTIVITY 10

Identify the subject and the predicate in each of these sentences. Draw one line under the subject and two lines under the predicate. Be prepared to distinguish between simple and complete subject and between simple and complete predicate.

1. The glowing ball of fire appeared suddenly in the eastern sky.
2. Mr. Lewelyn was confused by the barrage of questions fired at him by the panel concerning what he had seen while working at the plant.
3. Running five miles every morning will certainly keep you in shape.
4. To everyone's amazement, the party had been going on since Friday and showed no signs of slowing down.
5. The weatherbeaten miner carefully built a small fire using twigs and leaves for fuel.
6. Calmly, the manager of the large department store carefully explained to her staff what to expect.
7. A most important decision was made about the timing of the grape harvest.
8. The old oak near the farmhouse had been struck repeatedly by lightning.
9. The team's new quarterback was inconsolable after the loss.
10. Because she was not a union member, the carpenter was not allowed to work on the new building project.

ACTIVITY 11

Revise each of the following sets of short sentences into a single, effective sentence. You may combine sentences, add words, change the form of words, delete words, and make other changes that will produce effective sentences. Avoid using *and, but, or* to string ideas together.

1. Something shot out of the shadows. It was a power boat. It was sleek. The shadows were under the willows. The boat sliced across the lake. It went in an arc. The arc was clean. It was curving.
2. Whoever it was would claim it. It was the treasure. It belonged to the pirate. Someone must first find it. Someone must bring it to the surface. It was the sunken chest.
3. The children were on our block. They had friends from the next street. They conspired to meet somewhere. It was in our backyard. They put on a carnival. It was of unimaginable noise and confusion.

5c Complement

A complement "completes" the sense of the verb. A complement may be a direct object, an indirect object, a predicate noun, or a predicate adjective: The President is *unusually busy today*.

5d Direct object

Some verbs (called *transitive*) take objects: the object "receives" the action of the verb. For example: "The arrow hit *the target*." The direct object is usually a noun or a noun substitute such as a pronoun, gerund, or noun clause. The direct object answers the question "who" or "what" after the verb; for example:

> We saw the *President* on television. [The direct object here is the noun *President*.]
> We saw *him* on television. [The pronoun *him* is the direct object.]
> We all enjoy *swimming* at the beach. [The gerund *swimming* is the direct object.]
> I understand *what you mean*. [*What you mean*, a noun clause, is the direct object.]

Not all verbs take objects. Some verbs are "intransitive," meaning they do not express an action toward an object. See **4c**.

TRANSITIVE (OBJECT PRESENT)
The two boys fought each other. [The verb *fought* is transitive here; its object is *each other*.]

sent el   INTRANSITIVE (NO OBJECT PRESENT)
The two boys fought. [The verb *fought* is intransitive here; there is no object to receive the action.]

5e Indirect object

Sometimes a verb may have two objects, one which receives the action of the verb and a second *to whom* or *for whom* the action is done. For example: "We sent him a letter." In this sentence, the *letter* is the thing actually sent—the letter receives the action of the verb and is the direct object. But note that the letter was sent "to him": *him* is the indirect object. Note the same sentence with a prepositional phrase instead of an indirect object: "We sent a letter *to him.*"

INDIRECT   DIRECT
OBJECT   OBJECT
John's mother bought   *him*   a new *calculator*.

INDIRECT   DIRECT
OBJECT   OBJECT
We all gave *Annella* a surprise *party*.

INDIRECT DIRECT
OBJECT OBJECT
We finally found   *Ted*   a *date* for the dance.

5f Predicate noun

After linking verbs (that do not express action, and cannot therefore take objects), nouns in the object position are called *predicate nouns:* "The senator was *a powerful speaker*." Predicate nouns are sometimes called *predicate nominatives*.

Note the difference between predicate noun and direct object:

PREDICATE NOUN	DIRECT OBJECT
John is a Senator.	John saw a Senator.
Vivian became an ambassador.	Vivian married an ambassador.
Studying is work.	Studying precedes work.

5g Predicate adjective

After linking verbs, adjectives that refer to the subject are called *predicate adjectives*.

All the students were *terrified*.
After dinner we became *ill*.
The ground feels *moist*.

Because *predicate adjectives* and *predicate nouns* refer to the *subject* of a linking verb, they are somtimes called *subjective complements*.

ACTIVITY 12

Identify the complements in the following sentences. Underline and label direct object, indirect object, predicate noun or predicate adjective.

1. Give me a minute and you will have the results.
2. The hairdresser was delighted about the trend to punk styles.
3. Jane gave herself plenty of time before trying the shot.
4. Although Norm was a teacher, he voted against the millage.
5. Tell me, Doctor Codell, how can you be so knowledgeable in so many areas?
6. Slowly, she sipped her coffee and became more and more pensive.
7. Swallows and gulls were the only ones he could name.
8. Arcade games gave him pleasure despite their cost.
9. The film was fantastic, but Marge did not see it.
10. The breeze swept the aroma of freshly mown grass through the windows of the school.

ACTIVITY 13

Revise each of the following sets of short sentences into a single, effective sentence. You may combine sentences, add words, change the form of words, delete words, and make other changes that will produce effective sentences. Avoid using *and, but, or* to string ideas together.

1. I was pulling on the rod. I did it fiercely. I brought up something. I did it slowly. It was a boot. It was an inner tube. It was part of a 1947 Desoto.

sent el

2. Matlock once sent us something. He was my great uncle. It was a tiki. It was old. It was wooden. He had found it somewhere. It was on his travels somewhere. It was to the islands.
3. There was the box. It was mysterious. It was cardboard. It contained something. It was a dollar's worth of something. It was assorted nails and tacks. It was a feather boa. The boa was long. It was from the twenties.

5h Phrase

Any group of words acting as a unit can be called a *phrase* so long as the group lacks either a subject or a predicate. There are several kinds of phrases: *absolute*, a noun followed by a modifier; *prepositional*, a preposition followed by its object; *verb*, a main verb and its auxiliary verbs; *verbal*, a gerund, infinitive, or participle and the words associated with it.

Absolute phrases modify entire clauses instead of individual words. Absolutes are created by deleting the main verb or the helping verb of a simple sentence, or by substituting the present participle for the main verb:

His job completed, Stacy left.
They remained seated, *the bomb ticking loudly*.
The children finally asleep, she sat down to rest.

Prepositional phrases are used like adverbs and adjectives; occasionally they may be used like nouns. The prepositional phrase is composed of a preposition and its object.

After the interview, the mayor relaxed.
My father was a Colonel *during the last war*.
Where you should put your money is *in the bank*.

Verb phrases are formed by verbs and their helping verbs.

The shot *had been fired*.
We *did see* him just a moment ago.

Verbal phrases are verb forms and their complements used like nouns or modifiers. Verbal phrases include gerunds, participles, and infinitives.

Gerunds are verbal phrases used like nouns. A gerund is the *sent el* present participle of a verb. The gerund may have modifiers or, because it is a verb, objects.

Swimming in the ocean takes courage.
Jogging is good for you.
The best part of the show was *Jason's singing*.
Her closing the drapes was a signal to call the police.

Infinitives are formed with the word *to* and a verb: *to go, to talk, to think*. An infinitive may have its own complement. The infinitive phrase functions like a noun or a modifier.

To be champion was her goal.
I need a place *to park my car*.
It is time *to go*.

Participles are used like adjectives and are formed with the past or the present participle of a verb. Participial phrases may have modifiers and objects.

Cracked in many places, the vase was completely worthless.
The whistling wind rattled the eaves of the house.

5i Clause

A clause is a group of words containing a subject and a verb. A simple sentence is an *independent clause;* it can stand alone. Clause types: *independent* (also called *main* or *base*) and *dependent* (also called *subordinate*)—*adjective, adverb,* and *noun clause*. Dependent clauses have subjects and verbs, but are not complete sentences because they do not express a complete thought.

An independent clause has a subject and a verb; every complete sentence is an independent clause. Each of the following groups of words is an independent clause, and therefore a sentence, because it contains a subject and a verb and makes a complete statement:

       SUBJECT VERB
The great   *ship*   *sailed* out to sea.

SUBJECT VERB
  Dogs *bark*.

sent el

VERB
Stop! [*You*, although unexpressed, is the subject of this sentence.]

Each of the following groups of words is a dependent clause because it contains a subject and verb but does not make a completed statement:

       SUBJECT   VERB
Where   *we*   *were going* . . .

     SUBJECT   VERB
That   *she*   *can swim* . . .

            SUBJECT   VERB
Until the *problem is solved* . . .

Adjective clauses are dependent clauses used like adjectives, to modify nouns and pronouns and other nominals. Adjective clauses begin with relative pronouns (and are therefore sometimes called relative clauses) or the subordinators *when, where,* or *why.* See **4b**.

We found a man *who would cut the grass for us.*
One poem *that you should read* is "Ozymandias."
Now is the time *when we must all work together.*
Is there any reason *why their bus is late?*
It was she *whose money we had spent.*

Writers frequently omit the relative pronoun of an adjective clause: The card *we gave to John* was inexpensive.

Adverb clauses are dependent clauses used like adverbs. In addition to time, place, manner, and degree (see *Adverb*), adverb clauses can be used to show cause, comparison, concession, condition, and purpose. Adverb clauses begin with subordinate conjunctions. See **4f**.

When the rain stops, we can go.
We are going to the show *after we finish dinner.*
Since you have the car, you get to pick our destination.
This is tougher *than it looks.*
Although they had very little, they shared half their food.
Unless you object, we will stay the weekend.

Noun clauses are dependent clauses used like nouns, as subjects,

sent el

objects, and predicate nouns. Noun clauses begin with relative pronouns or the subordinators *when, where, why.* See **4b**.

NOUN CLAUSE AS SUBJECT
Why we had to go to war was never explained.

NOUN CLAUSE AS OBJECT
We gave them *what they wanted*.

NOUN CLAUSE AS PREDICATE NOUN
She was not *whom we expected*.

ACTIVITY 14

Identify the type of phrases and clauses italicized in the following sentences.

1. Near the clearing by the stream *Jack built the blind.*
2. *Running quickly around the corner,* the small boy ducked into the sports shop, *which was luckily still open.*
3. Since recent studies have determined *that cigarette smoking is even more harmful than previously believed,* the Surgeon General wants to word the warnings on cigarette packs and in print advertisements more strongly.
4. That the seals are endangered seems not to bother those *who hunt them.*
5. The students *of his class* were chosen first because they had studied that period *of history* most closely.
6. *Hitting a golf ball 250 yards* requires skill in timing and coordination.
7. In the meantime, read the next two chapters *because they will be on the exam.*
8. *To want to do well* is not enough.
9. Although home computers are enthusiastically endorsed by many, *some people question their effects on family relationships.*
10. Having spent all week in the museum, Phyllis had a good idea of *where the different schools of paintings were hung.*

ACTIVITY 15

Identify the sentence elements in the following sentences.

1. The old couple bought Ellen flowers for her birthday.
2. After the ceremony the mothers and fathers were too tired for the party.

3. When the noise began, all the children ran home and screamed, "Run!"
4. Whoever broke the window should confess.
5. Anyone who smokes should be aware of the dangers.

ACTIVITY 16

Identify the italicized sentence element in each of the following sentences.

1. The *citizens* of a democracy must participate in government.
2. Each night the students *spent* hours in the library.
3. Nancy's computer was extremely *fast*.
4. Iggy's mother sent *him* ten dollars for his birthday.
5. The most popular film was *Indiana Jones*.
6. They were required to buy a *diskette* for the English class.
7. She wanted to know *what was required*.
8. *To be a biophysicist* was Lorna's only ambition.
9. Just before the game, half the team became *ill*.
10. As soon as the car *stopped*, Wally and Janelle *jumped* onto the roof.

ACTIVITY 17

Revise each of the following sets of short sentences into a single, effective sentence. You may combine sentences, add words, change the form of words, delete words, and make other changes that will produce effective sentences. Avoid using *and, but, or* to string ideas together.

1. It was on the morning. It was the second day. It was in July. We heard the sounds. They were choked. Someone was gargling. It was in the closet. The closet was little. It was behind the kitchen. The kitchen was in Granny's cabin. It was little. It was in the woods.
2. They were disturbed by the rumors. The rumors were about war. It was impending. The students wondered. Who would remain in school? Who would join the army?
3. He was to bake it. It was a lemon pie. It would win a ribbon. The ribbon was blue. Doc Cassaway knew something. He would need something. It was help. Whatever he could get.

ACTIVITY 18

Write ten sentences of your own demonstrating subject, predicate, direct object, indirect object, predicate noun, predicate adjective, phrase, and clause. Underline and label the sentence elements. Each of your sentences may illustrate more than one sentence element, if you like.

6 SENTENCE TYPES

Sentences can be classified on the basis of their purpose: *declarative, interrogative, imperative, exclamatory*. Sentences can also be categorized according to their structure: *simple, compound, complex,* and *compound/complex*. One of the marks of experienced writers is their ability to use a variety of sentences, to create various structures in their sentences in order to avoid falling into the pattern of writing only the simplest kinds of sentences. It is important, therefore, that you understand and be able to use all the variations of sentences to improve your writing. This understanding becomes particularly helpful during the revising stage when you examine your sentences for repetitious patterns.

6a Sentence purpose

Declarative sentences make statements; they are used to express facts, opinions, propositions. The declarative sentence conveys information to readers.

It is twelve o'clock.
London is the capital of England.
I like pizza.
Germany lost the war because Hitler was insane.

Interrogative sentences ask questions; they are used to request information or permission or to express interest or affirmation. An interrogative sentence ends with a question mark. (Any sentence ending with a question mark is interrogative.)

How much does an Epson QX–10 computer cost?
May I go to the show after dinner?
Do you enjoy needle work?
You bought that scarf at the rummage sale, right?
The apple trees are in full bloom?

73

sent
type

Imperative sentences state commands or requests; they are used to give orders or directions.

> Put your books on the shelf.
> Turn left here.
> Please send me a dozen brochures.

Exclamatory sentences indicate strong feelings; they are used to express surprise, anger, fear, joy, and other emotions. Exclamatory sentences end with an exclamation mark. (Any sentence ending with an exclamation mark is exclamatory.)

> The bear is out of its cage!
> Don't you ever speak to me that way again!
> Five people will never fit into that car!

6b Sentence structure

A simple sentence is one independent clause. "Simple" need not refer to shortness or simplicity of structure. For example, the following are simple sentences:

> Birds sing.
> The Italian government cracked down on underworld gangsters.
> The members of the House of Representatives had undertaken a serious proposal, a matter of great urgency, and something of a unique challenge.

These sentences are classed as simple because each contains only one subject and one main verb. Note that there may be compound elements in a simple sentence. Contrast these simple sentences with the compound and complex sentences below.

A compound sentence contains at least two independent clauses, but no dependent clauses. The independent clauses of a compound sentence must be joined with a comma and a coordinate conjunction

or with a semicolon or colon.

The bread was stale, and the tea was weak.
At eight o'clock the whistle blew shrilly, but the men still refused to go down into the mine.
We must never fear to speak against tyranny, for tyrants use fear as a weapon.
The night grew suddenly intimidating; smokey clouds drifted down to the trees.

The two independent clauses of a compound sentence could be written as separate sentences.

AS COMPOUND SENTENCE

We called Kitty for hours, but she refused to answer.

AS SEPARATE SENTENCES

We called Kitty for hours. She refused to answer.

Independent clauses may also be joined by a semicolon and a conjunctive adverb (see Glossary).

We filled up the tank; however, we soon ran out of gas.
Be sure to wear high boots in the woods; otherwise, you may tempt a snake to bite you.
Otto was only five foot three; nevertheless, he was the star of the basketball team.

A complex sentence contains one independent clause and at least one dependent clause. All clauses must have a subject and a verb, but only the independent clause could be written as a separate sentence:

INDEPENDENT CLAUSE
The men began coming up out of the mine after the whistle blew.
Until Castro changes his tactics, *Cuba must be watched carefully.*
Although Miss Emily was poor, *she remained proud.*

A compound-complex sentence contains two (or more) independent clauses, and one (or more) dependent clauses.

DEPENDENT CLAUSE   INDEPENDENT CLAUSE
After the whistle blew, the men began coming up, and
     INDEPENDENT CLAUSE
their wives hurried to meet them.

The Prime Minister met with her cabinet, and *together they worked out a plan while the nation waited.*

ACTIVITY 19

Identify the following sentences as simple, compound, complex, or compound-complex.

1. The old B-52 bomber is too slow for today's rockets.
2. Since all the students have gone home, the university will close the dormitories for the summer.
3. They had sent spies into Tunisia before, but none of them ever came back.
4. When the danger was noticed, they opened all the safety valves, and the temperature gauges slowly returned to normal.
5. Long into the night the enemy guns pounded away at the forward lines, the supply depot, and our western gun emplacements.

ACTIVITY 20

Revise each of the following sets of short sentences into a single, effective sentence. You may combine sentences, add words, change the form of words, delete words, and make other changes that will produce effective sentences. Avoid using *and, but, or* to string ideas together.

1. We bought a goat for Sarah. It was young. We bought it after she broke her arm. It was really a pet. But it grew older. As it did so it became obnoxious. It was so obnoxious that we considered something. We were serious. We would butcher it.
2. The china was fancy. Aunt Vivian's silver was an heirloom. They were laid out for company. However, Bootsy jumped up on the table. It was at the last minute. She shed something everywhere. It was cat hairs.
3. The tank was faster than any other armored vehicle. Its firing system was more effective than any other mobile weapon. The system was computer controlled. The government refused to buy the tank. It was too heavy. It could not cross bridges.

ACTIVITY 21

Write two sentences of your own for each of the sentence types above. Write two simple sentences, two compound sentences, two complex sentences, and two compound-complex sentences.

ACTIVITY 22

Write a short composition of three or four paragraphs about an experience from your life. Assume you are writing to someone in a foreign country who will enjoy your use of language as well as the information in your paragraphs. Revise for appropriate grammar; create effective sentences.

Sentence Errors

frag   Your writing will be judged on how effectively and how correctly you construct your sentences. Readers expect you to write complete, accurately punctuated sentences. The parts of a sentence must be consistent with each other. Subjects and verbs must agree in number. Pronouns must match their antecedents in number, must be in the appropriate case, and must make clear reference for your reader. Verb forms must be appropriate for their context. Adjectives and adverbs must be used carefully. Revise your writing to eliminate sentence errors.

7 SENTENCE FRAGMENTS

Formal writing requires complete sentences. A sentence fragment is incomplete; the writer has written only a "fragment" of a sentence. Make sure that each of your sentences has a subject and a verb and can stand alone as an expression of an idea. This is a general guideline for all sentences except those deliberately written as fragments for special effect. Revise fragments to form complete sentences.

Though fragments are most often punctuation errors (see **26a**), they can sometimes be the result of sentence length. In a long sentence the writer may accidentally omit a word:

INCOMPLETE

The long line of gray ships passing across the horizon on the way to a rendezvous somewhere at sea with a carrier task force and the reserve squadron of the Pacific fleet.

REVISED

The long line of gray ships *was* passing across the horizon on the way to a rendezvous somewhere at sea with a carrier task force and the reserve squadron of the Pacific fleet.

When sentences are grammatically complete, they will make sense, even out of context, and this is the test for completeness: sentences must sound complete and make sense *by themselves*, without the context of other sentences. You can use this fact to test your sentences for completeness. Read each sentence aloud by itself. If you have any doubts about the completeness of a sentence, read it aloud to a friend. For example, read each of these sentences aloud, one at a time.

> Sesu was overcome with curiosity about the great snake his brother had brought home in the basket. Although he knew such snakes could be very dangerous. The scratches and swishes coming from the basket as the snake moved were too exciting to ignore.

In the context of other sentences, the fragment may temporarily seem to make sense. However, when read aloud by itself, the fragment sounds incomplete: "Although he knew such snakes could be very dangerous." Clearly these words are only part of a sentence; they must be connected either to the preceding sentence or the following one:

> Sesu was overcome with curiosity about the great snake his brother had brought home in the basket, although he knew such snakes could be very dangerous.

> Although he knew such snakes could be very dangerous, the scratches and swishes coming from the basket as the snake moved were too exciting to ignore.

7a Avoid punctuating parts of sentences as complete thoughts.

Prepositional phrases should not be split off from the words they modify. (4g.)

PREPOSITIONAL PHRASE FRAGMENTS
We all stood quietly. *In the shadow of the old oak.*
The children played out in the yard. *Without a care in the world.*

REVISIONS
We all stood quietly in the shadow of the old oak.
The children played out in the yard without a care in the world.

Verbal phrases (gerund, infinitive, and participle phrases) should not be split off from the words they modify. (5h.)

79

SENTENCE FRAGMENTS

VERBAL PHRASE FRAGMENTS

Citizens have a major responsibility. *Voting in each election.* (See gerund, **5h.**)
The troops had been sent to Grenada. *To rescue American medical students.* (See infinitive, **5g.**)
Lenore created quite a stir. *Wearing a scarlet cape.* (See participle, **5g.**)
The admiral stared out over the water. *The light beginning to fade.* (See absolute, **5g.**)

REVISIONS

Citizens have a major responsibility: voting in each election.
The troops had been sent to Grenada to rescue American medical students.
Lenore created quite a stir wearing a scarlet cape.
The admiral stared out over the water, the light beginning to fade.

Dependent clauses should not be written as fragments. (5i.)

DEPENDENT CLAUSE FRAGMENT

Bankruptcy forced the closing of the newspaper. *Which had been published for ninety years.* (See adjective clause, **5i.**)
Since I have been taking this class. My knowledge of physics has increased one hundred percent. (See adverb clause, **5i.**)
Given the cost overruns, it is no wonder. *That the missile is expensive.* (See noun clause, **5i.**)

REVISIONS

Bankruptcy forced the closing of the newspaper. It had been published for ninety years. (The fragment is revised by writing the second clause as a complete sentence.)
Since I have been taking this class, my knowledge of physics has increased one hundred percent. (The fragment is revised with punctuation.)
Given the cost overruns, it is no wonder that the missile is expensive.

Appositives should not be split off from the words they identify.
An appositive renames or re-identifies a preceding word. (21c.)

APPOSITIVE FRAGMENTS

Before the judge and jury he stood with his head down. *The defendant.*
Aunt Katerina was an angel of gentleness and strength. *A proud Dutch woman capable of rearing thirteen children.*

Young Sebastian was driven by some inner demon. *His raging passion for order.* *frag*

REVISIONS

Before the judge and jury he, the defendant, stood with his head down. [The appositive is inserted into the preceding sentence and set off with punctuation.]

Before the judge and jury he stood with his head down, the defendant. [The appositive is attached at the end of the preceding sentence with punctuation.]

Aunt Katerina was an angel of gentleness and strength, a proud Dutch woman capable of rearing thirteen children. [The appositive is attached to its sentence with punctuation.]

Aunt Katerina was an angel of gentleness and strength. She was a proud Dutch woman capable of rearing thirteen children. [The appositive is revised into a complete sentence with its own subject and verb.]

Young Sebastian was driven by some inner demon—his raging passion for order. [The appositive is joined to its sentence with punctuation.]

Young Sebastian was driven by his raging passion for order, his inner demon. [The appositive is revised into an independent clause.]

Other word groups should not be written as fragments.

VERB PHRASE FRAGMENTS

The author wanted to work with a photographer. *Searching for the best one available.*

We had plans for a gala night at the school. *Would have been the biggest party ever!*

REVISIONS

The author wanted to work with a photographer. She searched for the best one available. [The verb phrase is revised by writing the fragment as a complete sentence.]

We had plans for a gala night at the school. It would have been the biggest party ever! (The verb phrase is revised into a complete sentence.)

We had plans for a gala night at the school; it would have been the biggest party ever. (The verb phrase is revised into a complete sentence and joined to the preceding sentence with punctuation.)

We had plans for a gala night at the school, the biggest party ever. [The verb phrase is revised to an appositive and attached to the preceding sentence with punctuation.]

We had plans for a gala night, the biggest party ever, at the school! **81**

frag

[The verb phrase is revised to an appositive and embedded in the preceding sentence.]
We had plans for the biggest party ever, a gala night at the school. [The verb phrase becomes the independent clause.]

COMPOUND PREDICATE FRAGMENTS

The snowblower picked up the snow. *And kicked it out through its nozzle.* [The predicate is composed of the two verbs *picked up* and *kicked.*]
The magician created many illusions. *And astounded the audience.*
They sent all the packages by registered mail. *But got them back marked "Undeliverable."*

REVISIONS

The snowblower picked up the snow and kicked it out through its nozzle. [The predicate is revised by connecting the fragment to the independent clause.]
The magician created many illusions and astounded the crowd. [The predicate is revised by connecting the fragment to the independent clause.]
They sent all the packages by registered mail but got them back marked "Undeliverable." [The fragment is attached to its sentence.]
They sent all the packages by registered mail. But they got them back marked "Undeliverable." [The fragment is revised by changing the predicate into an independent clause.]
All the packages they had sent by registered mail were returned marked "Undeliverable." [The fragment becomes the main verb of the revised sentence.]

COMPOUND COMPLEMENT FRAGMENTS

Naturally the suspicion fell on Butch Lashwell. *And his younger bother, Otto.* [The fragment is part of a compound object. See **5d.**)
At the end of the election, Oona had become president. *And secretary too!* [The fragment is part of a compound predicate noun. See **5f.**]
Bettina knew herself to be clever. *And not at all shy with strangers.* [The fragment is a part of a compound predicate adjective. See **5g.**]

REVISIONS

Naturally the suspicion fell on Butch Lashwell and his younger brother, Otto.
At the end of the election, Oona had become president and secretary too!

Bettina knew herself to be clever and not at all shy with strangers.

frag

ACTIVITY 1

Revise the following sentences; turn sentence fragments into complete sentences. Supply needed punctuation, change the wording, or supply additional words.

1. The clouds assume the faces of hermits or of nuns or sometimes look like sad dog acts. Hurrying off into the wings over the horizon.
2. Large pieces of broken cement falling from the medieval fretwork high above the entranceway where the King would soon make his appearance.
3. After struggling with it for hours, we finally gave the bolt a yank. And pulled it free.
4. Unless Congress can find some way to cut spending on social programs like Medicare and Aid to Dependent Children. The budget deficits will continue to escalate.
5. Another scene in *The Gold Rush*, which was invented on the same principle as the boot dinner, the one where the big gold miner, half crazed with hunger, suddenly sees Charlie as a fowl and tries to catch him and eat him.
6. The old engine strained mightily. Climbed slowly up the grade past the old train station. Chuffing like an overweight athlete in an endurance test.
7. From the magic wish catalog we each were allowed to select a gift for ourselves. And some small gift to be used as a present for a family member of our choice.
8. The youngsters on the team were exhausted from exertion. Too tired even to take showers and go home.
9. During prohibition, a large number of respectable, conservative Americans dutifully broke the law. In defense of what they regarded as an inalienable human right.
10. Alfred was brought in. A frail young fellow, delicate, two wings fluttering behind his pale-blue shoulders, rippling with rosy light like two doves playing in heaven.

ACTIVITY 2

Read the following paragraph carefully. Test each sentence by reading it aloud by itself. Revise any fragments with punctuation or by changing wording. You may revise any way you like as long as you do not produce any awkward sentences nor leave any fragments punctuated as sentences.

```
   Touch typing is an important skill. For those who
plan to be writers. Although you may not intend to
```

frag

become a professional writer. You will probably need to
type your papers in school. And perhaps in your work
after you graduate. That you will have some experience
with a keyboard. Is almost certain. Nearly all students
today will learn to use computers. Whose keyboards are
very similar to a typewriter's. Unless your situation is
very unusual. You will almost certainly do some typing.
Or keyboarding. In your life. Therefore touch typing can
be very helpful to you. Looking at the keys while
typing. Slows down anyone. Even skilled typists. It is
worth the time it takes. To teach your fingers to do the
work. To strike the right keys automatically without
looking. Soon you will be able to type like a
professional. Without looking at the keys. And without
thinking about what you are typing! Once trained, your
fingers will fly over the keyboard. Faster than you can
say the words. That you are typing. You will have become
a skilled typist. A touch typist.

7b Some fragments are conventional and acceptable.

Fragments can be essential in dialogue that imitates speech:

"Hey, Jefferson!"
"What?"
"Going to the show?"
"What show?"
"At the Twin Cinema."
"Nope. Seen it."

Fragments are used in impressionistic style, emphasizing key
elements of description (but this style is seldom used in formal,
academic writing):

The evening sun slid into the trees. Red now. Glowing with fires of
heaven or hell. The long fingers of pine stretching out. Grasping.
Stroking. Gray bones of a life not quite human fondling the light.

Fragments can be used to ask and answer rhetorical questions:

What is the end of life after all? The grave?
Should we, then, give up hope? Not very likely.

Fragments sometimes appear as transitional expressions:

So much for the background.
Now for an example.
At last, the main event.

A few fragments are familiar expressions:

The bigger the better.
Foiled again!
Happy New Year!
Thank you.
Amen.

Fragments may be used to create heavy emphasis:

Suddenly we all remembered at once. The baby!
We stared at the gauge in disbelief. Out of gas.
He vowed never to return. Nor did he. Not ever.

8 COMMA SPLICES AND FUSED (RUN-ON) SENTENCES

Two errors that require your attention are joining two independent ideas with a comma (a comma fault or comma splice), and fusing two complete ideas together with no punctuation at all (a fused or run-on sentence). Proofread your writing carefully to catch and correct them.

COMMA SPLICES

The kangaroo is the world's largest marsupial, it is native to Australia.
Great-grandfather hid his money in trees and under rocks, no one has ever found any of it.

cs,
fs,
ro

George Washington wore ill-fitting wooden teeth, his lips protruded slightly.

Columbus set out for the new world with his three little ships, they were a gift from Queen Isabella of Spain.

Hemingway wrote several novels, *A Farewell to Arms* is one of his finest.

REVISIONS

The kangaroo is the world's largest marsupial, and it is native to Australia. [The comma splice has been revised by joining the two independent clauses with a comma and the coordinating conjunction *and.*]

Great Grandfather hid his money in trees and under rocks; no one has ever found any of it. [The comma splice has been revised by joining the two independent clauses with a semicolon.]

George Washington wore ill-fitting wooden teeth; hence, his lips protruded slightly. [The comma splice has been revised by joining the two independent clauses with a semicolon and a conjunctive adverb.]

Columbus set out for the new world with his three little ships. They were a gift from Queen Isabella of Spain. [The comma splice has been revised by punctuating the two independent clauses as separate sentences.]

Hemingway wrote *A Farewell to Arms,* one of his finest novels. [The comma splice has been revised by rewording the two independent clauses.]

RUN-ON SENTENCES

It is easy run the machine just turn the dial and hit the button.

Each of the girls was issued a rifle and a uniform they were marines now.

October was always the best month the trees turned brilliant shades of yellow, gold, brown, and red.

Heavy wagons rumbled through the streets under cover of darkness the dead bodies within jostled against each other at every thump.

REVISIONS

It is easy to run the machine; just turn the dial and hit the button. [The run-on has been revised by separating the two sentences with a semicolon.]

Each of the girls was issued a rifle and a uniform: they were marines now. [The run-on has been revised by separating the two independent clauses with a colon. The colon is an option when the second clause complements the first.]

October was always the best month. The trees turned brilliant shades of yellow, gold, brown, and red. [The run-on has been revised by punctuating each independent clause as a separate sentence.]

As the heavy wagons rumbled through the streets under cover of darkness, the dead bodies within jostled against each other at every thump. [The run-on has been revised by rewording the sentence; one of the independent clauses has been reduced to an introductory adverb clause.]

cs, fs, ro.

ACTIVITY 3

Revise the following sentences to eliminate run-on sentences and comma splices.

1. The rain pelted the marathon runners they were wet, cold, and exhausted.
2. After conducting the experiment, the chemist was sure that he had made an important discovery, he immediately phoned one of his colleagues with the results.
3. Michael had laboriously prepared breakfast, no one was interested.
4. He had taken the car to the shop three times to have the automatic choke repaired the mechanics had still not solved the problem.
5. Dogs and little children brought out his tenderness about cats he maintained a different attitude.
6. The whole family conspired to send mother a ticket had been secretly purchased for her trip.
7. Estelle was a habitual liar, indeed, no one trusted her at all.
8. Rutherford, for whom we had worked so hard all night, failed to show up, he had evidently fallen in with a company of carousers.
9. Sadly we set the little cage on the windowsill where the bird was, no one knew.
10. A little brass hook kept the lid up the tissue paper hid the gems.

ACTIVITY 4

Revise the following paragraph carefully. Remove each comma splice or run-on by changing the punctuation or changing the wording of the clauses. You may revise any way you like as long as you do not leave any comma splices or run-on sentences.

Odysseus was a clever man, he was renowned for his wit and ingenuity. It was his plan to fool the Trojans. The plan was to create a giant wooden horse it would be left on the beach. The Trojans, he said, would find the horse, they would assume it had been left as a peace *agr*

offering. The Greek ships sailed away out of sight the
great wooden horse was left behind. Into the city of
Troy, behind their impenetrable walls, the Trojans
pulled the wooden horse, its wooden wheels sank into the
sand from its great weight. Late that night, as the
Trojans slept, the Greeks came out of the horse Odysseus
had hidden them within, they slew all the Trojans.

---

9 SUBJECT-VERB AGREEMENT

Any verb must match its subject in number and person.

The *sound* of the airplane *upsets* the dog.
Everyone wants his or her name to appear.
The *report* of the combined committees *contains* unfavorable information.
He and she, the ones who are not present, *love* to create problems.
[The dependent clause "who are not present" has its own subject,
who, and verb, *are*. See **5i** and **9e**.]

Number refers to singular and plural. Most nouns form their plurals by the addition of *s* or *es: trees, dishes*. Some nouns change spelling to form plurals: *man/men, mouse/mice, child/children*. A few nouns are the same in the singular and plural: *moose/moose*.

Person refers to the speaker (first person), the person or thing spoken to (second person), and the person spoken about (third person). All nouns are third person and require third person verbs.

Verbs add *s* only in the third person *singular*, not in the plural, and only in the *present tense:* a man *runs*, she *has* a job, a student *works*. There are some exceptions to these conventions; for example, the verb *to be* is unusual in English (and most languages): I *am*, you *are*, he, she, or it *is*, we *are*, they *are*, I *was*, you *were*, he, she, or it *was*, they *were*. See Subjunctive, **13a, 13b**, for other exceptions.

Usually your own sense of language will tell you which verb form

agrees with the subject of your sentence, but there are some special *agr*
cases in formal writing you may need to review.

9a In general, two or more subjects joined by *and* take a plural verb.

Football and baseball were his favorite sports.
Athletic ability and keen eyesight are necessary in sports.
Sheila and he are running for office.
You and I were selected.

Some subjects joined by *and* are considered a unit and take a singular verb, units such as *ham and eggs, horse and buggy*. Occasionally *and* indicates a single concept:

My secretary and friend, Jack, *is* going to the conference for me.
[One individual has two roles.]

9b Two or more singular subjects joined by *or* or *nor* take a singular verb.

Nora or Ellen is available to take Mary's place.
Neither *he nor she* has been infected by the flu bug.

Plural subjects joined by *or* or *nor* require a plural verb.

The *soldiers or* their *commanders were* expected to carry the plans.
Neither the *frogs nor* the *snakes are* able to withstand such low temperatures.

When *or, nor, either . . . or, neither . . . nor, not . . . but,* joins a singular subject to a plural subject, the verb should agree with the closer one.

Neither the dog *nor* the cats *were* responsible for the mess in the garage.
Not the daughters *but* the son is taking over the family business.

9c Collective nouns and certain other subjects take singular or plural verbs depending on meaning.

In general, use a singular verb when you refer to the whole group represented by a collective noun, such as *orchestra, class, family.*

The *family holds* its reunion every five years.
The *committee meets* on the first Tuesday of each month.
The *orchestra is* playing a waltz.

To suggest individual action of the members named by a collective noun, however, you may use a plural verb.

The *family want* Andrew to give up hang-gliding.
The *faculty have argued* among themselves for years over the issue of merit pay.

Some concepts may be either singular or plural.

The noise and confusion *was* unbearable. [*Noise and confusion* identifies a single concept: a general uproar.]
The noise and confusion *were* unbearable. [*Noise and confusion* are meant as two different things, so the verb must be plural.]

In general, words like *all, half, any, more, part, none, some* require singular verbs when they refer to singular words, and they require plural verbs when they refer to plural words.

SINGULAR REFERENCE
Half of the team *has* the flu.
All the corn *was bought* on credit.
All was as it should be.

PLURAL REFERENCE
Half the contestants *are* sure they will win.
All of the children *were* excited about the picnic.
All were eager to begin.

Certain subjects, plural in form but singular in meaning, take
90 singular verbs:

Economics is required of all business students.
No *news is* good news.

9d *Each, every, everybody,* and most other (See 4b) indefinite pronouns require singular verbs.

Each of these men *was* given a different order.
Every student *thinks* his or her answer is best.
Everybody is concerned about the environment.
Anybody knows not to play with matches.
Neither of the boys *was* willing to admit the truth.
Either child *is* a good choice for the part.
One of the cars *was* stuck in the soft snow.

9e After *who, which,* or *that,* the verb agrees with the pronoun's antecedent.

A pronoun's antecedent is the word the pronoun identifies. Often the antecedent is the word immediately preceding the pronoun.

```
        PLURAL          PLURAL
        ANTECEDENT      VERB
```
He knows the *entertainers who sing* the old songs.

She signed *contracts that give* her artistic control.

In California, coastal waters, *great white sharks, which attack* more humans every year, have scientists as well as television reporters interested.

She is one of those *women who earn* high salaries. [Compare with: She is *the only one* of those women *who earns* a high salary.]

9f Neither inverted word order nor words that come between the subject and its verb affect agreement.

The *boy* together with his parents *is* going to the camp.
The *books* as well as the author *were* on display in the library.
The President's *decisions* concerning the tax cut *surprise* me.
Are the *ones* we want as expensive as the others?

9g When a sentence begins with *here* or *there* followed by a verb, the subject comes after the verb.

There goes the fox; here come the hounds.
Here are the book, the paper, and the blanket you asked me for.
There were only two of us who could continue.

9h The verb agrees with the subject rather than with a complement. (See 5c-5g.)

The winning *couple was* Ian and Loreen.
Iran and Loreen were the winning couple.

9i Noun clauses as subjects require singular verbs. (See 5i.)

That they still suspected us of cheating on tests seems unfair.
What we must give our laborers is recognition for their effort.
Why there were so many unsold chickens, goats, and pigs was what worried us.

9j Titles as subjects take singular verbs.

The Grapes of Wrath is Steinbeck's greatest novel.
"Three Blind Mice" *has* been a nursery tune for generations.

9k References to numbers as amounts usually take singular verbs.

The number of people at the game *is* ten thousand.
Three plus five *is* eight.
Four minus three *is* one.

Three times five *is* fifteen.
Twenty acres *is* a lot of land for a lawn.
Five dollars and sixty-five cents *is* a ridiculous price
for a pound of flounder.

agr

BUT

A *number* of people *are* coming to dinner tonight.
Three fives *are* fifteen.

ACTIVITY 5

Select the appropriate word in the following sentences.

1. Each of them (was/were) certain the other (was/were) wrong.
2. A trainload of nuclear wastes (is/are) expected through here in twenty-four hours.
3. Neither the library nor the English department (was/were) able to provide any information about the new poet.
4. A number of ideas (is/are) available to those who learn proper research techniques.
5. The horse and buggy (was/were) a main source of transportation in the last century.
6. The young actor in the lead, however, was one of those youths who (is/are) always in a hurry for success.
7. The years dedicated to education (is/are) paid back with interest in later life.
8. It seemed that the students' behavior (was/were) a sign of their uncertainty about world events.
9. A number of issues (remain/remains) to be negotiated.
10. There (was/were) a desk, a cot, and a bookshelf in the room.

ACTIVITY 6

Revise any errors in subject-verb agreement in the following sentences. Be prepared to explain your answers.

1. The size of my father's sweaters are large.
2. Carlos and his brother is going to play music at our party.
3. The present and immediate past president, Karyn, impress everyone with her authority and dignity.
4. Our mare or her foal are sure to be winners.
5. Neither poker nor bridge are allowed at church picnics.
6. Either the students or their professor are responsible for these poor test results.
7. General Motors this year are making an enormous profit at last.

agr

8. Some of the tubes in our old TV set was replaced with new solid state resistors.
9. Each of the students in this room are soon to receive an unexpected reward.
10. We lost one of the new cars that was bought last year.
11. Not only the busses but also the train have stopped running.
12. Our hobby together with our jobs were not enough to use up all the free time in the summer.
13. There in the cellar is grandmother's wedding dress and grandfather's cane.
14. The most enjoyable pair are a trusted friend and a loyal supporter.
15. What you must tell your friends and your parents are the truth and nothing but the truth.

ACTIVITY 7

Revise any errors in subject-verb agreement in the following paragraph.

The war, breaking suddenly and furiously around the people of Cambodia, were ruining that once peaceful nation. Everybody caught in the path of the advancing communists were terrorized by the savagery of the soldiers. Neither any parents nor any child were spared. What the dreaded Khmer Rouge leaders wanted were the total destruction of the society and its culture. The fighting for the control of the cities and the national government were both merciless and mindless. Each of the peasants who managed to escape the horrors have told the same tale. The land as well as the people were reduced to a primitive state. There was, by conservative estimation, three million people massacred. One of Asia's most beautiful countries, whose people produced much of the rice of the continent, were destroyed. What the devastation of Cambodia shows are that none of us are safe from the inhumanity of warfare.

10 PRONOUN CASE AND REFERENCE

Pronoun case shows how pronouns are used in sentences. They can be used as subjects (the subjective case), as objects (the objective case), and they can be used to show possession (the possessive case). Pronoun reference means that a pronoun must agree with its antecedent in number.

If a sentence is written in a "normal" order, that is, subject-verb-object, it is usually easy to determine a pronoun's proper case:

SUBJECT VERB   OBJECT
The *pilot flew* the experimental *shuttles*.

The subject does the acting, the verb names the action, and the object receives the action. If pronouns are substituted for the nouns in the sentence, a subjective pronoun must be chosen for *pilot* and an objective pronoun for *shuttles*.

She flew *them*.

A problem arises when, for variation, the sentence is in atypical order. Then it is necessary to analyze the sentence to determine mentally its normal order so that the proper case of the pronoun can be chosen.

ATYPICAL ORDER
OBJECT SUBJECT
These *flowers we* plant every spring.

NORMAL ORDER
SUBJECT   OBJECT
 We plant these *flowers* every spring.

When the sentence is in normal order, it is easier to see that a pronoun for *flowers* should be in the objective case.

We plant *them*.

case   **PRONOUN CASE**

PERSONAL PRONOUN CASES

	FIRST PERSON		SECOND PERSON		THIRD PERSON	
	SINGULAR	PLURAL	SINGULAR	PLURAL	SINGULAR	PLURAL
SUBJECTIVE	I	we	you	you	he, she, it	they
POSSESSIVE	my	our	your	your	his, her,	their
	mine	ours	yours	yours	hers, its	theirs
OBJECTIVE	me	us	you	you	him, her, it	them

RELATIVE OR INTERROGATIVE PRONOUN CASES

SUBJECTIVE	who	whoever
POSSESSIVE	whose	whosever
OBJECTIVE	whom	whomever

10a Use the subjective case for pronoun subjects and for pronouns that follow forms of the verb *to be.*

PRONOUN SUBJECTS
Gladys and *he* think alike.
We and *they* traveled in Mexico last summer.
We children stayed in our rooms and waited for Santa.

Forms of *to be (am, is, are, was, were, be, being, been)* do not take objects; in formal writing, use *subjective* pronouns after these verbs.

PRONOUNS AFTER *TO BE*
It is *I* [not *me*].
The one they wanted was *she* [not *her*].

10b Use the objective case for pronouns used as direct or indirect objects and after prepositions.

We all saw *him*. [The pronoun *him* is a direct object.]
The President has found *us* a home. [The pronoun *us* is an indirect object.]
There were no secrets *between him and me*. [*Him* and *me* are objects of the preposition *between*.]
Life was hard *for us civilians*, too, during the war.

ACTIVITY 8

Select the appropriate pronoun in the following sentences.

1. The ones they accused were Alice and (I/me).
2. She said the note was intended for (he/him).
3. We all wondered whether (she/her) and her brother would soon leave.
4 The letter said, "Let's keep this just between you and (I/me)."
5. When they announce the winner, do you think it will be (she/her)?

ACTIVITY 9

Write ten sentences of your own, five each showing appropriate use of pronouns used after verbs and after prepositions.

10c Pronouns used as appositives take the same case as the word they refer to.

The job was offered to the two students on the left, *him* and *her*. [Because *him* and *her* refer to the *the two students*, the object of a preposition, the objective case is required for the pronouns.]

The class representatives, Lionel and *she*, have been invited to speak to the faculty. [The pronoun refers to the subject; the subjective case is required.]

10d Before a gerund, pronouns require the possessive case.

His playing the guitar is what started all the trouble.
Everyone applauded *her* reading of the poem.
The doctor was insulted by *our* questioning his bill.

case

Note that a gerund is a verbal used like a noun (see **5h**). However, the following sentence illustrates a participle, a verbal used like an adjective (see **5h**.)

> The commander caught him *wearing* a civilian necktie. [*Him* is the direct object of *caught;* the participial phrase is an adjective describing *him.*]

ACTIVITY 10

Select the appropriate pronoun in each of these sentences. Be prepared to explain your choices.

1. Our teachers, (they/them) who had taught so well, finally became our students.
2. The captain said the enemy might attack (we/us) marines in the night.
3. The audience insisted on (his/him) doing an encore.
4. Margoe said she would divide the cake between Kyle and (I/me).
5. Those two children, (he/him) and (she/her), will say the Pledge of Allegiance.
6. The one who needed it most was (she/her).
7. It seems apparent that my brother and (I/me) are to do the work.
8. No one understood (him/his) leaving the cat out all weekend.
9. The person we need for this job is (he/him).
10. Someone saw the Joneses and (I/me) preparing to leave for Paris last summer.

10e Distinguish between *who* and *whom.*

Whom is rapidly disappearing from oral English. But in formal writing, writers still maintain the distinction between *who* and *whom.*

Who and *whoever* are the subject forms; *whom* and *whomever* are the object forms. The proper case depends on how the pronoun is used in its clause.

Find the subject and the verb in the clause. If there is no other subject, *who* is correct. If there is a subject, *whom* is right.

> *Who* is responsible for this damage? [There is no other subject.]
> *Whom* are you calling? [*You* is the subject; *whom* is correct.]
> To *whom* did you give the gift?

Whom usually follows prepositions, as in the third example. But note a sentence in which a preposition introduces a clause with *whoever* as its subject: *Give this message to **whoever** answers the door.*

To test any *who/whom* question, mentally convert the question into a statement using some other pronoun. If a subject pronoun is appropriate, the sentence requires *who*. If an object pronoun is appropriate, the sentence requires *whom*.

> Who/Whom made that noise? [*He* made that noise. A subject pronoun is required; *who* is appropriate.]
> Who/Whom did you invite? [You did invite *her*. An object pronoun is required; *whom* is appropriate.]

ACTIVITY 11

Explain the pronoun choices in these sentences.

1. *Who* owns this car?
2. *Whom* are they questioning?
3. To *whom* is this addressed?
4. We know *who* opened the wine.
5. *Who* do you think she is?

Reducing complicated sentences to basic ones in your mind can also help you to choose correct pronouns.

WHO/WHOM SENTENCE	ANALYSIS
The soldiers (who/whom) we thought were responsible have been punished.	The soldiers have been punished. We thought *they* were responsible. [A subject pronoun is required; *who* is appropriate.]
The students have identified the girl (who/whom) they want for president.	The students have identified the girl. They want *her* for president. [An object pronoun is required; *whom* is appropriate.]

It is often possible to substitute some other pronoun to determine whether *who* or *whom* is required.

> I see (who/whom) is using the chainsaw. [*I see **he** is using the chainsaw*. A subject pronoun is required: *who*.]

case

ACTIVITY 12

Select the appropriate word in the following sentences. Be prepared to explain your choices.

1. (Who/Whom) is going to win the race?
2. Send the answer to the ones (who/whom) asked for it.
3. (Whoever/Whomever) needs the blood should report to the clinic.
4. They knew (who/whom) they would find in the car.
5. They thought they had observed the one (who/whom) had been doing the damage.
6. The winner will be (whoever/whomever) they select.
7. They tried to find the one (who/whom) they wanted to do the work.
8. (Who/Whom) do you think is going to win?
9. This is the type of person (who/whom) we want for class treasurer.
10. They asked whether she was (who/whom) he said she was.

ACTIVITY 13

Write five sentences of your own illustrating appropriate use of *who, whom, whoever, whomever.*

ACTIVITY 14

Revise the following paragraph to eliminate problems with pronoun case.

In a letter to his sister, a young soldier discussed the war in Vietnam and what it meant to he and his buddies. ''Many of we guys in the corps have talked about what this war means. Who can we turn to? I'm glad my buddies and me think alike on this question, but just between you and I, it's not easy to know who's right. Our Captain says we are helping our South Vietnamese friends, and if there is anyone who should know what he's talking about it's him. Him and me don't get along too well; he's always yelling at my friend Al and I. But I respect his opinions, and I think he respects us, Al and I. Him saying the communists are all wrong doesn't make it so, of course, but us questioning him all the time about what we're doing here doesn't seem to bother

him. The ones who we really hate are whomever started
all this mess in the first place. Who we should attack
and who we should defend—these are tough questions for
we guys.''

PRONOUN REFERENCE

The *antecedent* of a pronoun is the word to which the pronoun
refers. Make sure pronouns agree with their antecedents.

The *car* had *its* undercarriage lowered to within three inches of the
ground. [*Car* is the antecedent of *its*.]
Michael applied for the job, but *he* was turned down. [*Michael* is the
antecedent of *he*.]

10f Collective nouns are singular and require singular pronouns.

Collective nouns identify groups: the *army*, the *band*, the *corporation*, the *faculty*, the *Ford Motor Company*, the *generation*, the *majority*, the *team*, and so on.

The *company* knows what *it* is doing.
The *navy* aims *its* recruitment campaign at high school graduates.

10g In general, use a singular pronoun to refer to an indefinite singular pronoun.

Indefinite pronouns are words such as *one, anyone, everyone, anybody, everybody, each, neither, either.* See **4b**.

Everybody in the Boy Scouts earns *his* merit badges the hard way.
Each house was constructed with *its* own design.
Neither of the girls was allowed to bring *her* pet to camp.
Either of the men could have lifted *himself* over the barricade.

10h Avoid the use of masculine pronouns when *both* sexes are implied.

For example, when a team contains both men and women, you should indicate that fact.

Each player should bring *his* or *her* own towel.

To avoid awkwardness or too much repetition of *his/her*, write in the plural.

Players should bring *their* own towels.

10i Use a plural pronoun to refer to antecedents joined by *and*.

Fred and Velma had a fine time on *their* vaction.

10j Use a singular pronoun to refer to singular antecedents joined by *or* or *nor*.

Was it *Michigan or Illinois* that recalled *its* governor?

When *or* or *nor* joins a singular antecedent to another that is plural, the pronoun should agree with the closer one.

Neither *John nor the twins* had *their* applications in on time.
Neither *the twins nor John* had *his* application in on time.

It is often better to revise such sentences to get rid of the confusing pronoun problem entirely.

John did not have *his* application in on time, nor did the twins.

ACTIVITY 15

Select the appropriate word in the following sentences. Be prepared to explain your choices.

1. Each of the boys had (his/their) gloves autographed by Trammell.
2. The jury chose not to continue (its/their) deliberations.
3. Everybody has to make up (his/their) own mind.
4. Michelle and Kathy both wanted (her/their) own way.
5. Neither the garden nor the orchard showed (its/their) best after the drought.
6. He is one of those athletes who (drives himself/drive themselves) too hard.
7. None of these films has enough excitement in (it/them) to make the price of a ticket worthwhile.
8. Either mom or the kids had to show (her/their) drawings.
9. Was it General Motors or AT&T that had (its/their) sharpest decline in years?
10. The team had (its/their) finest season in a long time.

ACTIVITY 16

Revise the following sentences to eliminate problems in pronoun reference. It may be necessary to change verbs along with pronouns. You may revise any way you like as long as you do not create any awkward sentences or leave any pronoun problems.

1. We have to believe that a big company like Ford Motor knows what they need to do to win new customers.
2. Each of the young men on the drill squad has their own ideas for winning the games.
3. Anyone who wants to get a scholarship should start making their preparations early in high school.
4. Every student should develop his own study habits.
5. A good microcomputer and a big mainframe both do similar work for its users.
6. The faculty senate or the board of regents will announce their new guidelines in April.
7. Neither my brothers nor my sister wanted their rooms painted orange.
8. Either of these cats can catch their own supper, mice.
9. Some of us wanted to have a party, but the majority had their own reasons against it.
10. Everybody in the house had their pajamas on when the fire alarm went off.

ref

10k Avoid using ambiguous pronouns.

When a pronoun seems to refer to more than one antecedent, the reference is ambiguous.

AMBIGUOUS

Don't put your feet into new boots when *they* smell bad.

REVISED

Don't put on new boots when they smell bad.

Don't put on new boots when your feet smell bad.

10l Avoid using vague pronouns.

A pronoun should always refer to a single nearby antecedent—never to an implied idea or a group of words.

VAGUE (ANTECEDENT UNCLEAR)

We have to write Aunt Esther a thank you letter, *which* is not easy for me.

REVISED

We have to write Aunt Esther a thank you letter, but letter writing is not easy for me.
We have to write Aunt Esther a thank you letter, but it is not easy for me to write to her.

VAGUE (ANTECEDENT NOT EXPRESSED)

My Labrador retriever is very intelligent, but she doesn't always show *it*. [*Intelligent* is an adjective and cannot be the antecedent of a pronoun.]

REVISED

My Labrador retriever is very intelligent, but she doesn't always seem bright.
My Labrador retriever has a great deal of *intelligence*, but she doesn't always show *it*.

VAGUE (ANTECEDENT NOT EXPRESSED)

Tuition was suddenly raised, which surprised everyone.

REVISED (ANTECEDENT SUPPLIED)

Tuition was suddenly raised, *a fact* which surprised everyone. [The sentence is revised by supplying an appropriate antecedent for the pronoun *which*.]

10m Use *who, which,* and *that* to make appropriate reference to humans, animals, and objects.

Use *who, whom, whoever, whomever* to refer to humans.

Clyde is a young man *who* knows what he wants.
Jean Edgars is the one *whom* we want for mayor.
The criminal must be *whoever* left the lights on.

Occasionally it may be necessary to use *who* to refer to an animal: *My dog, Barney, who has been with me for ten years, is still the best mouser in town.*

Some writers use *whose* to avoid awkward or wordy pronoun constructions.

This is an argument *whose* ending is certain. [*Whose* replaces *the ending of which.*]
Romeo and Juliet is a drama *whose* love story is timeless. [*Whose* is more economical than the very formal *in which the.*]

Use *which* to refer to animals, objects, and ideas, especially in nonrestrictive clauses (see **21e**).

The opposum, *which* is the only American marsupial, has a prehensile tail.
Chicago, *which* knows what winter is all about, has begun to dig itself out of drifts unsurpassed in this century.
We are studying nihilism, *which* is the theory that life has no purpose or meaning.

Use *that* to refer to animals and objects, especially in restrictive clauses (see **21e**).

Any dog *that* barks at night may be picked up by the dog catcher.
Crime and Punishment is a novel *that* presents the psychology of the criminal.

ref

10n Avoid using an excessive number of pronouns.

Too many pronouns will sound repetitious and may produce an immature tone.

EXCESSIVE

The boy knew *he* should go, and *he* thought *he* should say so, but *he* held back because *he* was afraid of what might happen to *him*.

REVISED

Although *he* knew *he* should go and thought *he* should say so, the boy held back out of fear.

ACTIVITY 17
Select the preferred sentence in the following pairs. Be prepared to explain your answers.

1. *A.* Science is a very difficult subject, which I realized almost immediately.
   B. Science is a very difficult subject, a fact which I realized almost immediately.
2. *A.* The fact that our entire family has inherited great grandfather's nose is considered a genetic accident.
   B. Our entire family has inherited Great-grandfather's nose, which is considered a genetic accident.
3. *A.* Aunt Wilma asked mother whether she might wear a light-blue dress to the funeral.
   B. Aunt Wilma asked mother whether it might be appropriate to wear a light-blue dress to the funeral.
4. *A.* My brother took dancing lessons with his girlfriend, not that it helped him much.
   B. My brother took dancing lessons with his girlfriend, but he didn't learn to dance very well.
5. *A.* The boys knew the girls had their keys.
   B. The boys knew their keys had been taken by the girls.

ACTIVITY 18
Write sixteen sentences of your own, two each to illustrate appropriate pronoun reference for the topics in 10e through 10m.

ACTIVITY 19

Revise the following sentences to remove pronoun problems of case and reference. It may be necessary to change verbs when you change pronouns. You may revise any way you like as long as you do not create any awkward sentences nor leave any pronoun problems.

1. Any dog which can fetch and do tricks is all right with me.
2. Each of these ten children have lost their mother.
3. The one who we set to guard the jewels turned out to be the thief.
4. You should never put braces on your teeth when they are rusty.
5. All of the dogs had developed an infection in its paw.
6. Someone will have to tell Ralph his dog has been killed, which is very unpleasant.
7. A monkey who wants a banana is likely to do anything you say.
8. The soldiers who the nation honored were those who had served bravely.
9. After hearing legal precedent and argument, the grand jury announced that the guilty one was me.
10. Gretch wanted her mother to give her her allowance instead of her promise to find her a job.
11. We painted the barn bright red, but it didn't help.
12. The bank sent a letter saying that we had overdrawn our checking account, which was a great surprise to us.
13. Make sure you speak firmly to whomever is making all the racket out there.
14. The class attempted to interrupt him lecturing in a monotone by asking questons.
15. Between she and I there is a long standing friendship and trust.

11 VERB FORMS

Verbs have four forms: present, past, past participle, and present participle. Some have alternate forms; a few have repeated forms. Some troublesome verb forms:

PRESENT	PAST	PAST PARTICIPLE	PRESENT PARTICIPLE
awake	awoke, awaked	awaked, awoke	awaking
awaken	awakened	awakened	awakening
begin	began	begun	beginning

vb form

PRESENT	PAST	PAST PARTICIPLE	PRESENT PARTICIPLE
break	broke	broken	breaking
bring	brought	brought	bringing
buy	bought	bought	buying
dive	dived, dove	dived	diving
draw	drew	drawn	drawing
drink	drank	drunk	drinking
freeze	froze	frozen	freezing
get	got	got, gotten	getting
go	went	gone	going
know	knew	known	knowing
lay	laid	laid	laying
lie (recline)	lay	lain	lying
lie (tell a lie)	lied	lied	lying
make	made	made	making
set	set	set	setting
sing	sang	sung	singing
sink	sank	sunk	sinking
take	took	taken	taking
wake	woke, waked	waked, woken	waking
wear	wore	worn	wearing

The past participle and present participle are used to form the *perfect* and *progressive* tenses. They are used with forms of *to be (am, is, are, was, were, be, being, been)* and with forms of *to have (have, has, had)*.

> Michael *is making* dinner.
> The world *has known* about her secret for months.
> I *have been sitting* here for hours.
> You *will have worn* that coat twelve times if you put it on again.

11a Avoid slang verbs in formal writing.

In less formal writing, slang verbs can be appropriate, but for formal writing, slang should be avoided: *busted, rappin', frosted* (for *frozen*), *croaked* (for *died*) and so on.

vb form

11b Avoid nonstandard verb forms in formal writing.

Nonstandard verb forms may be acceptable in conversation or quoted dialogue but should be avoided in formal writing.

NONSTANDARD
The ship *had sank* in deep waters. The ship *sunk* in deep waters.

REVISED
The ship *had sunk* in deep waters. The ship *sank* in deep waters.

NONSTANDARD
They *snuck* out of the house after curfew.

REVISED
They *sneaked* out of the house after curfew.

11c Avoid inventing verb forms.

INVENTED VERB
You *have tooken* to much time.

REVISED
You *have taken* too much time.

11d Use lie/lay and sit/set correctly.

Lie and *lay* have different meanings. *To lie (lie, lay, lain, lying)* means "to be at rest, to recline." *To lay (lay, laid, laid, laying)* means "to put something somewhere." *Sit* and *set* have different meanings. *To sit (sit, sat, sat, sitting)* means "to be in a seated position." *To set (set, set, set, setting)* means "to place in position."

The pairs of words are also different *grammatically. Lie* and *sit* never take objects. They are usually followed by *place* expressions: *lie down, lie on the bed, sit up, sit on that chair. Lay* and *set* always take objects: *lay the book down; lay it on the bed; set the pencil over there; set it on the counter.* Note the past tense of *lie:*

Today I *lie* down; yesterday I *lay* [not *laid*] down.

vb form

ACTIVITY 20

Select the appropriate verb choice in the following sentences.

1. To maintain dignity, never (lay/lie) your hands on your opponent.
2. She said our papers have been (sitting/setting) there all day.
3. (Lay/Lie) a measuring tape along the edge of the wall.
4. They (lay/laid) in bed until noon yesterday.
5. That dog has (sat/set) there all day.
6. If you're tired, you ought to (sit/set) down for a while.
7. The letter is (sitting/setting) right there in front of you.
8. They have (laid/lain) tracks right across our field.
9. After the game they (lay/laid) on the grass, enjoying the weather.
10. Better let sleeping dogs (lie/lay).

ACTIVITY 21

Write twelve sentences, three each illustrating appropriate use of *lie, lay, sit,* and *set.*

ACTIVITY 22

Revise the following sentences to eliminate any verb problems.

1. "Don't you dare lay down in your bed until you have cleaned that room," mother shouted.
2. The boys were too wasted to answer the policeman's questions.
3. If we had stayed another few minutes I could have drank my coffee.
4. I must have lain my glasses down somewhere, but I can't find them now.
5. "Sit that pitcher a little nearer to the center of the table, please," mother said.
6. It looked like father had drug out everything in the house for spring cleaning.
7. I wanted Dennis to help me wash the car, but instead he just laid down on the grass and pretended to be asleep.
8. Grandfather would ask anyone who came to the door to set and rest a spell.
9. After the diamond was lain out in the dust, we started the ball game.
10. The child nearly drownded itself in the shallow pond near the house.

12 VERB TENSE

Verb tense indicates when an action takes place: past, present, or future.

The **past tense** indicates action that has been completed and habitual action in the past.

> The Premier *vetoed* the bill.
> The Pistons *won* the game.
> Festus *whistled* whenever he saw a pretty girl.

The **present tense** indicates action occurring in the present, generalizations, and habitual or continuing behavior.

> The group *is* ready to begin its performance.
> Pollution *causes* acid rain.
> Most humans *need* companionship.
> John *clears* his throat before talking on the phone.

The **future tense** indicates that an action will occur in the future.

> It *will snow* tomorrow.
> The space shuttle *will land* next week.

The old tradition (observed by very few people today) called for a complicated distinction between future tense and intent or determination. To indicate future time, first person pronouns used *shall:* **I shall** [or *we shall*] *be 65 next year.* The other pronouns used *will* to indicate future: **You will** [*he, she,* or *it will, they will*] *be in Washington by noon.* However, to indicate intention or strong determination, the use of *shall* and *will* were reversed: **I will** [*we will*] *prevent anyone from entering the center after hours.* **You,** [*he, she, it, they*] **shall** *certainly be punished.* These distinctions between *shall* and *will* are seldom observed today, even in formal writing.

Each tense has a **perfect** form to help show complex time relationships.

The **past perfect tense** describes action completed prior to another action in the past.

t shift

The government *had fallen* long before the truth was revealed.
Jeff *had been asked* for the solution, but another student came up with the answer.

The **present perfect tense** describes action that began in the past and is continuing or action that took place at an indefinite in the past.

The armed services *have recruited* specialists in the field of electronics.
He *has pondered* long and hard for many years.

The **future perfect tense** describes action that will be completed before another action.

She *will have finished* before you.
The protestors *will have spoken* for three hours by the time we get to the rally.

Verbs also have **progressive** forms that indicate ongoing action:

I *am writing* a letter.
You *were working* very late last night.
He *will be dancing* a new number in the show.
She *had been teaching* for thirty years in the same school.

Any tense that fits your purpose is suitable, the past, present, or future. The key is to be consistent, to follow a logical sequence. The past tense is appropriate for most formal writing, but certain kinds of expression conventionally take the present tense. Often the present tense is used to describe what an author accomplishes in his or her works or to describe the actions of a character.

Shakespeare *creates* a symbol of evil in the play *Othello*.
Huck Finn eventually *escapes* from Pap.

12a Avoid unjustified shifts in tense.

The tense of the first verb in a sentence sets up a reference for the rest of the verbs in that sentence. If the reference is to the present, for example, make sure the other verbs in the sentence conform.

SHIFT FROM PAST TO PRESENT

The company's common stock *split* last December as production costs *decrease*.

REVISED FOR CONSISTENT TENSE

The company's common stock *split* last December as production costs *decreased*.

SHIFT FROM PRESENT TO PAST

Susan *is waiting* for the proper moment, but John suddenly *annouces* he *was* leaving.

REVISED FOR CONSISTENT TENSE

Susan *was waiting* for the proper moment, but John suddenly *announced* he *was* leaving.

12b Avoid inappropriate past tense.

When writing in the past tense, avoid using the simple past to indicate one event occurring before another. Use the past perfect tense for the earlier event:

INAPPROPRIATE PAST TENSE

We knew the bird *escaped* when we saw that its cage door *was* ajar.

REVISED TO SHOW ONE EVENT OCCURRING EARLIER

We knew the bird *had escaped* when we saw that its cage door *was* ajar.

13 VERB MOOD

The mood of a verb suggests whether an action should be considered a statement of fact (indicative mood), a command (imperative mood), or a wish, a doubt, or a condition contrary to fact (subjunctive mood). The indicative mood is the most common, but the subjunctive mood is observed in a few situations in formal writing.

mood

13a Use the subjunctive to express doubt, wishes, probability, conditions contrary to fact, or conditional statements.

The most common subjunctive forms are *be* and *were*. Others are formed from the plural present tense (without the *s*).

We insist that you *be* present.
If I *were* you, I would not get there too early.
He wished he *were* an astronaut.
She insisted that Henry *deliver* the manuscript.
Were it true, I would have told you so.

The subjunctive is still appropriate for conditional statements.

If you *were* to do it, you would be penalized.

However, this use of the subjunctive is passing out of style. The indicative mode is often used now; the result is more direct, less tentative.

If you *do* it, you *will be* penalized.
If you *have done* it, you *will be* penalized.
If you *did* it, you *will* [or *would*] *be* penalized.
If you *had done* it, you *would have been* penalized.

Avoid using a redundant conditional (If you *would* do it, you *would* be penalized). Use *will* or *would* only for the consequence, not the condition.

13b Use the subjunctive for demands, preferences, or requests introduced by *that.*

He insists that she *do* it by herself.
It is important that you *be* accurate.
They ask that she *come* as soon as possible.
We would prefer that he *sleep* in the garage.

mood

ACTIVITY 23

Select the appropriate verb in each of the following sentences. Be prepared to explain your choices.

1. Their house (sits/sets) in the middle of their property.
2. After the tree died, we discovered its roots (were/had been) eaten away by moles.
3. Her fried chicken was the best we had ever (ate/eaten).
4. After the dance, the guests (lay/laid) around on the lawn.
5. By twelve o'clock, they will (be/have been) flying across the Atlantic for six hours.
6. Would you lend him money if he (was/were) to ask you?
7. We quickly found our row and (took/take) our seats.
8. The papers have been (lying/laying) on the floor since you left them there.
9. I wouldn't accuse him if I (was/were) you.
10. If you break the window, you (would/will) have to pay for it.

ACTIVITY 24

Write five sentences of your own correctly using present, past, and future perfect verbs and subjunctive verbs to express a conditon and to express a demand, preference, or request.

ACTIVITY 25

Revise the following sentences to eliminate any problems in verb tense or mood. You may need to change other words when you revise verbs. You may revise any way you like as long as you do not create any awkward sentences nor leave any verb problems.

1. It seemed the burglars had took everything of value in the house.
2. The cornered rat glared at us and gritched its teeth in anger.
3. Soon everyone was tired of hearing Nan pop off with irrelevant questions every few minutes.
4. Mom's cooling pies set precariously on the window ledge.
5. We yelled at Arfy to get out of the way, but he just laid there on the driveway.
6. It looked like the cannisters busted their seams when the temperature rose too high in the storage room.
7. Our surveyors had lain out the lot lines too close to the river bank.
8. If Jack was able to get through the snow, he would be here now.
9. Our dog likes to sleep in the house, but father prefers that it sleeps in the barn.
10. By morning we had sang every song we could think of.
11. Of course I wish I was a millionaire, doesn't everyone?

act/pass

12. Yesterday I just laid in bed all day thinking about my problem.
13. I knew that even if I would memorize all the words, I would never be able to win the spelling contest.
14. His majesty the king commands that you are present at the royal ball next week.
15. When we examined the pictures, we realized immediately that Winnona drew them.

---

14 ACTIVE AND PASSIVE VOICES

The voice of a verb indicates whether its subject acts or is acted upon. When the verb is active, its subject is the actor in the sentence. When the voice is passive, the subject is acted upon.

A passive sentence reverses the order of the logical subject and object. In an active sentence, the subject is the actor in the sentence. In a passive sentence, the subject is acted upon or receives the action of the verb. If the actor is expressed, it appears in a *by* phrase: (See Transitive, **4c;** Direct Object, **5d.**)

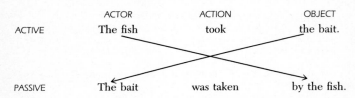

	ACTOR	ACTION	OBJECT
ACTIVE	The fish	took	the bait.
PASSIVE	The bait	was taken	by the fish.

The logical subject in the passive sentence is still *the fish* (the fish is the actor in this sentence), but the *grammatical* subject is now *the bait*. Passive conveys the sense of being acted upon: *My apartment has been robbed six times in three years.* It deemphasizes an actor: *The experiment was conducted over a two-month period.* The passive voice is sometimes used for writing about scientific subjects. Its generally distant and depersonalized sound may be undersirable for academic writing in nonscientific fields.

PASSIVE
Heavy books are seldom read by students.

ACTIVE

Students seldom read heavy books.

PASSIVE

That immunological activity is increased by raising the body's temperature is concluded by Smith.

ACTIVE

Smith concludes that raising the body's temperature increases immunological activity.

ACTIVITY 26
Revise each of the passives below to active.

1. The grass had been cut by Anne.
2. Several experiments were finished after the grant had been received by us.
3. Emergency procedures should be taken whenever gas is observed to be leaking.
4. An angry letter had been sent by the President to Congress.
5. The doctor left the office after her last patient had been seen.

ACTIVITY 27
Revise the following paragraph to eliminate any problems with verbs. It may be necessary to change other words when you revise the verbs. You may revise any way you like as long as you do not create any awkward sentences nor leave any verb problems.

```
     During President Carter's administration the Shah of
Iran was ousted by conservative moslems. After the Shah
had been driven out, the leadership of the country was
given to the Ayatollah Khomeini. One of the first acts
of the new government under the Ayatollah was to nab the
American embassy. Embassy workers and some civilians
were held hostage by the Ayatollah's revolutionary
guards. President Carter had gave orders to work
patiently to free the hostages and not to hassle the
Iranians too much. He felt that if we would treat the
Iranians with respect, they would respond in kind.
```

However, it finally dawned on him that the Iranians aren't going to release our people. He ordered that a helicopter raid was made on the embassy, but this plan fell through when sand gummed up the engines of the helicopters. The staging area for the helicopters laid out in the desert. An entire year of negotiations with the Iranians fails to release any prisoners. The Iranians are blaming America for the tyranny of the Shah, who had been supported by us. They imagined we are planning to sit him back on the throne. Then too, having America as the "enemy" allowed the revolution and control of Iran to be maintained by the Ayatollah; the people had been united with him against a common "threat" from America.

15 ADJECTIVES AND ADVERBS

Adjectives modify nouns and pronouns. Averbs modify verbs, adjectives, and other adverbs. (See **4d, 4e.**)

Adjectives and adverbs have degrees of comparison, from least to most. The degrees of comparison are positive, comparative, superlative.

POSITIVE	COMPARATIVE	SUPERLATIVE
angry	angrier	angriest
angrily	more angrily	most angrily
bad	worse	worst
fast	faster	fastest
good	better	best
happily	more happily	most happily
slow	slower	slowest
well	better	best
young	younger	youngest

A few modifiers are considered **absolute.** Words like *incomparable*, *total*, and *unique* suggest qualities that have no degrees of comparison; they are absolute. Avoid expressions like *more unique*, *most incomparable*.   *adj/adv*

Use the comparative degree for comparisons between two things, not the superlative: "He is the *younger* [not the *youngest*] of the two boys."

15a Avoid redundant, invented, or otherwise faulty comparatives and superlatives.

REDUNDANT OR FAULTY COMPARATIVES

It is *more better* to win than to lose.
Lonnie works *slowlier* than anyone else.
This pie is *more good* than the other.

REVISED

It is *better* to win than to lose.
Lonnie works *more slowly* than anyone else.
This pie is *better* than the other.

REDUNDANT OR FAULTY SUPERLATIVES

Alicia is the *most prettiest* girl I have ever seen.
Professor Glade is the *bestest* teacher I know.
He gives the *goodest* grades of all.

REVISED

Alicia is the *prettiest* girl I have ever seen.
Professor Gade is the *best* teacher I know.
He gives the *best* grades of all.

15b Avoid dropping -*ly* from adverbs.

Most words ending in -*ly* are adverbs, especially when the -*ly* is a suffix added to a root word. The suffix -*ly* added to the adjective *quick* produces the adverb *quickly*. (Not all words ending in -*ly* are adverbs: *motherly*, *priestly*, and *scholarly* are not adverbs. See **4e**.)

The car rides very *smoothly* [not *smooth*].
Walk *quietly* [not *quiet*] so you don't disturb anyone.

15c Use adjectives after linking verbs, adverbs after action verbs.

These apples *taste delicious*. [The predicate adjective, *delicious* describes the subject.]
We *tasted* the wines *carefully*. [The adverb *carefully* describes *tasted*, the verb.]
Your new haircut *looks youthful*.
Everyone *looked intently* at the insects.

15d Use adjectives to modify objects, adverbs to modify verbs.

They found their new puppy *clever*. [The adjective, *clever*, describes the direct object, *puppy*.]
The found their new puppy *cleverly*. [The adverb, *cleverly*, describes the verb, *found*.]

15e Use *bad, badly, good, well* appropriately.

Bad is an adjective.

This is a *bad* day for swimming.
The doctor felt *bad*. [Linking verbs take predicate adjectives; *bad* describes *doctor*.]
Fish and guests smell *bad* after three days.

Badly is an adverb.

The car was *badly* damaged in the accident.
She fell *badly* on the ice.

Good is an adjective.

Mother makes *good* desserts.
The flowers look *good* in that old pot.

120   *Well* is both an adjective and an adverb.

I hope we all remain *well* during the flu season. [*Well* is a predicate adjective after the linking verb *remain*.]
She paints *well* for such a young child. [*Well* is an adverb after the action verb *paints*.)

ACTIVITY 28

Revise the following sentences to remove any problems with adjectives and adverbs. You may need to change other words when you revise modifiers. You may revise any way you like as long as you do not create any awkward sentences nor leave any faulty adjectives or adverbs.

1. Father looks awfully in the morning before he has shaved.
2. He does good for a person with little formal education.
3. You have to do your work quick if you want to have any time for fun.
4. Our dog was hurt bad when the car struck it a glancing blow.
5. Benny is the most coolest teenager in our class.
6. It will be more better for you to have the milk than coffee.
7. Between Felicia and Dawn, I think "Dawn" is the prettiest name.
8. "The Windhover" is the most unique poem I have ever heard.
9. I felt badly about losing the lottery.
10. Chester is hopefullier than I am about our winning the game.

SECTION REVIEW

ACTIVITY 29

Select the appropriate word in the following sentences. Be prepared to explain your answers.

1. Each of us wants (his/their/our/his or her) relatives to think well of us.
2. Long after the exam was over, he (lay/laid) in bed for hours wondering whether he had passed.
3. She had written in the last page of her diary, "It is (they/them) who will be sorry."
4. They boasted that they could have (swum/swam) all night.
5. She knew this was a message for (whoever/whomever) would feel guilty about it.
6. The expensive wine will be (drank/drunk) by all the guests at the main table.
7. Speaking of Cyril and Deliah, the latter is certainly the (strongest/stronger) of the two.

adj/adv

8. You have to work (slow/slowly) if you want your work to be perfect.
9. If the truth (was/were) known, she would never have allowed him to go.
10. The police insisted that he had (laid/lain) the luger there purposely to mislead them.
11. Lonnie was more (optimistic/optimistical) than I about winning the game.
12. "The girl in the saffron dress," she wrote, "was (I/me)."
13. The President asked whether he was one of those aides who (tell/tells) everything you say to them.
14. Sally Mae is the (youngest/younger) of my two sisters.
15. We found one of those trashy novels which (is/are) full of romantic nonsense.
16. The note said the police insist that he (come/comes) to the station immediately.
17. Each of the young marines (was/were) going to be tested for the first time under fire.
18. Everyone will be (more better/better) off with a little exercise.
19. *Time* magazine writes (its/their) stories for maximum reader interest.
20. We were told that she had a mad aunt (who/whom) it was not easy to get to know.
21. The rules required a penalty if the player (was/were) unable to offer a counterbid.
22. We knew that if we (were/would be) late we would be punished.
23. Either his friends or his wife (is/are) going to tell him the truth.
24. We cleaned the rug extra (careful/carefully) before returning it.
25. The Chinese abacus works as (good/well) as an electric calculator.

REVISION PRACTICES

ACTIVITY 30

Revise each of the following sentences.

1. You really have to look careful to see the bird move.
2. Everyone needs friends in their life sometime.
3. Neither the city nor the town were ready to raise taxes.
4. The reward was that if we would cross the line first we would gain a point.
5. The letter said this was to be kept just between she and I.
6. It is a mistake to put the dog near the cat if it is excited.
7. He is one of those men who has a good time no matter what.
8. The statement that the Russians' newest weapons were more powerful than our rockets were disturbing to our leaders.

9. Either their materials or their craftsmanship are the reason for *adj/adv* the high quality of the work.
10. Our certainty was more absolute than ever after we saw the town in flames.
11. My brother was the only one of those applicants who were qualified for the job.
12. When they asked her who had done it, she said that it was her.
13. Why do you want to know whom is going to win the race?
14. You cannot get the thread through the needle when it is wet.
15. There is without a doubt endless supplies of solar energy.

ACTIVITY 31

Using the rules and guidelines in this section, eliminate all sentence errors in the following composition. You may revise any way you like as long as you do not create any awkward sentences nor leave any sentence errors.

The Pride of Germany

The great zeppelin, *Hindenberg,* was the pride of Germany. The enormous airship was a luxurious liner for wealthy travellers. And considerably faster than ocean liners. It could be flown between Lakehurst, New Jersey and Frankfort, Germany, in 50 hours, or less. It was one of the safest means of travel, the number of miles it had been flown without an accident were over 100,000, which was surprising. The Germans whom were responsible for the ship were justifiably proud. Everyone connected with the ship were knocked out about it.

The *Hindenberg* was eight hundred feet long and more tall than a ten-story building. Its dangerous hydrogen gas keeped the ship above clouds and bad weather it flew absolutely smooth without vibrations at speeds in excess of 60 miles an hour. It was truly one of those luxury class ships that provides passengers with all the comforts of an ocean liner as well as allowing them to set and enjoy spectacular views of the ocean far below. The ship was considered more totally safe than any other

123

form of travel, even though hydrogen is highly explosive. Nonexplosive helium is not used, because it was available only in the United States, and it is terrible expensive to use it. However, it was assumed that when properly handled, there was no need to fear hydrogen, of the two gasses, it was thought to be the most practical. That any accidents could befall the ship or its people were unthinkable.

Unfortunately, the *Hindenberg* became one of the worst disasters in aviation history on May 6, 1937. A black day for Germany and for aviation too. The ship arrived in the United States during a severe storm. Although the powerful ship was capable of landing in any kind of weather. It was wisely decided by the captain to cruise about for several hours, giving the passengers an unexpected sight—seeing tour of New York while they waited for the storm to subside. If anyone would be careless with the *Hindenberg*, it would not be him. Finally, many hours more later than normal, the monstrous craft began to descend slow at Lakehurst. Everybody on board was making their preparations to disembark the ground crew were pulling in the mooring lines. Each of the people involved were attending to their own duties and interests. Perhaps it was the activity of them getting ready to leave which led to the subsequent events. Perhaps not. Radio commentators were on hand for live interviews with passengers returning from vacations in Europe. Neither the passengers nor the captain were expecting anything unusual to happen.

Suddenly, the *Hindenberg* burst into flames. The hydrogen fuel exploded, enveloped the ship in a fireball, and spilled sheets of liquid fire on the ground crew whom were below. Terrified passengers leaped from the windows of the ship while they were yet too high in the air. The radio commentator shrieked and cried while he attempted to describe the horror he witnesses. He was the most hystericalest announcer anyone had ever heard. He gave his report tearful. He made even the audience feel bad about the fate of the people. The broadcast allowed listners to share the terror with he, the young newsman. The burning craft sunk quick to the earth where it laid burning fiercely. The fire was so hot that the steel girders inside the ship melted. If it was any hotter, the ground too would have melt. There had been 97 passengers and crew members on the ship, most of who were severely burned. The ship together with thirty-five people who died, were lost forever. The end of the *Hindenberg* marked the end of airships. They were too dangerous and too slow for a world that was entering the age of the propeller planes. The end of the pride of Germany. It was a great tragedy for whomever was there that day.

Sentence
Structure

coord,
sub

A primary consideration in writing is readability. Nothing else matters very much if the reader cannot understand your sentences. *Readability* refers in part to the ease with which readers can get information from your sentences. Effective writing must be clear, concise, and accurate.

Readability does not, however, imply merely the ability to "decode" a sentence. After all, elementary books are "readable" in their childish simplicity: "See Dick run. Run Dick. Run, run, run." But the *effect* on a mature reader of this kind of simplicity is tiresome and possibly insulting. You must balance simplicity and other strategies for effective sentences.

16 COORDINATION AND SUBORDINATION

Coordination and subordination refer to the balance between clauses in a sentence. Clauses of equal emphasis are connected by coordinating words (see **4f**) or punctuation. When one clause is given less emphasis than another, the lesser clause is *dependent* and is introduced with a subordinating word (see **4f**).

COORDINATE CLAUSES

The plumber soldered the pipes, but he forgot to turn the water back on. [The two clauses share equal emphasis and are joined by the coordinating conjunction *but*.]

The gourmet restaurant served only the finest food; however, the owners had misjudged their market and were forced to close. [Two clauses are given equal emphasis and are joined with a semicolon and a conjunctive adverb. See **23b**.]

Snoopy is more than a dog: he is Charley Brown's alter ego. [The two clauses are closely related and joined with a colon. A semicolon would also be possible here. See **24c, 23a**.]

SUBORDINATE CLAUSES

Since the race was to be run over a longer track, the filly was now considered the favorite. [The first clause is dependent, receives less emphasis, and is introduced by the subordinating conjunction *since*.]

Questions should be saved until the President's speech is over *be-*

cause he might otherwise lose his train of thought. [Here the main clause comes first followed by a dependent clause introduced by the subordinating conjunction *because*.]

Every tree *that we plant today* may one day provide fuel, paper, or shelter for our children. [The dependent clause begins with the relative pronoun *that* and is embedded in the main clause.]

16a Avoid excessive coordination.

As sentences grow longer, a number of problems can arise. Mere length by itself is not the goal. By stringing together phrases and clauses with *and, but,* and *or* you will succeed in producing a long sentence, but it may become unreadable. Avoid the overuse of coordinating words.

EXCESSIVE COORDINATION

My car is a Chevrolet, *and* it has a six cylinder engine, *and* it gets twenty miles to the gallon, *and* it is a hot rod.

REVISED FOR BETTER COORDINATION

My car, a hot rod Chevrolet, has a six cylinder engine *and* gets twenty miles to the gallon. [One clause has been reduced to an adjective; another has been reduced to a compound predicate.]

Excessively coordinated sentences sound immature. Readers perceive such strings as separate sentences tacked together with *and*'s, as indeed they are.

16b Avoid faulty coordination.

In informal English, the additive conjunction *(and)* is frequently used to join coordinate clauses, even when the clauses are contrastive.

CONFUSING COORDINATION

He drank the poison, *and* he didn't die.

REVISED FOR CONTRAST

He drank the poison, *but* he didn't die.

sub

16c Avoid excessive subordination.

Too many words indicating subordination or relationship can make a sentence hard to read or confusing.

EXCESSIVE SUBORDINATION

When they opened the package *after* it arrived, they knew it was dangerous *even though* they weren't afraid of it *although* they should have been.

At the end of the semester I found out *that* the essay *that* had been selected as the winner hadn't been mine.

REVISED FOR CLARITY

They opened the package when it arrived. Although they knew it was dangerous, they weren't afraid of it.

At the end of the semester I found out *that my essay hadn't won.*

At the end of the semester I found out *that the winning essay wasn't mine.*

16d Avoid faulty subordination.

Only the writer can decide which ideas are greater in importance, which lesser. But sometimes the reader may be presented with a puzzle in which it can seem that the wrong idea has been subordinated, that the relationship is unnatural, or that the connecting word is inappropriate.

FAULTY SUBORDINATION

Grandfather had been a wealthy man, although we were surprised to discover that he had died penniless.

SUBORDINATION REVERSED

Although grandfather had been a wealthy man, we were surprised to discover that he had died penniless.

FAULTY SUBORDINATION

When the children had caused the fire, we were certain they had been playing with matches.

RELATIONSHIP CLARIFIED

Because the children had been playing with matches, we were certain they had caused the fire.

FAULTY SUBORDINATION

The storekeepers put up security shutters as the citizens threatened to riot.

CONNECTIVE IMPROVED

The storekeepers put up security shutters *after* [or *because*] the citizens threatened to riot.

ACTIVITY 1

Revise for clarity. Edit the sentences to eliminate errors of coordination and subordination. In some cases you may wish to create more than one sentence.

1. Because we were frightened, we saw the snake crawling toward the baby.
2. Until the engines of the plane are started by the man who is to be the pilot until the real pilot arrives, the man that is standing by must wait until it is ready.
3. The red hint of dawn was showing a pale line, and it was below the clouds, and they were at the horizon, and it was just beyond the dark string of islands.
4. After two men had died there while they were trying to cross the swamps that were full of traps that you couldn't get out of because they had quicksand in them that most people just sank down and died in, a warning sign was put up.
5. The door had locked itself from the inside since we had to stay outside all night.

---

17 ILLOGICAL SENTENCES

Illogical sentences do not make clear sense. Writers must make sure their sentences are complete and conform to the expectations of educated readers. The patterns of oral English, faulty comparisons, inexact appositives, faulty predicates, illogical prepositions, garbled sentences will be confusing to educated readers. Revise your writing to eliminate any illogical sentences.

17a Revise faulty comparisons.

Avoid the inexact use of *than*.

ILLOGICAL

She is *stronger than any* swimmer in the meet. [This sentence is acceptable only if the subject, *she*, is not in the meet or is not a swimmer.]

REVISED

She is the *strongest* swimmer in the meet. [Or] She is *stronger than any other* swimmer in the meet.

ILLOGICAL

The smell of cigarette smoke is more disgusting than a cigar. [The sentence illogically compares an odor with an object.]

REVISED

The smell of cigarette smoke is more disgusting than *the smell of cigar smoke*.
The smell of cigarette smoke is more disgusting than *that of a cigar*.

Avoid faulty interruption of comparisons.

ILLOGICAL

Steel is as strong, *if not stronger*, than iron. [If the interrupter, *if not stronger*, is removed, the remaining statement is not grammatically acceptable: *Steel is as strong . . . than iron.*]

REVISED

Steel is as strong *as, if not stronger than*, iron. [Removing the interrupter leaves a grammatically acceptable statement: *Steel is as strong as . . . iron.*]

ILLOGICAL

Abraham Lincoln was one of the greatest, *if not the greatest*, President we ever had. ("One of the greatest" cannot describe "President.")

REVISED

Abraham Lincoln was one of the greatest Presidents, *if not the greatest*, we ever had.

17b Revise faulty apposition.

An appositive renames or reidentifies whatever it refers to. Make sure the appositive is a synonym for its referent.

ILLOGICAL

All week he had received only one job offer, a clerk. ["A clerk" is not a job offer.]

REVISED

All week he had received only one job offer, a clerk's job.

ILLOGICAL

He said he had finally realized his life's ambition, a skydiver. ["A skydiver" is not an ambition.]

REVISED

He said he had finally realized his life's ambition, to be a skydiver.

17c Revise faulty predication.

Be sure your predicates match their subjects. See Agreement, **9.**

ILLOGICAL

The design of the building was too close to the street. [The sentence says the design, not the building, was too close to the street.]

REVISED

The design of the building *placed it* too close to the street.

ILLOGICAL

The little trees were knocked over and the large oak damaged. [Plural *trees* and singular *oak* cannot both be subjects of the plural verb *were.*]

REVISED

The little trees *were* knocked over, and the large oak *was* damaged.

Avoid illogical predicate nouns. See **5f.**

flty
prep

ILLOGICAL

Her job was a welder. [A welder is a person, not a job.]

REVISED

Her job was welding.
She was a welder.

ILLOGICAL

Lifting weights is where you strengthen your muscles. [Clauses be-ginning with *where* can rarely be used as predicate nouns; they should be used only when they refer to a *place*.]

REVISED

Lifting weights strengthens you muscles.

ILLOGICAL

Argumentation is when you try to convince someone of your point of view. [Clauses beginning with *when* can rarely be used as predi-cate nouns; such clauses must be used only when they refer to *time*.]

REVISED

Argumentation is an attempt to convince someone of your point of view.

ILLOGICAL

The *reason* the campaign was such a success was *because* of the many contributions. [*Because* is redundant when used as a predicate noun for *reason*.]

REVISED

The campaign was such a success because of the many contributions.
The reason the campaign was such a success was *that* there were so many contributions.

17d Revise illogical prepositions.

You must make sure that your prepositions match both elements of a compound prepositional phrase.

ILLOGICAL

She said she had been simultaneously worried and delighted *with* her new neighbor.

REVISED

She said she had been simultaneously worried *about* and delighted *with* her new neighbor.

17e Revise garbled sentences.

Missing elements, transposed elements, faulty predication—many things can go wrong in a garbled sentence. In editing a sentence you may accidentally delete something or move things around so that the end result is gibberish.

GARBLED

Only minutes before the bear was tearing up our supplies by the huge sharp claws that we had stowed carefully with the cartons in the remaining supplies.

REVISED

With huge, sharp claws, the bear tore open our cartons, trying to get at the remains of the supplies we had carefully stowed only minutes before.

ACTIVITY 2

Revise each of the following sentences.

1. In a few minutes we had with the help of our field glasses spotted standing near a cave an old grizzly in the face of the cliff just below the plateau above.
2. She said Bobo was as tall, if not taller, than Ernie.
3. In a short time Helga had asked and received her tax refund from the IRS.
4. I think Tolstoi's *War and Peace* is longer than any book in the library.
5. Clarissa had the best costume at Halloween, a witch.
6. One kind of poetry is when the words rhyme.
7. All the children were huddled in a corner and their teacher too.
8. We eat our own corn more often than our pigs.
9. The new teacher was as young, if not younger, than some of her students.
10. The meaning of the book was a love story between an older woman and a young man.

ACTIVITY 3

Revise each of the following sets of short sentences into one longer effective sentence. You may add, delete, and shift words; change the forms of words; and change punctuation. You may combine sentences any way you like as long as the result is a *single* effective sentence for each set. Avoid overusing *and* to string words together.

1. Somebody told Bruce to go home. It was because his family needed him. Something had happened at home. There had been an accident. His father had been working on the roof. The shingles needed repairing. His father had fallen. He was badly injured. Bruce's English professor gave him the news.

2. We were conducting experiments with rats. This was in our psychology class. Rats normally live together in colonies. They live in harmony. The experiment was to see how they would behave. We forced them into a very confined space. There the rats grew aggressive. They attacked each other.

3. This semester we are studying communism and we are learning how the conditions were bad in Europe in the nineteenth century and how Marx wanted to make reforms. He felt the workers were oppressed. He felt they were exploited. He believed they should own everything collectively.

18 MODIFIERS

Modifiers describe or limit their referents. Careful use of modifiers can add power and color to your writing; however, you must avoid common problems like dangling modifiers, ambiguous modifiers, split infinitives, and awkwardly placed modifiers. Revise your sentences to eliminate problems with modifiers.

18a Revise dangling modifiers.

Modifiers that do not clearly attach to anything in a sentence often attach themselves to something unintended. To avoid the problem, place modifiers next to what you intend them to modify, or supply a suitable subject within the modifier itself.

DANGLING MODIFIER

The doctor examined my ears *looking through his machine*. [The sentence says "my ears" were "looking through his machine.]

REVISED

Looking through his machine, the doctor examined my ears. [The modifier is moved next to what it describes.]

DANGLING MODIFIER

Swinging the axe with all my strength, the old tree fell toward me.

REVISED

Swinging the axe with all my strength, *I* realized the tree was falling toward me.
While *I* was swinging the axe with all my strength, the tree began falling toward me.

DANGLING MODIFIER

We all brought gifts with us for the orphan children *in our cars*. (The sentence says the children were "in our cars.")

REVISED

We all brought gifts with us *in our cars* for the orphan children.

DANGLING MODIFIER

Everett gave a model ship to his father *that he had made with his own hands*.

REVISED

Everett gave a model ship that he had made with his own hands to his father.

18b Revise ambiguous modifiers.

Avoid ambiguity with movable modifiers (*almost, just, only,* and so on). For example, "I only washed the cups" can be interpreted "I merely washed them, I didn't dry the cups," or "I washed only the cups, the saucers I left for you." Place the modifier next to the word it modifies and, when necessary, give the reader additional information to make your meaning clear:

mm

AMBIGUOUS	REVISED
I just rented a summer cottage.	I rented a summer cottage just now.
	I just rented a summer cottage; I didn't buy one.
Everyone doesn't become senile in old age.	Not everyone becomes senile in old age.

Squinting modifiers seem to modify two words at once. Move the modifier next to the word you intend to modify.

SQUINTING	REVISED
The professor asked them *frequently* to review Homer's work.	The professor frequently asked them to review Homer's work.
	The professor asked them to review Homer's work frequently.

18c Revise split infinitives.

An infinitive is the word *to* plus a verb *(to miss, to go, to understand)*. Putting a modifier between *to* and its verb is called "splitting the infinitive" *(to easily miss, to quickly go, to really understand)*. In formal writing, the split infinitive is usually a mistake; it is always a mistake when it sounds unnatural.

SPLIT INFINITIVE	REVISED
You have *to usually work* hard in college.	You usually have to work hard in college.
You need *to slowly develop* your stamina.	You need to develop your stamina slowly.

18d Revise awkwardly positioned long modifiers.

Placing long modifiers between major sentence elements such as between the subject and its predicate or between a verb and its complement or between the parts of a verb phrase can produce an *mm*

awkward sentence. Such lengthy interrupters may confuse your readers. Revise your sentences to eliminate problems with lengthy modifiers.

LONG MODIFIER INTERRUPTS SUBJECT AND PREDICATE

The President and other members of his administration, *since many complaints had been received from the news media about improper use of public money,* spent less money redecorating their offices.

REVISED

Since many complaints had been received from the news media about improper use of public money, the President and other members of his administration spent less money redecorating their offices.

LONG MODIFIER INTERRUPTS VERB AND COMPLEMENT

Lord Victor felt, *without the support of the bankers who had helped him rise to power,* powerless.

REVISED

Lord Victor felt powerless *without the support of the bankers who had helped him rise to power.*

LONG MODIFIER INTERRUPTS VERB PHRASE

We believed our team would, *despite what appeared to be the obvious advantages of our opponents,* be victorious.

REVISED

We believed our team would be victorious, *despite what appeared to be the obvious advantages of our opponents.*

ACTIVITY 4

Revise the following sentences to eliminate errors in modification.

1. Racing down the street and shouting for the driver to stop, the midtown bus slowly drew away from me.
2. Too tired to work anymore, the office suddenly looked hostile and uninviting.
3. Disgusted with its ugly appearance and expensive maintenance, the old car was ready for the junk yard.
4. We just told them to leave their shoes outside.
5. We tried to evenly spread the mixture over the surface of the wood.

dm,
mm

6. Tall, muscular, and good looking, her hair glistened in the afternoon sun.
7. The window faced a brick wall through which the sunlight streamed.
8. She swore she had, just where you and I are standing now under this old willow, seen grandfather's ghost.
9. Everybody isn't too young to remember Elvis.
10. Hooking him with my best fly, the fish proved quite a catch.

ACTIVITY 5

Revise the following paragraph for clarity. Combine sentences; add, delete, and shift words; change the forms of words; and make punctuation accurate. You may revise any way you like as long as you do not produce any garbled, illogical, or ineffective sentences. Revise so that the paragraph contains several sentences; avoid overusing and *to string words together.*

The Platypus

The platypus is a unique animal and it is a mammal and it is a primitive creature. It has a bill like a duck's which is like leather and it has a body which is covered by hair which is brown. It has a tail which is as flat, if not flatter, than a beaver's, although it does not have teeth since it only has short claws. The male has a spur that is made of material which is similar to a horn that is near each foot. It uses this spur to only defend itself. This spur contains poison. The poison is from a sac although it will not kill human beings. Being scratched by a platypus is when you will get ill. The reason the poison will not kill a person is because it is not strong enough. However, everyone doesn't react the same way to platypus poison. Since they are used for swimming, there are webs on its feet. Being a mammal, its milk feeds their young although they do not have real nipples. Oozing from a gland, the hair of the platypus becomes wet with milk. Because it is different from other mammals, it lays eggs. The platypus lives in a burrow and it eats bugs and it eats small shell fish and it eats worms. This animal is stranger

than any living creature. Being about two feet long, its
head is part duck. Its tail is more like a beaver. Its
burrow protects it like a mole. Truly the unique parts
of this creature puzzle for science that lives on
despite comic mismatch of features may be nature's joke
on it.

---

19 SENTENCE CONSISTENCY

Make sure your word choices are consistent with the grammar of
your sentence; avoid distracting shifts in verbs, levels of formality,
viewpoint, pronoun number, and conjunctions. Revise your sentences to eliminate any problems in sentence consistency.

19a Avoid shifts in voice, mood, person, number.

Avoid shifting conditional verbs. Avoid mixing *can* with conditionals: *might, could, should, would.*

SHIFTING CONDITIONAL
The silk *might* be purchased for less if you *can* go directly to the
manufacturer.

REVISED
The silk *might* be purchased for less if you *could* go directly to the
manufacturer.

Avoid shifting voice.

SHIFT FROM ACTIVE TO PASSIVE
He first *writes* his essay, and then it *is revised.*

REVISED
He first *writes* his essay, and then he *revises* it.

shift   **Avoid shifting mood of verbs.** Mood refers to manner or type of statement: imperative, indicative, interrogative, and subjunctive moods.

SHIFT FROM IMPERATIVE TO INDICATIVE
Now *read* your books and then you *will write* an essay.

REVISED
Now *read* your books and then *write* an essay.

SHIFT FROM SUBJUNCTIVE TO INDICATIVE
It is necessary that he first *clean* his boat and then *paints* it.

REVISED
It is necessary that he first *clean* his boat and then *paint* it.

SHIFT FROM INDICATIVE TO INTERROGATIVE
They *said* he *was* a respectable citizen and *why would* we *think* otherwise?

REVISED
They said he was a respectable citizen, and *they wondered* why we would think otherwise.

19b Avoid shifting the level of formality.

Choose words consistent with your stance and avoid shifting unnecessarily from one level to another.

SHIFT FROM FORMAL TO INFORMAL
The psychologist's profile and the evaluation of Harry's analyst established conclusively that he was a nut case.

REVISED
The psychologist's profile and the evaluation of Harry's analyst established conclusively that he had severe mental problems.

SHIFT FROM INFORMAL TO FORMAL
It was a complete turn on—out-of-sight jams, foxy looking women, and stimulating beverages.

REVISED
It was a complete turn on—out-of-sight jams, foxy looking women, and good juice.

19c Avoid shifting the point of view.

Keep your point of view consistent. The less formal approach is to use *I* or *you;* more formal is the third person, *she, he, they,* or *one*. Most formal is not using personal pronouns at all. Consistency is the key: if you begin writing from the point of view of *I*, stick to it.

SHIFT FROM FIRST TO THIRD PERSON
I have difficulty writing a paper when *one* does not understand the assignment.

REVISED
I have difficulty writing a paper when *I* do not understand the assignment.

SHIFT FROM INDEFINITE PRONOUN TO PERSONAL PRONOUN
One should be extra careful when *he* drives with bald tires.

REVISED
One should be extra careful when *one* drives with bald tires.

Drivers should be extra careful when their tires are bald.

19d Avoid shifting pronoun number.

SHIFT
The dog is man's best friend, and *they* will never let you down.

REVISED
The dog is man's best friend, and *it* will never let you down.

SHIFT
Nursing is a challenging career, and *they* receive good wages.

REVISED
Nursing is a challenging career, and *it* pays good wages.

shift

19e Avoid shifting conjunctions.

Keep subordinate conjunctions in compound expressions consistent.

SHIFT

Because we had paid in advance, and *since* we couldn't get our money back, we decided we had better go.

REVISED

Since we had paid in advance, and *since* we couldn't get our money back, we decided we had better go.

ACTIVITY 6

Revise for consistency.

1. That computer might be the best buy if you can increase its memory storage.
2. The lobster is considered a delicacy, but I know many people who won't eat them.
3. The instructor assigned the paper, and the student writes it.
4. It is imperative that Louis win the long jump and then runs the 100 yard dash.
5. After he had finished typing and since he had proofread the paper, Michael handed it in.

ACTIVITY 7

Revise the following paragraph to make sentences consistent. Combine sentences; add, delete, and shift words; change the forms of words; and change punctuation. You may revise any way you like as long as you do not produce any garbled, illogical, or ineffective sentences. Revise so that the paragraph contains several sentences; avoid overusing *and* to string words together.

```
                    The Jester

     The fool was known in ancient times. The fool was an
entertainer. If someone could be clever then they can
pretend to be stupid in a way that will amuse people.
Playing the fool is hard work, and they are respected by
their audiences. The professional fool is called a
```

jester, and sometimes they were a musician, sometimes
poets and philosophers. Some jesters became famous. They
are remembered in history. Because some jesters were
dwarfs, and since people thought dwarfs brought good
luck, there is a long tradition of dwarf jesters.
European fools wore a cap with bells on it. They dressed
in a suit of many colors. In France there was a Feast of
Fools. It was celebrated at Christmas. Church members
behaved like buffoons at the Feast; they flapped around
like ninnies. Wealthy people and royalty kept fools.
Some fools became wealthy themselves. Some famous fools
appear in literature. The most famous appear in
Shakespeare's plays. They are <u>As You Like It</u>, <u>Twelfth
Night</u>, and <u>King Lear</u>. The fool in literature represents
someone who sees the truth; they can see through
pretenses. Most people try to live with dignity. They
overlook or deny things that make life undignified. One
is reminded by the fool that they are humiliated by
life.

20 EMPHASIS AND VARIETY

Too much of anything looks like a fault in writing. Too many
sentences that sound alike or look alike will produce a monotonous
effect on the reader. You can achieve variety through a number of
options.

20a Make writing emphatic by being economical.

Often sentences become unclear, illogical, or rambling because
they are not economical, that is, because of the *extra* words in
them. However, economy in writing is not always related to sen-   145

emph tence length. Even short sentences can be wordy: *Her hair was blond in color. The tile was rectangular in shape.* Remove any word that does not contribute to the effect you are trying to achieve.

WORDY
Our determination of the situation has been that in the matter of the death of the rat, it was the dog that should be blamed or credited as the case may be.

REVISED
The dog killed the rat.

REPETITIOUS
I've been reading this book; this book is very interesting; it is about Napoleon.

REVISED
I've been reading a very interesting book about Napoleon.

REDUNDANT
The authors have managed to condense all this information into a two-page article which is straight to the point and wastes no words!

REVISED
The authors have managed to condense all this information into a concise two-page article.

ACTIVITY 8

Edit to make the following sentences economical.

1. We must read our past history to learn from the words on the printed page those events that happened long ago.
2. In the consequence of a terminal sequence having been reached it is advisable if not altogether necessary that there be a cessation of forward progress.
3. After she said her name orally, I asked her the question if she would please repeat it again.
4. The car came into view; it was a red Corvette; it was going flat out; it came over the hill; it was leading a police car by half a mile.
5. The young knight suffered a mortal wound and then died.

emph

ACTIVITY 9

Revise each of the following sets of short sentences to produce a longer, more effective sentence. You may add and delete words, shift words around, change the forms of words, and change punctuation. You may combine sentences any way you like as long as the result is a *single* effective sentence for each set. Avoid overusing *and* to string words together.

1. The tank is an armored vehicle. The tank's armor is heavy. The tank's armor will stop a bullet. The tank was used in World War One. The tank revolutionized warfare.
2. Gregor woke up suddenly. He was lying on his back. He looked down at his body. He saw dozens of tiny legs. They were wiggling. They were waving in many directions. Gregor had been changed. He was a bug.
3. Commander Lucifer took a long puff. He was smoking his pipe. He blew out the smoke. The smoke made a dense cloud. He turned to stare. His manner was absent-minded. He saw the young sailor. The sailor steered the ship.

20b Make sentences emphatic by subordinating material.

One way to connect short sentences to each other is through subordination. "Subordinate" means "lower in order"; it means a complete idea or complete sentence has been reduced to a dependent (subordinate) clause. Connect lesser ideas with subordinate conjunctions (**4f**).

Although the fire destroyed the house, we managed to save our business records.

Though it might seem to us that saving the records is less important than loss of the house, only the writer can make this judgment. Perhaps the writer thinks that the house can be replaced but business records cannot.

Although we saved our business records, the fire destroyed the house.

emph   Here the writer has decided that the loss of the house is the more important idea. Note that the independent clause comes last when the writer is trying to emphasize the most important idea.

Avoid faulty subordination.

SUBORDINATE CLAUSE IN EMPHATIC POSITION
The fire destroyed the house, *although we saved our business records.*

Putting business records in the subordinate clause is a signal that this is the lesser idea, but putting it last, in the most emphatic position makes an ambivalent effect. Occasionally the writer may wish to create a deliberately ambivalent effect:

Melvina lost the contest, although she was the most beautiful girl in it.

However, in most nonfiction writing, ambivalence and ambiguity are errors.

This problem arises because in oral English *though* and *although* are frequently treated as equivalent to *but* or *however:*

The fire destroyed the house, *but* we saved our business records.
The fire destroyed the house; *however,* we saved our business records.

The two ideas are relatively similar in importance, the writer merely indicates the contrast.

ACTIVITY 10
Revise the following sentence sets to produce greater emphasis and rhythm. Connect some or all of them any way that produces more readable, less choppy writing.

1. We slept in the sand. It was close to the water's edge. It was between two protecting boulders. They took care of the stormy night winds for us.
2. I must have been asleep. All of a sudden there was the moon. It was a huge moon. It was framed in the window.
3. Eva was shy. She was chinless. She would be straining her upper

emph

lip. It would be over two teeth. They were enormous. She would sit in corners. She would be watching her mother.

4. It is the most defenseless of animals. It is a grounded primate. It is the baboon. The baboon has preserved himself. He has been developing nature's instrument. It is developed to a high degree. It is the most sophisticated instrument. It is for defense. The instrument is society.

5. That was the first day. My mother dressed me. I was neat-as-a-pin. I was in a starched shirt. I was in creased trousers. She had brushed my hair. She sent me off to school. It was in a taxi.

20c Use effective repetition for emphasis.

Repetition is one way to achieve emphasis within a sentence, as long as you don't create the impression of redundancy.

UNEMPHATIC

In every time, tongue, lonely, troubled corner on earth, this bewilderment has been uttered.

REVISED

In every time, in every tongue, in every lonely, troubled corner of the earth, this bewilderment has been uttered.

Benjamin Kogan, *Health*

UNEMPHATIC

Society is sustained by communication, which makes human life possible.

REVISED

Society is sustained by communication: communication makes life possible.

Peterson, Goldhaber, Pace, *Communication Probes*

ACTIVITY 11

Write five sentences of your own illustrating effective repetition. Repeat key terms, phrases, and so on. For example: *Their work took them beyond science, beyond imagination, beyond human understanding.*

emph

ACTIVITY 12

Revise the following paragraph for clarity. Combine sentences, add and delete words, shift words around, change the forms of words, and change punctuation. You may revise any way you like as long as you do not produce any garbled, illogical or ineffective sentences. Revise so that the paragraph contains several sentences; avoid overusing *and* to string words together.

Quebec

Quebec is a province of Canada, and it is the largest one. There are 10 provinces in Canada although the capital of Quebec is Quebec City, although Montreal is Quebec's largest city. Most people in Quebec speak a language which is French because it shares a boundary with Maine, New Hampshire, Vermont, and New York. It is popular with hunters. It is popular with fishing enthusiasts. It is popular with tourists. Since it was called New France, Quebec was originally a French possession. In the eighteenth century France ceded it to England. The reason was because of the French and Indian War. This was where the French Canadian farmers kept their farms. They held much of the land. Being merchants, England supplied many new people. Others came from Scotland when they became merchants. They controlled most of the trade. The language and customs of Quebec remained French conflict which between French Canadians and English Canadians warfare. The French Canadians mostly were Catholic. They were farmers; they speak French. The English Canadians were mostly Protestant. They were merchants. They spoke English. In 1867 French Canadians won the right to survival as a culture; their language and religion had been protected. They were higher than a kite about it. Today you can see Quebec has become much more industrial. Its people now live primarily in, if not entirely, the cities. It has a parliamentary government like Britain's. Like the rest

//

of Canada, its government is part of the monarchy, the
Queen of England. Canada is our neighbor, and they are
good friends of the U.S.A.

20d Use parallelism for emphasis.

Parallelism is a basic concept in writing. Similar concepts should
be written in similar forms; that is, they should be parallel. Parallelism is a form of repetition.

NONPARALLEL
I like *fishing and to ski.*

REVISED
I like *fishing and skiing.*

NONPARALLEL
We selected plants that were *tall and which were full of strength.*

REVISED
We selected plants that were *tall and strong.*

NONPARALLEL
They said they wanted to know *who he was, who his backers were,*
and *the names of his friends.*

REVISED They said they wanted to know *who he was, who his backers*
were, and who his friends were.

Avoid problems with parallelism. Incorrectly parallel expressions are confusing for readers.

CONFUSING
The short-order cook had to be *a fryer and baker* of bread. [Is he
frying and baking the bread?]

REVISED
The short order cook had to *fry hamburgers and bake bread.* [The
two actions have been separated.]

//

CONFUSING

They showed their appreciation *by eating and washing* the dishes.

REVISED

They showed their appreciation *by eating dinner and washing the dishes*.

CONFUSING

Doctors need blood plasma *not only to treat emergencies but also operations*.

REVISED

Doctors need blood plasma *not only in treating emergencies but also in doing operations*.

Avoid problems with *who, which,* and *that*. Clauses beginning with *and which, and who,* or *and that* require a preceding *who, which,* or *that* clause to achieve proper parallelism.

CONFUSING

We ordered a powerful new sports car with an overhead cam, *and which* would go 200 miles an hour.

REVISED

We ordered a powerful new sports car *which* had an overhead cam *and which* would go 200 miles an hour.
We ordered a powerful new sports car with an overhead cam and a 200 mile an hour top speed.

CONFUSING

She seemed to be the kind of executive employees found decisive *and who* would be fair.

REVISED

She seemed to be the kind of executive *whom* employees found decisive *and who* would be fair.

ACTIVITY 13

Revise the following sentences for effective parallelism.

1. We hired ourselves out that summer as trash haulers, lawn mowers, and guys to paint houses.
2. In less than two weeks we had covered neural, epidermal, and intestine disorders.

3. They were sent to prison for stealing and shooting a policeman.   *var*
4. These goggles are designed not only to protect women's eyes but also men.
5. The mail order house has sent us a set of wrenches we can't use, and which we didn't order.

20e Use contrast for emphasis.

You can emphasize an idea by contrasting it with another.

WITHOUT CONTRAST
The black-eyed ermine stole seemed to suggest that Etka had arrived directly from Minsk so that the fact that she had actually made many moves was concealed.

REVISED
Etka from Minsk had arrived *not* directly from Minsk, as the black-eyed ermine stole seemed to suggest, *but* after many moves.
Laura Cunningham, "The Girls' Room"

WITHOUT CONTRAST
By some chance they and we may become friends of the heart or within six months or two years we will probably be erased from each other's thoughts.

REVISED
Six months or two years will probably erase us from each other's thoughts, *unless* by some chance they and we have become friends of the heart.

Jane Howard, *Families*

20f Vary sentence beginnings.

Your sentences will sound monotonous if they all follow standard *subject-verb-object* sentence order. There are several options for variety in sentence beginnings.

Begin with absolute constructions. Absolutes look like sentences with deleted verbs. Because absolutes do not occur very often and because they sound unusual (the verb "missing"), an occasional sentence starting with an absolute is both varied and emphatic.

153

His hands in his pockets, the boy stood shyly waiting for her. [His hands *were* in his pockets; the boy stood shyly waiting for her.]
The elephant suddenly looming up above her, Casey backed into a corner.
His face looking tired, he watched the children at play. [His face *was* looking tired; he watched the children at play.]
His rod lying out on the logs, Nick tied a new hook on the leader, pulling the gut tight until it grimped into itself in a hard knot.

Ernest Hemingway, "Big Two-Hearted River: Part II"

The first plan failing, she tried an alternative. [The first plan *failed;* she tried an alternative.]

Begin with adjectives or adverbs.

Red, the evening sun glowed mysteriously.
Small, dirty, and *pathetic*—the puppy was irresistible.
Swiftly, silently the hawk dived on the pigeon.

Begin with appositives. The appositive is a synonym, an identifying name or label for a noun or pronoun. It can come before or after its noun or pronoun: *A **bluish green haze**, oxidation*, gradually transforms copper exposed to air. *Oxidation*, **a bluish green haze**, gradually transforms copper exposed to air.

A spaniel, my dog enjoyed the water as much as I did.
Supermarket shelves, the great barometer of what America eats, all seem to be colored brown now.

Ruth Gay, "Fear of Food," *The American Scholar,* Summer 1976

The national sport, politics keeps everyone in a turmoil over the state of the nation.

Begin with infinitives.

To be or not *to be,* that is the question.
To try, with gritted teeth and girded loins, is after all American.
To save his house was his only thought.

Begin with modifying clauses. A clause (unlike a phrase) has both
a subject and a verb. Start adverb clauses with a subordinator (*after,*

although, as, as if, because, before, if, since, though, unless, until   *var*
when, whenever, wherever, while).

> *After the guns had stopped,* we found soldiers everywhere.
> *Before the fire reached the barrels,* we had connected the second hose.

Begin with noun clauses. The noun clause (with its own subject and a verb) is used like a noun.

NOUN AS A SUBJECT   PREDICATE
The bread thief   must have been hungry.

NOUN CLAUSE AS SUBJECT   PREDICATE
Whoever stole the bread   must have been hungry

Noun clauses start with relative pronouns or certain subordinators (*that, what, whatever, when, where, wherever, which, who whoever, whom, whomever, whose, why*).

> *Why the villagers would do such a thing* tormented the priest.
> *Who we were* was her biggest worry.
> *That such a crime could be committed here* baffled our local police.

Begin with prepositional phrases. The prepositional phrase contains a preposition and its object, with optional modifiers for the object; a phrase does not have a subject or predicate.

> *In July,* they left for Paris.
> *At dawn,* we turned the dogs loose in the yard.
> *Near the bank of the river,* a great old willow had stood for fifty years.

Begin with participles. The present and past participles are the *-ing* and *-ed* forms of regular verbs.

> *Tilting* heavily toward the shore, our raft began moving off into the current.
> *Twice elected* to the Presidency, the second time in a record landslide, Mr. Nixon seemed immune from serious challenge.

> *The End of a Presidency*

> *Cracked,* the mirror seemed a portent of evil.

var

Begin with similes. A simile is a comparison using the words *like* or *as*.

Like a badly rusted hinge, the huge rocket groaned ominously and slowly leaned off perpendicular.
Like amoebas splitting, one dishwasher becomes two, one vacuum cleaner becomes two, one television becomes two.

Lionel Tiger, "Omnigamy: The New Kinship System,"
Psychology Today, July 1978

ACTIVITY 14

Write sentences of your own illustrating each of the ten variations above. Write one sentence beginning with an absolute, one beginning with an adjective (or several), and so on.

ACTIVITY 15

Revise the following paragraph for emphasis and variety. Combine sentences, add and delete words, shift words around, change the forms of words, and change punctuation. You may revise any way you like as long as you do not produce any garbled, illogical or ineffective sentences. Revise so that the paragraph contains several sentences; avoid overusing *and* to string words together.

Plastic

Plastic is not a natural substance. It is made by humans. It is a remarkable substance. Its products will have strength. It can be formed into any shape. It is used in toys. It is used in household goods. It is used in industrial products. It can be found, too, in clothing and all kinds of packaging. It is used in just about everything. Ballpoint pens are made of plastic. Plastic is in false teeth. It is used for photographic film. Billiard balls and plumbing pipe have plastic in them. Plastic is in paint and thread and even in things that make you healthy and for grooming. Plastic is lighter, if not the lightest, of many natural materials. It is stronger. It does not rust like metal or wood. And

it seldom deteriorates as rubber does. And its
conductivity of electricity is as low, if not lower,
than anything. Plastic does not absorb water. Plastic
can be molded. It can be cut. It can be fused together.
It can be made stiff and hard. It can be made soft and
pliable. Some plastic will not burn. It can be produced
in long sheets and which are as thin as paper. It can be
produced in liquid form. It is used for lacquer. It can
be produced in any color. It can also be transparent
like glass. It resists wear. It is relatively
inexpensive. Without plastic the modern world could not
exist.

20g Vary sentence types.

Writers can fall into the habit of writing the same type of sentence over and over again. If many of your sentences are alike in
structure, make some variations by using simple, compound, complex, or compound-complex structures.

SIMPLE SENTENCE

The simple sentence is "simple" only in a grammatical sense: it
has only one subject-predicate relationship. But there are several
options for variety with simple sentences.

Use compound subjects. Two sentences expressing similar ideas
can often be revised into one sentence with a compound subject.

TWO SENTENCES
The motorcycle is a noisy road vehicle. Old cars with faulty mufflers
are also noisy road vehicles.

REVISED WITH A COMPOUND SUBJECT
Motorcycles and old cars with faulty mufflers are noisy road vehicles.

Use compound predicate. Two sentences about the same subject
can often be revised into one sentence with a compound predicate.

157

TWO SENTENCES
The boys designed their own clubhouse. Then they built it.

REVISED WITH A COMPOUND PREDICATE
The boys *designed and built their own clubhouse*.

Use compound complements. Sentences with the same verb can often be revised as one sentence with a compound complement.

TWO SENTENCES
The youths painted the old house. Then they painted its garage.

REVISED
The youths painted *the old house and its garage*.

Use other compounds. Other possibilities for compound elements within the simple sentence include compound adjectives, compound adverbs, compound prepositional phrases, and so on.

SIMPLE SENTENCE WITH COMPOUND APPOSITIVE, DIRECT OBJECT
The old horse and its companions, a dog and a cat, hauled paper, junk, and sometimes furniture.

ACTIVITY 16

Write five simple sentences of your own illustrating variety through compound elements. Refer to the examples above. Write one simple sentence with no compound element, one simple sentence with a compound subject, one with a compound predicate, and so on.

COMPOUND SENTENCE

The compound sentence looks like two sentences joined with one of the coordinate conjunctions: *and, but, or, nor, so, for, yet*. It is composed of two independent clauses—two clauses, each with its own subject-predicate relationship, and each of which could be written as a separate sentence.

TWO INDEPENDENT CLAUSES
The planes landed. [and] The passengers got off.

REVISED AS A COMPOUND SENTENCE
The planes landed, *and* the passengers got off.

Note the difference between a compound sentence and a simple sentence with compound predicate:

COMPOUND SENTENCE
SUBJECT + PREDICATE + SUBJECT + PREDICATE
The planes landed, and they taxied down the runway.

SIMPLE SENTENCE WITH A COMPOUND PREDICATE
SUBJECT + PREDICATE
           VERB   +   VERB
The planes landed and taxied down the runway.

Not only can the sentence itself be compound, but you can compound any of the elements within it to produce variety:

COMPOUND SUBJECT
The guards and prisoners

COMPOUND PREPOSITIONAL PHRASE
in the building and out in the yard

COMPOUND PREDICATE
worked together and came to be friends,

COMPOUND VERB
for they *had much in common and seemed to share the same fate.*

ACTIVITY 17

Identify each of the following sentences by type by writing C beside compound sentences and S beside simple sentences.

1. The boys were playing basketball, and the girls were playing football.
2. Mini drove into the parking lot at top speed and stopped just short of the mailbox.
3. January and February are the two worst winter months here, and March is not much better.
4. We had planned to stay all night, but the furnace quit at 7:00.
5. Two captains and their general hopped in a jeep and headed for town, but only after evening prayers.

COMPLEX SENTENCE

The complex sentence has one (and only one) independent clause but at least one dependent clause. There are many opportunities for variety with complex sentences.

INDEPENDENT
They bought plain white dishes
DEPENDENT
because they planned to serve very simple dinners.

Dependent clauses start with subordinate conjunctions—*after, because, since,* and so on—or one of the relative pronouns—*who, which, that.* **4b.**

SUBORDINATE CLAUSE FIRST
Although they said they supported the ceasefire, they worked to sabotage plans for the peace talks. [Note the comma with the subordinate clause first.]

SUBORDINATE CLAUSE LAST
They worked to sabotage plans for the peace talks *although they said they supported the cease-fire.* [When the subordinate clause follows the independent clause, the comma is sometimes optional, depending on meaning.]

ACTIVITY 18

Write five complex sentences on your own. Write some sentences in which the dependent clause comes first, some in which it comes last, some in which it interrupts. See 4f, 4b for subordinate conjunctions and relative pronouns.

COMPOUND-COMPLEX SENTENCE

The compound complex sentence contains two or more independent clauses and at least one dependent clause.

INDEPENDENT
The puppy chased its tail awhile,

DEPENDENT
and *when it tired of that,*

INDEPENDENT
it tried to wriggle into an old slipper.

ACTIVITY 19
Write five compound-complex sentences of your own. See 4f, 4b for subordinate conjunctions and relative pronouns.

ACTIVITY 20
Revise the following paragraph for variety in structure and sentence type. Combine sentences, add and delete words, shift words around, change the forms of words, and change punctuation. You may revise any way you like as long as you do not produce any garbled, illogical or ineffective sentences. Revise so that the paragraph contains several sentences; avoid overusing *and* to string words together.

The Eye

The eye is nature's triumph. It is one of the great works of nature. It works like a camera. The outer cover of the eye is the cornea. It is transparent. Between the cornea and the iris is a liquid. It is called aqueous humor. The iris surrounds the pupil. The pupil is the opening of the eye. The rest of the eye is filled with another liquid. It is called vitreous humor. There is a lens right behind the pupil. This lens is focused by muscle action. This action allows us to focus on near and far objects. This lens gets less flexible as we grow older. It also becomes less transparent. Light enters the eye. The amount of light is controlled by the colored part of the eye. It is called the iris. The light falls on the back of the eye. This is called the retina. The lens of the eye reflects light from above on the lower part of the retina. It reflects light from below upon the upper part of the retina. Then objects on the retina are upside down. The retina is stimulated by the light. This is transmitted to the optic nerve. It has nearly a million fibers in it. The nerve transmits the message to the brain. The brain interprets the message from the eye. Then we see things properly. They appear right-side up in the brain.

var

20h Vary sentence patterns

Different sentence patterns create different impressions on your readers. If all your sentences use the same pattern, the effect on your readers will be monotonous. Vary your sentence patterns with loose or cumulative, periodic, and balanced patterns.

Use loose sentences. The typical English sentence is called the loose or cumulative sentence. It generally identifies a subject, followed by some statement (the predicate) about that subject, adding modifiers and qualifiers at the end. The sentence unfolds in "normal" or "natural" order as the writer thinks through his or her thought.

> The last decade has made a large number of men more uneasy about what to wear than they might have believed possible.
>
> > Anne Hollander, "Clothes Make the Man—Uneasy,"
> > *The New Republic*, 7 (Sept. 1974)

In a loose sentence, the writer spins out details. Such a sentence is built by addition, adding modifiers to the main clause.

> The grasshopper took hold of the hook with his front feet, *spitting tobacco juice on it.*
>
> > Ernest Hemingway, "Big Two-Hearted River: Part II"

> We rode all night, *our horses panting and soaked in sweat, to reach our post ahead of the messenger.*

ACTIVITY 21

Revise the following short sentences to longer, sentences. Reduce some of the sentences to participles or adjectives. Combine sentences where appropriate.

EXAMPLE

The house became ominous at night. It creaked. It popped. It moaned softly.

REVISED

The house became ominous at night, creaking, popping, moaning softly.

1. She stood at the end of the pier. She looked out to sea.
2. They laughed. They joked. They jostled each other. The boys made their way toward the store.
3. The car was full of possibilities. It was a 1970 Pontiac. It was rusted. It was dented. It was sagging on its springs.
4. She was tall. She was stern. She was intimidating. Miss Marsh waited for the class to settle.
5. The little boat bobbed at the end of its tether. The boat was gay. It was in its new paint. It was red, white, and blue.

ACTIVITY 22
Write five loose sentences of your own.

Create variety with periodic sentences. The periodic sentence is an inverted structure. The main clause or the predicate is withheld until the end. While the loose sentence pattern is the most common one in English, too much of a good thing—too many loose sentences in a row—can produce negative effects on the reader. If *all* your sentences are like these, your writing will have a "loose" and perhaps monotonous sound to it. One way to avoid this monotony is to revise to create periodic sentences.

STRING OF LOOSE SENTENCES
I had left home late in the afternoon to go for a walk along the banks of the river. I had no real plans for getting home in time for dinner. I began to think of food more and more as the day wore on.

REVISED TO A PERIODIC SENTENCE
Having left home late in the afternoon to go for a walk along the banks of the river and having no real plans for getting home in time for dinner, I began to think of food more and more as the day wore on.

Periodic sentences can be constructed in a number of ways:

MAIN CLAUSE AT END
In a score of small things of no advantage to him, in the hair and the direction of the hair upon his limbs, for example, *he recalls the ape.*

H. G. Wells, *The Outline of History*   **163**

var

After a decade of heavy losses, labor troubles, and mediocre management that almost drove it into the ground, Italian auto giant *Fiat is once again on the fast track in the European auto market.*

"Fiat Slims Down to Get Back into the Black,"
Business Week, 4 (July 1983)

PREDICATE WITHHELD UNTIL THE END

The minister, worried about the souls of his parish and fearful that many of them might already have been lost to the forces of temptation, *gave a sermon on the return to faith.*

ACTIVITY 23

Write five periodic sentences of your own, some in which modifiers, phrases, dependent clauses come first and the main clause comes last, and some in which the subject and predicate are interrupted by modifiers.

Create variety with balanced sentences. The balanced sentence has a formal elegance; for this reason it is often used in public oratory. The balanced sentence is crafted by balancing similar ideas in similar words and structures.

WEAK

And so my fellow Americans when you want to know what your country can do for you, just ask yourself that question the other way around.

REVISED AS BALANCED SENTENCE

And so my fellow Americans, ask not what your country can do for you; ask what you can do for your country.

John F. Kennedy, Inaugural Address

WEAK

It is no vice to be extreme in defending liberty; and . . . to pursue justice only moderately lacks virtue.

REVISED AS BALANCED SENTENCE

Extremism in the defense of liberty is no vice; and . . . moderation in the pursuit of justice is no virtue.

Barry Goldwater, Acceptance Speech

WEAK

The only way to win is through perseverance; however, if you quit, obviously the victory will not be yours.

REVISED AS BALANCED SENTENCE

Winners never quit; quitters never win.

ACTIVITY 24

Revise the following weak sentences as balanced sentences.

EXAMPLE

Life is not long enough for all the things we do, but then there isn't much reward in taking the time to do most of the things anyway.

REVISED AS BALANCED SENTENCE

Life is not long enough for all the things we do, and the things we do are not reward enough for all the time they take.

1. It doesn't do much good to say how many problems you have that might overcome you; it's better to say if you can overcome your problems.
2. The truth never diminishes the strong, and strong people don't try to cut down things that are true.
3. If you are spending all your earnings you will end in poverty, but if you take in as much as you spend, this is the way to be successful.
4. Curiosity begets understanding, and the more you learn the more curious you will be.
5. America must defend her children, but then they have a duty to do the same for their country.

ACTIVITY 25

Write three balanced sentences of your own.

ACTIVITY 26

Revise the following paragraph for varied sentences. Combine sentences, add and delete words, shift words around, change the forms of words, and change punctuation. You may revise any way you like as long as you do not produce any garbled, illogical or ineffective sentences. Revise so that the paragraph contains several sentences; avoid overusing *and* to string words together.

var

The Death of Socrates

Socrates was a great man. He was a philosopher. He lived in Greece. He was born about 469 B.C. He was the wisest man of his time, probably. He was physically unattractive. Some people called him ugly. He was fat. He was bald. He liked to read. He was also a teacher. He taught by questioning. He would ask people what they believed. Then he would ask why they believed it. Then he would ask how it was possible to believe such a thing. Then he would ask if they could believe things that were contradictions. This way he made people understand. His questions caused them to examine their beliefs. It also caused them to analyze their logic. Many people were unhappy with his methods. They did not like to be forced to analyze themselves. They did not like to be forced to change their minds. The people of Athens decided to get rid of Socrates. They said he was not a religious man. They said he corrupted his students. They said he should be put to death for this. He went to trial. There were 501 jurors. Socrates was his own lawyer. He said none of his students were corrupted. No student testified against him. The jury convicted him anyway. He mocked the jury. He said his punishment should be a life-time pension. It should be a gift from the state for his good work. He was sentenced to die. He was forced to drink poison. It was hemlock.

Create emphasis by inverting sentences. Changing the usual order (subject-verb-object) of sentences can provide emphasis.

Gone was the sweeping mandate Mr. Nixon had won from the American Electorate in November, 1972. . . .

Staff of The New York Times, *The End of a Presidency*

ACTIVITY 27
Change the five loose sentences you wrote for Activity 22 to periodic, balanced, or inverted patterns. Then change each sentence once more to a new pattern.

20i Vary sentence lengths.

There is no rule in English concerning length of sentence. But if all your sentences are the same length, you may produce an unnaturally monotonous rhythm that suggests all the sentences are of the same importance, as in a list. Furthermore, it is true that professional writers tend—on the average—to write longer sentences than students do. For example:

> When he was done shaking hands with me, the Judge smoothed back his thick black mane, cut off square at the collar, like a senator's, put one had in his pocket, played with the half-dozen emblems and charms on his watch chain with the other, teetered from his heels to his toes two or three times, lifted his head, smiled at me like I was the biggest pleasure he'd had in years, and drew a great, deep breath, like he was about to start an oration. I'd seen him go through all that when all he finally said was, "How-do-you-do?" to some lady he wasn't sure he hadn't met before. The judge had a lot of public manner.
>
> Walter Van Tilburg Clark, *The Ox-Bow Incident*

Clark's first sentence is 85 words long. The unusual length was achieved almost entirely through the use of compound predicates and similes. Here the author is trying to create an image, building suspense with his long sentence. His second sentence is 26 words long, and the third is 8. The final very short sentence is emphatic by contrast. The interplay among long, medium, and short sentences sets up a rhythm that the reader is hardly aware of but that nevertheless helps to make the point.

Avoid rambling sentences. A sentence "rambles" when the writer strings ideas together in an unplanned stream, usually using too many coordinators or subordinators. Sometimes these rambling sentences can be revised by deleting irrelevant details, sometimes **167**

var   by breaking the sentence into smaller sentences. But sometimes it is necessary to rethink and start anew with a more controlled *idea*. Unless you are deliberately trying to create an image, as Clark did in *The Ox-Bow Incident*, revise excessively long sentences containing many connecting words.

RAMBLING (TOO MANY COORDINATORS AND SUBORDINATORS)
We went to the pond to do some fishing *because* we knew there were lots of good brim there *and* we didn't have much else to do *so* we decided just to take some time off *and* try to relax *and* have some fun for a few hours *until* we had to go home *and* get ready for work that night at the new factory *where* they were building the experimental car the government had promised last year in its budget proposal for restoration of small towns like ours *that* were in need of assistance to get out of the recession *and* put people back to work *so* they could have something to do besides go fishing all the time.

REVISED FOR EFFECTIVE LENGTH
As part of the government's small-town restoration proposal last year, the experimental car was being built at the new factory where we worked. There was a small pond near the factory, and since we had a few hours before work with not much to do, we went fishing for brim.

ACTIVITY 28
Write a long and short pattern of your own. Write a longer than average sentence, followed by a short one. Use the contrast between long and short to create emphasis.

Do not pad your sentences. It is possible but not advisable to lengthen sentences artificially simply by padding them. *Padding* means sticking in detail after detail, modifiers, phrases, and so on, in a mechanical fashion—whether they fit the context or not. This might be a good technique to generate material when freewriting, but in the revising stage you should decide precisely what details you want to emphasize and what effect you want to have on the reader. For example:

PADDED
Our dear little gray goose whose feathers shine so sleekly when they are wet, runs waddling fatly and honking brazenly around and about the yard until its poor frail webbed feet become shredded quite be-

yond repair on the sharp old fieldstones lying carelessly strewn here *var* and there in the outback without regard for the simple bird's comfort.

REVISIONS

We have a gray goose running free in our yard. [The emphasis is on the act.]

With feathers that shine sleekly when wet, our little gray goose waddles fatly about the yard, honking brazenly. [The emphasis is on appearance.]

We had strewn fieldstones here and there in the yard without regard to the little goose's webbed feet, which were soon shredded by the sharp stones. [The emphasis is on cause.]

Waddling about on the sharp fieldstones in the yard, our little gray goose's frail webbed feet have become shredded beyond repair. [The emphasis is on consequences.]

ACTIVITY 29

Revise these sentences. Edit out any padding (but try not to lose the central meaning).

1. It is probably true that the reason that we have not really conquered nature is because of the fact that we have not conquered ourselves.
2. There is an idea and it is about animals, namely that they have their own languages, and this idea is an old notion.
3. A female trunkback turtle is often a thousand pounds (half a ton) or more in weight and she is full of a kind of zeal that is fanatical and it is given from the glands, so that it would almost pass for something like ingenuity.
4. His father got up into the seat where the older brother already was sitting at and then he struck out at the two very thin-looking mules with two blows which were savage with the peeled willow stick but he didn't really put any heat into it.
5. The thing which is possible is that there will be a chief problem in the coming generation and it will be survival, no matter whether it will be from one thing or another; it could be from nuclear bombs, and it could also be from genocide; or, it might be from ecological disaster, or maybe it will be from starvation of masses of people or wars that keep going on and on without ending.

var

ACTIVITY 30
Write five sentences of longer than average length. Avoid stringing words together with coordinate conjunctions. Avoid padding your sentences. Strive for sentences that create effective images without giving the impression of being excessively wordy.

Avoid too many short, choppy sentences. Too many long sentences may put the reader to sleep. Too many short ones may irritate the reader. For example:

> Our cat is a Persian. Its hair is long. It is pure white. It has unusual blue eyes.

The reader may be able to read one or two sentences like this (that is, one after the other), but the third and fourth sentences begin to make a pattern of short, choppy, immature sentences. Because each sentence is a separate and unrelated idea (the relationship is not specified), they look like a list of random facts. There is no emphasis here to tell us that any of these ideas is more important than the others. Soon readers will stop following the ideas as the rhythm builds and overpowers the words, like the rhythm section of a band getting very loud and drowning out the melody. Few people enjoy the experience. Even if all the rest of the sentences have better rhythm, the memory of the faulty section will remain (like a misplaced cymbal crash). To revise for better emphasis, more natural rhythm, connect some of the sentences.

> Our cat, a long-haired Persian, is pure white and has unusual blue eyes.

The revised sentence not only has more mature rhythm, it actually contains fewer words than the four original sentences. Thus, while it is longer, overall it is also more concise.

ACTIVITY 31
Revise the following passage for effective sentence structure. Combine sentences, add information, delete redundant words, change the wording of the passage but try not to change the main ideas. Use this exercise to show how well you understand sentence structure.

Making False Teeth

The dentist first makes an impression. It is of the patient's bite line. The dentist does this with a pair of things that are shaped like the letter <u>U</u> made of rubber. They are impression trays. Once this activity of the dentist has been brought to a completion the models can be made and it is the usual thing for the dentist to pour the models. Or an assistant can. But usually the dentist does it. Sometimes they are sent to the technician since this is when the technician can construct them. A model is a replica of something. It is the patient's upper palate. Or it could be the lower palate. The model is made of plaster. First, there is excess rubber which is extra and must be trimmed away from the tray and this makes it easier to work with it. Mixing this stuff to a medium consistency, is a bowl of plaster. Plaster which is watery is difficult to work with because plaster which is stiff sets up too fast. The plaster must be thoroughly blended. Then the bowl of plaster must be tapped. Firmly. It is done on a hard surface. This is to force the air bubbles out or it will be ruined by air bubbles. The impression tray is filled with plaster by one using a small knife. Or you could do it with a spatula. Next a patty is made. This is done with the remaining plaster. A dentist if the patty should be about the size of a hamburger enjoy their work. Next the tray is set upside down on the patty. It is wiggled into the patty. Gently. It is done just so all the plaster in the tray is making contact with the patty. The tray should not be buried in the plaster. This would be a disaster. This has to dry completely. Then the tray can be pried off to carefully expose the model. Then the model is finished. Then the technician's work begins.

Punctuation

^
,

Accurate punctuation clarifies and emphasizes meaning and, for many readers, reflects the care you have given to a paper.

21 COMMA

The comma is the most frequently used mark of punctuation. It is chiefly used to set off one part of a sentence from another. In written English, the comma is a signal telling the reader to pause as if speaking.

21a Use commas to separate sentences joined by the coordinate conjunctions *and, or, nor, for, but, yet, so.*

Thousands of teenagers packed the concert, but they made hardly a sound as she finished the song.
The questions became more and more embarrassing, so he abruptly terminated the press conference.

If the sentences are very short, and there is no possibility of confusion, the comma is sometimes eliminated.

It rained and it rained.

Using only a comma to join two sentences creates a *comma splice,* a punctuation error unless the sentences are very short and similarly constructed.

COMMA SPLICE
The opponents of the new tax legislation were aggressive and bad mannered, they screamed obscenities and jammed their placards into the faces of the congressmen.

ACCEPTABLE
I came, I saw, I conquered. [The sentences are short and similarly constructed.]

A comma splice can be corrected by replacing the comma with a ⌃,
semicolon, a colon, or a period or by adding a coordinating conjunction immediately after the comma. (See **8.**)

ACTIVITY 1

Edit the following sentences; insert the proper punctuation and appropriate words; delete unnecessary punctuation.

1. Granger slowly lifted his head but he still could not see the buck.
2. Expanding rapidly, the star glowed brighter and brighter, it dominated its portion of the sky.
3. Bacon and ham sizzled on the grill, the rich smell of coffee floated into the room.
4. Since joining the circus, the Flying Fouret had mastered the difficult triple but he also had broken four ribs and an arm.
5. The cat yowled and the dog barked.

21b Use a comma after most introductory elements.

First, we must organize a committee of volunteers.
Besides John, there were three who refused to participate.
Near a great blue spruce, they set up a salt lick for the deer.
In spite of that decision, we shall continue to picket the Capitol.

The comma may be omitted if the introductory material is very short. The effect of leaving the comma out is to deemphasize the beginning. Be careful to use the comma if its omission makes the sentence ambiguous.

AMBIGUOUS

In time capsules accounted for 50 percent of sales.

CLEAR

In time, capsules accounted for 50 percent of sales.

If the sentence begins with a long introductory phrase or series of phrases, use the comma.

In the old barn across from the Smithers' rebuilt farmhouse, Jeremy sat and contemplated his future.

175

, If the introductory material contains a verb or verb form, use the comma.

> Since I arrived in town, property values have decreased significantly.
> Until the welders had secured the beams, no one was allowed near the scaffolding.
> Stumbling down the long hallway, Ruth kept muttering about staying up all night to study for a test that was cancelled.
> To run a business properly, you should have a sound accounting background.
> Ignoring me, the salesperson continued to chat with his friend.

ACTIVITY 2
Edit the following sentences; insert commas where appropriate.

1. In addition to Mary Jane was also added to the list.
2. Having carved the roast expertly Cynthia began to serve her guests.
3. I have heard what you had to say but I must follow my own feelings.
4. Slipping quietly into the back of the room the student slid noiselessly into his seat.
5. To run an effective program you must have a command of the proper sequence.

ACTIVITY 3
Edit the following paragraph to eliminate problems with commas. Add any needed punctuation; delete unnecessary marks.

Gladiators

In order to provide the deceased with an armed escort into the next world Roman gladiators fought at funerals; those who died became attendants for the deceased. Gladiators were very popular and performed for entertainment all over the Roman empire. Early emperors owned several hundred gladiators and later ones had several thousand. The gladiators marched into the arena in procession and then they handed their weapons over to be examined. Gladiators fought in pairs until one of them was wounded, the spectators then signalled whether

```
the wounded man should live or die. Thumbs up meant he
should live but thumbs down meant death and this is the
origin of our expressions ''thumbs up'' and ''thumbs
down.'' The word gladiator comes from a Latin word for
''sword,'' and survives today in gladiolus, a flower with
leaves shaped like swords.
```

21c Use commas to separate items in a series.

Jojo lost his glasses, his wallet, and his sunny disposition when the sailboat capsized.

Some writers consider the comma before the *and* to be optional when there is no possibility of misreading the series. However, retaining the comma is never wrong, and sometimes it is necessary for clarity. Students should mark each item in a series with a comma. For example:

Dan's favorite breakfast is coffee, orange juice, corn flakes and beer.

To make clear that Dan does not put beer in his corn flakes, use a comma before *and*.

When the series is the subject of the sentence, do not insert a comma after the last item. Do not separate the subject from its verb.

Dates, places, and the names of Presidents were all he could think of.

21d Use commas between movable adjectives.

If adjectives describe the same word and can be rearranged without loss of meaning, separate them with commas. A good test is to say the sentence with *and* between the adjectives; if the adjectives make sense with *and*, use commas.

ˆ
,

It was a long, arduous, depressing exam. [It was a long and arduous and depressing exam.]

When adjectives are not freely movable and cannot be separated by *and,* they have a cumulative modifying effect, and they should not be separated with commas.

She was an inquisitive but dedicated business major.
Jean reluctantly rapped on the door of the old, dilapidated Victorian mansion.

21e Use commas to set off "nonessential" elements in a sentence.

Nothing in a sentence is actually nonessential since every word and phrase conveys some meaning. But *nonessential* here means an element the elimination of which does not alter the meaning of the base sentence (the subject and its verb). Such elements are usually called *nonrestrictive;* they can be words, phrases, or clauses. They can be contrasted with *restrictive* elements, which are necessary to preserve the meaning of the base sentence. Nonrestrictive modifiers should be set off with commas from the essential parts of the sentence.

Set off nonrestrictive appositives. An appositive "renames" a preceding noun or pronoun. A nonrestrictive appositive provides added information but does not limit or restrict its noun or pronoun. Most appositives that follow full proper names are nonrestrictive because usually a proper name is the most specific limiting information there is.

Herman Melville, author of *Moby-Dick,* spent many years at sea.
A standing ovation was given to Jimmy Carter, former President of the United States.

Unless these sentences are directed at someone who knows two

Herman Melvilles or two Jimmy Carters, the appositives provide
nonessential information. The next two examples show the difference between a nonrestrictive appositive and a restrictive one that
identifies its noun or pronoun.

> Mike's brother Bob lives in California.
> Mike's brother, Bob, lives in California.

Without the commas, the writer is saying that Mike has more than
one brother, and the one named Bob lives in California. Contrast
this sentence with the one below it, which says there is only one
brother.

Set off nonrestrictive modifying phrases and clauses. The meaning of the sentence changes if the commas are left out. These examples assume the reader knows which group and which young man
are being discussed.

> The rock group, playing its final number, had been arrested in Lon-
> don last summer.
> The young man, who had just turned eighteen, entered the univer-
> sity instead of working for his father.

Set off contrastive elements.

> The issue is one of people, not of politics.
> A number of shareholders voted for the merger, but others wanted
> to maintain the status quo.

Set off explanatory and parenthetic material.

> The decision, it seems to me, was arbitrary and rash.
> The plan, or at least the latest version of it, was not well received by
> the group.

Set off transitional words and phrases.

> The harp seal, however, has been threatened for years.
> On the other hand, Sally is admirably suited to her job.

ACTIVITY 4

Edit the following sentences; insert commas where appropriate.

1. The breakfast orders called for an omelet waffles and ham and eggs.
2. John Renquist a minister in a local church wrote the article about boxing.
3. Maple oak walnut and cherry were all possibilities.
4. The women who joined the action crusade represented a cross-section of society.
5. Larry Holmes a heavyweight struggled to retain his title.
6. Ardently devoted to his wife Mary Lou telephoned every night when he was on the road.
7. The experiment by the way will be run three times not twice.
8. The sorority blackballed Muffin not Stephie for her actions at the party last night.
9. The lawn or what passed for one hadn't been mowed all summer.
10. John was an attractive bubbly six-year-old child.

ACTIVITY 5

Edit the following paragraph to eliminate problems with commas. Add any needed punctuation; delete unnecessary marks.

Computer

Our new computer is sophisticated, and fast. It keeps all the records for our athletic program, and even prepares our correspondence orders new supplies for the locker room, and regulates the temperature in the gym. Of course learning to use the computer has been a difficult tiresome and often frustrating task. The computer an Epson has dual disk drives a detachable keyboard and a dot—matrix printer that can print 160 characters per second. The floppy disks which hold approximately 100 pages of text are 5¼ inch squares. They are made of a flexible recording material plastic. Naturally the computer has some problems but not serious ones. It sometimes crashes refuses to function and loses material we have typed. Nevertheless by contrast with its predecessor the typewriter it makes our work much easier saving us time effort and money.

21f Use commas to separate dialogue from the rest of the sentence.

He asked, "How can you distinguish between the dancer and the dance?"
"It's not who wins," he commented bitterly, "but how much you get paid."

When quoted material ends with an exclamation point or question mark, the comma is redundant.

REDUNDANT
"Is everyone ready to go?", she asked.

CORRECT
"Is everyone ready to go?" she asked.

21g Use commas to set off names and titles in direct address.

Direct address means speaking to a person (directly addressing) and calling him or her by name, descriptive phrase, or title. It occurs in dialogue, letter writing, and sometimes in essays when the writer addresses the reader.

You see, Jill, losing your job doesn't mean the end of the world.
Doctor, how bad is it?
Say, man, what're you doing here?
So once again, citizens of America, the future lies in our own hands.
And please, Mandy, don't tell anyone about this until I get there.

21h Use commas correctly in dates and addresses.

He was born on November 16, 1939, at Letterman General Hospital. San Francisco, California, is still his permanent residence. [Notice especially the commas after *1939* and *California*.]

^
,

When the day precedes the month, military style, no commas are required:

He was born 16 November 1939.

No comma is used for a month-day combination:

He was born on November 16 in San Francisco.

Some writers omit commas for month-year combinations:

January 1985 is the date we expect the bill to come before the committee.

21i Use a comma after the salutation of informal letters and after the closing of any letter.

Dear Marcia,   Dear Dad,   What's happening, Babe,
Sincerely yours,   Love,   With best wishes,

21j Use a comma with a short interrogative at the end of a declarative sentence.

You're not going to go out with me, are you?
The Magna Carta was signed in 1215, right?

21k Use commas correctly with *too*.

When *too* is used to mean "also" at the beginning of a sentence, most writers set it off with a comma.

Too, an abstract must be submitted with the paper.

If *too* falls in the middle or at the end of the sentence, the use of commas depends on the emphasis you want to provide.

His mother, too, was going.
His mother too was going.
Willie wondered if his mother was going, too.

21l Use commas correctly with mild interjections and words like *yes* and *no*.

Yes, the cells have duplicated themselves.
Well, I'm not sure if that's true.

21m Use commas for clarity.

Sometimes, even if there is no specific rule for using a comma, one might be needed to prevent ambiguity or misreading.

AMBIGUOUS
Those who can teach the rest of us.
Eight months before I had taken the class.

CLEAR
Those who can, teach the rest of us.
Eight months before, I had taken the class.

ACTIVITY 6
Edit the following sentences; insert commas where necessary.

1. Stalley replied "I'm not sure sir. I thought I was only going fifty-five."
2. Attendance too was one of the requirements.
3. Yes quantities have been limited by the embargo.
4. Henry you're going to have to start coming to class more often.
5. The package was addressed to Mr. Daryl Groutt 5002 Chipwall Drive Weidman Michigan.
6. Dear Charlie
7. "That combination" Rachel said knowingly "will never work."
8. You go too okay?
9. The children were covered by the policy too.
10. Maria thought for a long time before saying "I just can't sell this property."

no $\overset{\curvearrowright}{,}$

ACTIVITY 7

Edit the following paragraph to eliminate problems with commas. Add any needed punctuation; delete unnecessary marks; make other changes if necessary.

Finches

```
    We encouraged everyone to look for the birds were
approaching the feeder. "Look" I said "They are
finches." "Finches?" Anna asked. "Yes finches." "But
they look like sparrows" said Quentin "dark and
dirty." "Maybe so Quentin" I said "but in the spring
they will turn bright yellow. They have been coming here
since March 1979 and they always turn yellow in the
spring. No they aren't sparrows." "The sparrows too
look better in the spring right?" Anna added. "Well I
wouldn't go that far" I said.
```

22 OVERUSE OF COMMAS

Sometimes problems arise not from failing to insert commas but from using too many. Here are some cases where commas may seem called for, but to use them is incorrect.

22a Do not separate a subject from its verb or a verb from its complement or direct object.

MISUSED The well-educated but naive attorney, could not understand why anyone would commit such a crime.

REVISED The well-educated but naive attorney could not understand why anyone would commit such a crime.

MISUSED The astronaut gave, fully detailed instructions to the ground crew.

REVISED The astronaut gave fully detailed instructions to the ground crew.

22b Do not use a comma before the first or after the last item in a series.

MISUSED Aunt Anne gave him, good advice, $300, and a sloppy kiss.

REVISED Aunt Anne gave him good advice, $300, and a sloppy kiss.

MISUSED They liked athletic, ambitious, intelligent, students.

REVISED They liked athletic, ambitious, intelligent students.

22c Do not use a comma to signal a series or list after *such as* or *like.*

MISUSED They were known to give tests such as, multiple choice, true/false, and essay.

REVISED They were known to give tests such as multiple choice, true/false, and essay.

MISUSED From a distance the birds looked like, children, flowers, ornaments.

REVISED From a distance the birds looked like children, flowers, ornaments.

22d Do not separate compound elements.

Many sentence elements can be joined (compounded) with conjunctions like *and* or *or.* No comma should be used with such compounds.

MISUSED We read essays by Lamb, and Montaigne.

REVISED We read essays by Lamb and Montaigne.

MISUSED The student typed her paper carefully, and handed it in two weeks late.

REVISED The student typed her paper carefully and handed it in two weeks late.

no ‸

ACTIVITY 8

Edit the following paragraph to eliminate problems with commas. Add any needed punctuation; delete unnecessary marks; rearrange the format of the sentences if necessary.

Guadeloupe

Our geography class, had been studying the Caribbean islands and I took notes from a lecture on Guadeloupe. Guadeloupe is a territory of the French Antilles, and consists of twin islands Basse-Terre and Grande-Terre. The two islands are separated by swamps, and a small inlet the Riviere Salee. Guadeloupe lies northwest of Marie-Galante, La Desirade and the Iles des Saintes and de la Petite Terre. The two parts of Guadeloupe are very different. Basse-Terre is mountainous and volcanic, Grande-Terre on the other hand is flat. ''You Mr. Adams would like Guadeloupe'' the professor said. Mr. Adams who was in the front row asked ''Why?'' ''Because its temperature is always very warm but seldom hot, it rarely gets above 85 degrees.'' ''Never?'' the same student asked. ''Well perhaps sometimes but you always have the mountains which are always cool.'' ''What about rain?'' someone asked. ''Ah there we have a different matter. The mountainous parts of Guadeloupe receive a great deal of rain hurricanes too. However the flatlands receive very little rain, and experience droughts in the dry season.'' Most of the class felt this was not enough information so we began asking questions about Guadeloupe. The professor explained that the mountainous side of the country was covered by a tropical rain forest, the flatland was only sparsely dotted with scrub wood. Despite these differences the islands are a tropical paradise. The people of Guadeloupe many of whom are descendants of slaves represent many races and cultures, their chief products are, sugar rum and bananas. Coffee and citrus fruits too are grown for

```
export. ''Guadeloupe is similar to many of the Caribbean
islands we have studied right?'' the professor asked.
Warm climates diverse populations and agricultural
exports, are common throughout the Caribbean.
```

23 SEMICOLON

The semicolon shares characteristics of the comma and the period. Like a comma it indicates a pause between sentence elements, but like a period it separates complete sentences.

23a Use a semicolon to connect two closely related sentences.

Quantities of the material were missing; only about one-third remained in the warehouse.
You must pay attention to detail; you must count the variations.

23b Use a semicolon to separate two sentences joined with conjunctive adverbs such as *however, therefore, indeed, moreover, then, consequently, nevertheless.*

The spacecraft was sighted by several different stations; moreover, it was headed straight for earth.
Johnson refused the transfer; indeed, he quit the company.

The comma after the conjunctive adverb may be omitted for less emphasis.

We found no difference in the rats; hence we abandoned the experiment.

187

;

23c Use a semicolon to separate two sentences joined with transitional phrases such as *as a result, on the other hand, for example, in fact, on the contrary.*

The experiment failed; as a result, the research grant was cancelled. Mary Jane has always been fortunate; for example, she won $10,000 in the lottery last year.

23d Use a semicolon to separate items in a series if the items are long or have internal punctuation.

The following were some of the guests: John Markham, President of United Endeavors; Fred Slasher, Vice-President of Consolidated Shipping; Paula Zunkel, Chairwoman of the Board, Products Unlimited.

23e Use a semicolon to connect compound sentences that are very long or that contain internal punctuation.

Sam had read a book about a dentist who owned a charter boat, *The Mystic Molar;* and he was now reading a book, a strangely written one, with a talking parrot as a heroine. [The comma rule says two sentences joined by *and*, as these two are, require a *comma;* but the semicolon rule says the semicolon may be used instead, to relieve the number of commas.]

23f Use a semicolon to separate multiple references in footnotes and endnotes.

[1]Chap II, pp. 6–13; Chap IV, pp. 78–81; Chap. IX, pp. 231–35.

[2]See Flint, 1980; Whetlock, 1982; Pangborne, 1985.

;

ACTIVITY 9

Edit the following sentences; insert semicolons where appropriate; delete or change errors in punctuation.

1. The reaction took place just as expected, in fact the result surpassed everyone's hopes.
2. The typewriter finally stopped working the keys were bent beyond hope.
3. He subscribed to three newspapers : *The Times,* which was conservative, *The Post,* which was extremely liberal in its views, and *The Standard,* which never took a firm stand either way.
4. The old man had been traveling for six days he was tired, bone tired.
5. Claudia got to her feet trembling inside, nevertheless, she spoke confidently and knowledgeably.

ACTIVITY 10

Edit the following paragraph to eliminate problems with semicolons. Add any needed punctuation; delete unnecessary marks.

Hiroshima

On August 6, 1945; the United States dropped an atomic bomb on Hiroshima Japan surrendered on August 15. This single nuclear device flattened the city; killing nearly 75,000 people, however, the surrender of Japan ended the war in the Pacific; and saved the lives of thousands of American and Japanese soldiers. The U.S. had ordered Japan to surrender, warning the Japanese of the consequence of a nuclear attack; and pointing out that the Japanese could no longer hope to win the war, but the emperor refused to give in and ordered Japanese military forces throughout the Pacific to die fighting, never surrendering an inch. Even after the destruction of Hiroshima; Japan still refused to surrender, it was necessary to drop a second nuclear bomb on Nagasaki. Today Hiroshima has been rebuilt, it has become a center for the study of research on nuclear radiation. It draws medical researchers from such distant places as; London, England, Los Angeles, California, Sydney, Australia.

:

24 COLON

The colon is a very formal mark of punctuation. It is chiefly used to introduce lists and examples; the colon is the preferred mark to introduce all illustrative material. However, like the semicolon, the colon can connect complete sentences.

24a Use a colon to introduce a series.

The following students must report to the office: Baines, Rhydall, Stelling, and Johnson.
The project demanded specific attributes: intelligence, endurance, adaptability, and courage.

In the first example the series is clearly signaled by the words *the following*. Other such signals are words like *as follows* and *namely these*. In the second example, the signal for a series is implied; the colon itself means *such as the following*.

Do not use a colon after forms of the verb *to be* nor after prepositions.

MISUSED My classes this semester are: math, history, Spanish, accounting, and English.

REVISED My classes this semester are math, history, Spanish, accounting, and English.

MISUSED I am enrolled in: math, history, Spanish, accounting, and English.

REVISED I am enrolled in math, history, Spanish, accounting, and English.

Do not separate a verb from its object with a colon.

MISUSED We initiated: Estelle, Irving, Denise, and Frank.

REVISED We initiated Estelle, Irving, Denise, and Frank.

24b Use a colon to emphasize an appositive at the end of a sentence.

We said that in America we are proud of our President's former career: acting.

24c A colon may be used between sentences when the second explains, illustrates, summarizes, or complements the first.

The photograph is unique: it is the only proof of the animal's existence.
A serious issue arises when one considers the side effects of the drug: we may be curing the disease at the cost of the patient's sanity.

24d Use a colon to introduce long or formal quotations without speaker tags.

He reminded me of Patrick Henry's words: "Give me liberty, or give me death." [No speaker tag is present.]
He reminded me that Patrick Henry said, "Give me liberty or give me death." [A speaker tag, *Patrick Henry said*, is present.]

Note that the first word of a quotation following either a colon or a comma is capitalized. For rules on long prose quotations, see **29c.**

24e Use a colon after the salutation of a formal letter.

Dear Ms. Atkins: Dear Sir: Doctor Charles: **191**

:

24f Use colons between chapter and verse of Biblical references and between hours and minutes (and seconds) in precise time references.

Luke 4:12   10:30 p.m.   1:06:32

ACTIVITY 11
Edit the following sentences; insert colons where appropriate; delete incorrect punctuation.

1. At 12 15 p.m. the following athletes should report to the starter Higgins, Roman, Hay, McClintock.
2. Shirley, shopping for the party, bought: pretzels, beer, potato chips, onion dip, and one bottle of diet pop.
3. She said that one requirement was absolutely necessary for working with the children, enthusiasm.
4. The winners of the spelling contest for the sixth grade are: Mary Jean Arch, Nancy Arbor, and George Johnson.
5. The small dog was absolutely ferocious, it bit seven people between January and March.

ACTIVITY 12
Combine the following sets of sentences using colons. You may add to, delete, or change the words in the sentences, but be sure to use a colon in your answer.

1. Anyone visiting America for the first time should be sure to see our capital. It is Washington D.C.
2. Robert Goodloe Harper is the author of the stirring American challenge to the French. He said, "Millions for defense, but not one cent for tribute."
3. There are several U.S. Presidents few people know very much about. Some of them are James Knox Polk, Zachary Taylor, Millard Fillmore, Franklin Pierce, and James Buchanan.
4. Many dangerous drugs are abused by large numbers of people. Some of them are LSD and heroin. Others include cocaine and amphetamines. Alcohol, too, is abused.
5. Fort Sumnter holds a unique position in American history. It was the site of the first shot in our Civil War.

25 DASH

--

The dash is a multipurpose mark of punctuation that has in itself no unique function. Rather, dashes can be used like strong commas, parentheses, colons, or ellipses. Too frequent use of the dash can be bothersome to the reader, but proper use can bring emphasis to your writing.

In typing, a dash is indicated by two hyphens with no additional space before, between, or after.

```
This is a typed dash--two hyphens.
```

25a Use a dash to indicate a sudden interruption in thought.

Let me explain my situation—but you don't care about that.
If the police found out—they were bound to find out—I would be a candidate for the mallard mortuary.

25b Use a dash for emphasis or clarification.

Each of the following could be punctuated with commas, but the dash adds emphasis.

There was only one thing Michael wanted in his life—love.
The mist stole eerily—remorselessly—into the blackened streets.
The second method—the deductive one—would not succeed.

25c Use a dash after an introductory series.

Furniture, the stereo, the television, the kitchen appliances—the burglar took them all.
Cigarettes, hamburger, potato chips, wine, beer—his shopping basket held his week's groceries.

-- Compare these sentences with one in which the series is the subject of the sentence (and not set off with a dash):

> Furniture, the stereo, the television, the kitchen appliances had all been taken by the burglar.

To produce a less formal tone, the dash can be used instead of a colon before a series.

> The prosecutor tried everything—intimidation, friendliness, cajolery, humor.

25d Use a dash to indicate faltering or abruptly ending speech.

> "Will you m—, m—, mar—, marry me?"
> "You stop that right now or I'll—." Tom had already run out of the house.

25e Words between dashes may take question marks or exclamation points, but not periods.

> The young princess—have you met her?—is having a party.
> The Russian KGB—torture is their main technique!—is made up of mentally defective killers.
> Hartley resigned—let younger men run the show—much earlier than was required.

ACTIVITY 13

Edit the following sentences; insert dashes and, if necessary, question marks or exclamation points with them, where appropriate.

1. The chihuahua who called a dog man's best friend chewed up my term paper and slobbered all over my pillow.
2. His life was devoted to the pursuit of the one thing he thought would make him happy money.

3. "The life span of the mayfly is" The professor stopped; Emily had fallen asleep again.
4. Race? He would race anything cars, boats, airplanes, skateboards.
5. Five dollars, ten, twenty, a hundred any amount would help.

ACTIVITY 14

Combine the following sets of sentences using dashes. You may add to, delete, or change the wording of the sentences if necessary. Make sure your answer uses a dash.

1. The wind was whipping the antenna back and forth. It had reached 70 miles per hour.
2. Captain Peabody showed up wearing a handlebar mustache. He was the one who had insisted on strict military dress.
3. Let me show you how. Watch out for the acid!
4. Sydney looked sadly at his brother. Sydney was the wiser twin.
5. Cheesecake, butter cookies, quarts of ice cream were the main ingredients. These were mainly our diet.

26 PERIOD

The period indicates a complete stop, a break between completed ideas. Its primary use is as a sentence end mark, but it can also be used to terminate other sentence elements.

26a Use a period at the end of a complete statement.

The quality of life is affected by the quality of one's natural environment.

A sentence embedded within another (set off with dashes or enclosed by parentheses) does not require a capital letter or a period:

We experimented foolishly—government regulations meant nothing to us then—with all sorts of dangerous substances.

• But embedded questions and exclamations retain their marks:

> We spent a fortune—doesn't everyone?—on our vacation.

SENTENCE FRAGMENTS

A sentence fragment is a group of words punctuated like a sentence but not expressing a complete idea. Although professional writers occasionally write fragments in fiction or informal writing, students are advised not to use them in academic writing. (See Section 7 for a complete discussion of sentence fragments.)

FUSED SENTENCES

Fused or run-on sentences are those that have been joined with no mark of punctuation; they are not necessarily long or "rambling." Fused sentences can result from a failure to recognize sentence boundaries, from faulty punctuation, or from not analyzing the relationship of one idea to another. (See Section 8 for a complete discussion.)

26b Use a period after an indirect question.

She asked why she had to supply everybody in the dorm with deodorant. [Compare *She asked, "Why do I have to supply everybody in the dorm with deodorant?"*]

26c Use periods after most commands and after requests expressed as questions.

Please sit down.
Will you please come this way.

Note that emphatic commands may use exclamation marks to convey tone of voice: *Shut up! Drop that immediately!* But writers may omit exclamation marks when no extraordinary emphasis is intended: *She looked him in the eye and said, "Shut up."*

26d Use a period for each item in a sentence outline or list of full sentences.

The employees had only a few minor complaints.
1. The working hours were too long.
2. The pay was too low.
3. The working conditions were too uncomfortable.
4. The boss was too arrogant.

In a list or outline of words or phrases rather than sentences, do not use periods. Avoid having both sentences and nonsentences in the same list.

26e Use periods with most abbreviations and initials.

A.D.	J.F.K.	Ms.	Dr.
e.g.	Inc.	Co.	km.

Do not add an additional period when an abbreviation or initial comes at the end of a sentence.

After eight years of postgraduate study, John finally earned his Ph.D.
We were set to go at 8:00 P.M.

Many abbreviations of well-known organizations do not require periods. Less well-known names can be given as initials without periods after you have once spelled out the full name: CIA, NCAA, NAACP, FBI, UNESCO, NHL.

The Government Printing Office (GPO) has published everything from menu-planning guides to instruction manuals for building nuclear bombs; the President was eager to cut back on the GPO's activities.

26f Use a period to express a decimal number.

.01   16.05   .007   3.14159

ACTIVITY 15

Insert periods where appropriate. If necessary, add material to create full sentences.

1. Will Ms Stegner and Dr Bale please come forward
2. Stepping carefully on the line of rocks across the stream, which was gurgling quietly
3. The quarterly report gave an optimistic account the company looked healthy at last
4. The deadline was 10:30 A M
5. The bus, which was usually overcrowded with schoolchildren that were bursting with laughter after a long day of classes.

ACTIVITY 16

Edit the following paragraph to eliminate problems with punctuation. Add any needed punctuation; delete unnecessary marks. You may need to make other changes, such as adding or deleting words.

Aida

Written to celebrate the opening of the Suez canal, Verdi's <u>Aida</u> remains one of the most popular operas in 1871 the premiere performance was held in Cairo Egypt. Aida, an Ethiopian slave loved by Radames captain of the Egyptian army. However, Radames is loved by Amneris Princess of Egypt, loves Ramades, she knows he loves Aida. Love jealousy, honor and death, the motifs of Aida. The Egyptians defeat the Ethiopians, and to reward Radames, the King of Egypt announces that Amneris will marry Radames how the lovers, Aida and Radames, will deal with this development the plot of the opera. Among the captured Ethiopians, Aida's father the King, Amonsaro. His plan to attack the Egyptians again depending on secret knowledge of the Egyptian battle plans. Torn between love of her country and Radames Aida tricks him as he tells her the secret, Amneris arrives and denounces him as a traitor to Egypt. Radames is condemned to be buried alive in his tomb he discovers Aida waiting for him the two lovers perish together.

27 EXCLAMATION POINT

Exclamation marks signal strong emotion. Use these marks infrequently and, for the most part, only with dialogue. Using more than one exclamation mark at a time is not appropriate in formal writing. *!!!!* is not more emphatic than *!*

Wow! Did you see what that guy did?
What a disgusting thing to say!

Avoid the use of exclamation marks for sarcasm. *The government's experts (!) have declared that tobacco smoking may have hidden benefits* is better without the exclamation mark's heavy-handed irony.

28 QUESTION MARK

The question mark, like the period and exclamation point, is primarily an end mark, signaling a question. It tells the reader not only how to interpret a sentence but also how to read it aloud.

28a Use a question mark after a direct question.

What are you doing here?
Can anyone tell me where the stadium is?

Notice the difference between direct questions and indirect questions (no question mark):

She wondered why nobody liked her.
She wondered, "Why doesn't anyone like me?"

Any statement can be made into a question with a question mark:
Go now? You're passing English?

A question inserted into a statement retains its question mark.

Hawthorne wrote *The Marble Faun*—was that his last novel?—while he was living in England.

"/"

28b Use a question mark for each item in a series of short questions.

Are you going to accept the manuscript? reject it? sit on it?
Is the body affected after one drink? two? five?

28c Use a question mark within parentheses to indicate uncertain information.

Quintillian was born in A.D. 35 (?) in Spain.

Avoid the sarcastic use of question marks to challenge an author's words or ideas: *Carstair's data (?) indicate that infantile paralysis is almost unknown in India.*

28d Use a question mark with an embedded question.

An embedded question is one set off by dashes or enclosed by parentheses within another sentence.

The novel, *The Right Stuff*—have you read it?—is a good example of the new journalism.

29 QUOTATION MARKS

Quotation marks signal spoken words or words copied from a written source. These marks are important, especially in academic writing, because they help to distinguish between words of one person and words of another. Use quotation marks carefully to make clear to the reader whose words belong to whom.

29a Use quotation marks correctly with direct quotations.

Direct quotations are the spoken or written words of others that you use in writing of your own.

He said, "A white dwarf is the corpse of a star."
"Not me," Mary screamed, "not in a hundred years."
"The question," Congressman Fields asserted, "is not only irrelevant but also impertinent. We cannot dictate our morality to nations receiving our aid."

Quotation marks enclose only the quoted words. The final quotation marks are withheld until the speaker finishes.

Use quotation marks for less than four lines of poetry, drama, or prose. Quotations of three or fewer lines of poetry, drama, or prose are not displayed; that is, they are not set off from your words by space and indentations. They *are* enclosed in quotation marks.

In his poem, "Peter Quince at the Clavier," for example, Wallace Stevens writes, "She felt, among the leaves, / The dew / Of old devotions."

The slash (/) shows line divisions; use a space before and after it.

The quotation of less than four lines of prose is handled in the same way, except that line divisions are not shown.

Thoreau states, "Old shoes will serve a hero longer than they have served his valet—if a hero has a valet—bare feet are older than shoes, and he can make them do."

29b Use quotation marks to indicate dialogue.

Paragraph indentation shows changes of speakers in dialogue.

"Seven."
"Naw, couldn't be more than five."
"Seven. I counted 'em twice."
"Get your eyes checked, man."

"Say, listen, there's seven of 'em," Hedley said, with some heat, "an' don't you tell me not."

I was in no mood to argue, so I allowed, "O.K. Seven."

"Right."

Thoughts and conversations one has with oneself (internal dialogues) are not usually enclosed in quotation marks.

Why me, I thought, as the ball bounced off my glove and rolled to the wall.

I asked myself, as Joan nodded and smiled, how could anyone be happier?

29c Use quotation marks around source material incorporated into your own sentences.

Calling her "guilty as Jezebel," the judge sentenced her to twenty years.

An incorporated quote does not create the need for a comma or a colon. Also, the incorporated quote usually does not require an ellipsis unless you think it is important to tell the reader that you have incorporated less than a full sentence.

29d Use quotation marks within quotation marks correctly.

Singleton said, "Have you read Melville's 'Bartleby the Scriviner'?"

"Audrey said, 'Do it yourself ' when I asked her to help me clean the room," Lee whined.

If something you want to quote is already in quotation marks, you must add your own set of marks to indicate that you are quoting a quote. (Some writers use only double marks when the context or reference note makes it clear that the original was quoted.)

ORIGINAL

Huttenlocher says, "Six seems to be a critical period, a time when the brain is especially receptive."

AS IT MIGHT APPEAR IN YOUR PAPER

Research shows that "'six seems to be a critical period, a time when the brain is especially receptive'" (qtd. in Campbell 143).

On rare occasions it may be necessary to use a third set of quotation marks. Quotations must always begin with double quotation marks; thereafter you may alternate single and double marks as often as needed.

ORIGINAL

"How dare you say, 'Horse tails,' to me," Lady Small cried.

AS IT MIGHT APPEAR IN YOUR PAPER

"'How dare you say, "Horse tails," to me,' Lady Small cried."

See **29e** for quotation marks in displayed (set-off) quotations.

29e Display long quotations correctly.

When typing prose, poetry, or drama quotations of four or more lines, do not add quotation marks. Triple space above and below the quotation. Indent all the lines of the quotation ten spaces from the left margin and double space the material. Do not indicate the beginning of a single quoted paragraph with indentation. However, if you display two or more full paragraphs, indent the first line of each an additional three spaces.

Last summer Jim was reading Robert Pirsig's <u>Zen and the Art of Motorcycle Maintenance,</u> and one paragraph really struck home:

> The real cycle you're working on is a cycle called yourself. The machine that appears to be ''out there'' and the person that appears to be ''in here'' are not two separate things. They grow toward Quality or fall away from Quality together (209).

"/"

If the original material contains quotation marks, you should copy them, but do not supply any additional marks.

ORIGINAL

At the same time, the brain of a six-year-old has a slower and more irregular activity than that of an adult, and this, too, increases the child's capacity to acquire and remember knowledge. Huttenlocher says, "One of the most interesting aspects of the six-year-old brain is that a child who has had little educational experience in this crucial year has tremendous difficulty in catching up later, even with a very good effort. Six seems to be a critical period, a time when the brain is especially receptive."

AS IT MIGHT APPEAR IN YOUR PAPER

Another cause of learning disabilities can be traced to delaying education until after the child's sixth birthday:

    "One of the most interesting aspects of the six-
    year-old brain is that a child who has had little
    educational experience in this crucial year has
    tremendous difficulty in catching up later, even with
    a very good effort. Six seems to be a critical
    period, a time when the brain is especially
    receptive" (qtd. in Campbell 142–3).

29f Use quotation marks with titles of short works.

Short stories, magazines and newspaper articles, most poems, book chapters, specific episodes of radio or television series, and short musical works require quotation marks.

"The Fog" is a Sandberg poem popular with our class.

Books of the Bible do not take quotation marks.

Michael was told to go to his room and read Leviticus.

29g Use quotation marks with words used with special meaning and with invented words.

His "forecast" had no relation to what eventually occurred.
Al called them "quiffs," and it wasn't complimentary.

Avoid using quotation marks around words to indicate irony or sarcasm: *She was a real "friend."*

29h Quotation marks may be used with words referred to as words and with letters and numerals referred to as symbols.

He called her "madam," not knowing how right he was.
"Mississippi" has four "s's" and four "i's."

See **36** for optional use of underlining here.

29i Use other punctuation correctly with quotation marks.

Commas and periods always go inside quotation marks.

"The Beatles," Tom said, "were just lucky."
She said her favorite word was "intimacy."
She liked to say, "Everything is so 'devious.'"

Colons and semicolons alway go outside quotation marks.

"The book was called *The Brave*"; it was less than a commercial success.

Question marks and exclamation marks go either inside or outside the quotation marks. If what you are quoting is a question or an exclamation, the mark goes inside, regardless of the rest of the sentence; if not, the mark goes outside.

How can you say, "The Beatles were just lucky"?
Her only response was, "Horse manure!"

Do not use quotation marks for indirect quotes.

Refusing to accept the transfer, Phil said he would rather quit. [Compare *Refusing to accept the transfer, Phil said, "I would rather quit."*]
He said that the big city was not for him or his family. [Compare *He said, "The big city is not for me or my family."*]

ACTIVITY 17
Edit the following sentences; supply quotation marks and appropriate punctuation where required.

1. James Joyce's short story Araby served as the basis for Jack's paper.
2. He's about as sensitive said Amy sacrastically as an armadillo.
3. Receive was misspelled fourteen times in the essay.
4. Genesis is the first book of the Old Testament.
5. I wonder said Steve to himself how I got myself into this mess.
6. What do you think of Emerson's essay Gifts? I asked.
7. Jeff said only time will tell.
8. He called his brief poem Jasmine; it was delicate and beautiful.
9. Did you enjoy Hammond's song A New Love asked Barb.
10. Chapter 7, Black Holes, was the most interesting to me.

ACTIVITY 18
Edit the following paragraph to eliminate problems with punctuation. Add any needed punctuation; delete unnecessary marks.

English Notes

As I look back on my English notes now, I wonder what some of them mean? One note says only ''Shakespeare!!!'' Someone has written in the margin, ''Homer's book-length poem, The Odyssey—have you read it—is about Odysseus' struggle to return home after the Trojan War.'' In another place, I find a cryptic reference to the first book of the Bible, ''See Genesis.'' Just below that there is a note from my professor: Your t's all look like l's, and your o's all look like q's. Inside the back cover, I

```
apparently copied part of a poem: Because I could not
stop for Death— / He kindly stopped for me—. They are
from Emily Dickinson's short poem, Because I could not
stop for Death. I've asked myself several times, How
could I have passed English with such meaningless notes?
A professor once told me I was an intuitive student, but
I think he was just using that word out of politeness.
On the back of my notes is a long quotation from the
Bible: ''And I looked, and behold a pale horse; and his
name that sat on him, was Death, and Hell followed with
him. And power was given unto them over the fourth part
of the earth, to kill with sword, and with hunger, and
with death, and with the beasts of the earth.'' The last
thing in my notes looks like a note from a classmate:
Stop asking him ''What do you mean when you say
Existentialism.''
```

30 SLASH

The slash, also called *solidus, virgule,* or *diagonal,* is used to indicate choices or to separate sentence elements. The slash is a relatively uncommon mark and must be used with care; it is not a substitute for a dash.

30a Use a slash to mark the division between run-in lines of poetry or drama.

Run-in lines of poetry or drama are those you quote but do not separate from your own words with space above, below, and at the left margin.

Hughes concludes his poem "The Lovepat" with the touching lines "It went far away, they could not speak, / Only their tears moved."

30b Use a slash to indicate fractions.

4/5   3/7

30c Use a slash to indicate a choice between terms.

pass/fail   either/or   and/or

31 ELLIPSIS

An ellipsis—three spaced dots—signifies an omission. The omission may be material deliberately excluded from a quotation, or it may be the missing words of an unfinished statement.

31a Use an ellipsis to show that material has been omitted from quoted material.

To show an ellipsis, type periods with equal space before and after each (. . .). The ellipsis tells the reader that a word or words, sometimes whole sentences, have been left out.

> As the Secretary of the Interior stated: "It is my intention to see that . . . the wetlands be incorporated into our National Park system."

If the omitted material is at the end of a sentence, use four periods, placing the first as you would a sentence-ending period, no space.

ORIGINAL

Watching him, the boy remarked the absolutely undeviating course which his father held and saw the stiff foot come squarely down in a

pile of fresh droppings where a horse had stood in the drive and ···
which his father could have avoided by a simple change of stride.

AS IT MIGHT APPEAR IN YOUR PAPER
```
Watching him, the boy remarked the absolutely
undeviating course which his father held and saw the
stiff foot come squarely down in a pile of fresh
droppings. . . .
```

If whole lines of poetry or prose have been omitted, indicate this with four periods (but remember that four periods must appear only at the end of a sentence, never within a sentence).

ORIGINAL
Out walking in the frozen swamp one gray day,
I paused and said, "I will turn back from here.
No, I will go on farther—and we shall see."
The hard snow held me, save now and then
One foot went through.
         From Robert Frost, "The Woodpile"

AS IT MIGHT APPEAR IN YOUR PAPER
```
Frost's ''The Wood-Pile'' uses many winter images:
        Out walking in the frozen swamp one gray
        day. . . .
        The hard snow held me, save now and then
        One foot went through.
```

31b Use an ellipsis to indicate a pause or an unfinished statement.

John began to count the money, "Let's see now. . . . "
The name was . . . he was unable to remember.

If necessary for clarity, you may use other punctuation with an ellipsis.

ORIGINAL
She said, but don't tell her I told you, "Rip out their eyes!"

WITH ELLIPSIS
She said, . . . "Rip out their eyes!"

ORIGINAL

His speaking style was full of shouts, whistles, laughter, animal noises, giggles, and obscene gestures.

WITH ELLIPSIS

His speaking style was full of shouts, whistles, . . . and obscene gestures.

ACTIVITY 19

Condense the following passage. Eliminate anything you can to reduce the paragraph to its bare message. Supply appropriate ellipsis marks.

Death

The traditional criteria for death are cessation of respiration and heart action, but modern technology can keep a patient breathing and his blood circulating long after his brain has died. Now a special Harvard University committee has recommended that brain death, or irreversible coma, be considered a definition of death and has drawn up a set of guidelines for determining when there is no discernible activity of the central nervous system. The 13-man committee, drawn from the faculties of medicine, public health, law, arts and sciences and divinity, was headed by Henry K. Beecher of the Harvard Medical School. Its report was published in the <u>Journal</u> <u>of</u> <u>the</u> <u>American</u> <u>Medical</u> <u>Association</u>.

From "Science and the Citizen: What is Death,"
© 1968 by Scientific American, Inc.

---

32 BRACKETS

Brackets, like commas and parentheses, are used to set off sentence elements from the rest of a sentence. In academic writing, they are chiefly used to set off a writer's words from source material or to give special clarifying or explanatory messages to the reader. If your typewriter doesn't have brackets, leave spaces for them as you type and later draw them in with a pen.

32a Use brackets around clarifying material you insert into quotations.

"They [Lewis and Clark] opened up the Northwest to the white man."

ORIGINAL
The tornado ripped through the village, destroying seventeen houses.

IN YOUR PAPER
"The tornado ripped through [Quentenville], destroying seventeen houses."

32b Use brackets with *sic* to indicate errors in quoted material.

To point out errors in fact, logic, grammar or spelling in source material, insert *sic* in brackets [sic] directly after the error. *Sic* means "thus" in Latin and tells the reader that you recognize the error. (You may correct minor typographical mistakes without using *sic*.)

"In 1982 [sic], Soviet athletes stayed away from the Summer Olympics, turning some of the American gold to brass."

Notice that *sic* is not followed by a period; it is not underlined, according to the 1984 MLA stylesheet.

32c Use brackets for parenthetical material within parentheses.

The defendants (Elsworth and Petry [Sommers was being tried separately]) were brought into court chained and handcuffed.

211

(1) As you can see, this is an awkward construction; and when you find yourself needing it, you should revise the sentence, if possible.

33 PARENTHESES

Parentheses are used to give incidental, clarifying, or explanatory material for the reader. Parenthetic material can usually also be set off with commas, but use of the parentheses gives stronger emphasis to such material.

33a Use parentheses to set off incidental or explanatory material and material not grammatically connected to the sentence.

Before the Civil War (1861–1865) was fought, the South relied heavily on slave labor.
The breakdown of the figures (see the chart on p. 17) shows population increasing exponentially.

33b Use parentheses to label items in a list.

In order to score well, you must (1) line up your shot, (2) assume the correct stance, and (3) execute the mechanics of the swing.

It is informal usage (not recommended) to use a half parenthesis: *1)*, *2)*, *3)*.

33c Use other punctuation correctly with parentheses.

The sentence-ending mark (period, question mark, and exclamation mark) falls outside the parenthesis. Even if the parenthetic material embedded within a sentence is a full sentence, neither a capital letter to begin nor a period to end is required.

The veteran thought about his struggle (it was too painful to speak), *(1)* but he tried not to be bitter.

If the parenthetic material is a question or exclamation, you need both the appropriate mark within the parentheses and a period outside.

Kyle kept telling the same story over and over (talk about boredom!).

If the parenthetic material begins after an end mark and is not part of another sentence, final punctuation goes within the parentheses.

Many professionals are in the top ten percent of the income scale. (Teachers are another story.)

A comma is not used before an opening parenthesis, but one may be required after a closing parenthesis.

Because the house was built on sand (poor choice, builders), it had a tendency to shift. [The parenthetical material is part of a long introductory clause, which must be set off from the rest of the sentence.]

ACTIVITY 20
Edit the following sentences; add parentheses and other punctuation where appropriate.

1. During the early part of the year Jan.-Mar. the Gross National Product rose four percent.
2. To assemble the swingset, you should 1 read the instructions carefully 2 try to follow the instructions exactly 3 call a professional 4 take an aspirin.
3. The author he did write well I guess spoke incoherently for two hours about his profession.
4. America's involvement in World War II 1941–1945 was costly in money and human life.

ACTIVITY 21
Edit the following paragraph to eliminate problems with punctuation. Add any needed punctuation; delete unnecessary marks. You may change the wording of the sentences if necessary. Use this paragraph as a review of the punctuation section.

Lincoln

Abraham Lincoln was born in 1809 in Kentucky. Though both his parents were probably illiterate and Lincoln himself is known to have attended formal school for less than a year he apparently taught himself to read, and went to great lengths to find books with which to educate himself. History shows that he read books like; "Robinson Crusoe" "Pilgrim's Progress" and, Aesop's "Fables". Though he did not have many books to read those that he had were read very carefully and thoroughly. Many historians believe he studied the <u>Bible</u> it was certain to be in any frontier home. From Kentucky the Lincoln family migrated first to Indiana, then to Illinois. The man was physically striking, he stood six feet four inches tall. While very lean and some said awkward—looking; the powerfully built young man with a reputation for log splitting. After many different jobs including state representative Lincoln determined to be a lawyer and taught himself to read law books. The records show that he was an effective and prosperous lawyer earning a better than average living. In later life Lincoln was fond of quoting often at length poets such as: Shakespeare, John Stuart Mill, Byron, and Robert Burns. He was not an abolitionist but over the issue of permitting the western territories to enter the union as slave states he said "A house divided against itself cannot stand. I believe this government cannot endure permanently half slave and half free". Throughout the Civil War, Lincoln avoided the slavery issue claiming his only interest was in preserving the Union. He declared "If I could save the Union without freeing any slave I would do it and if I could save it by freeing all the slaves, I would do it". Of the many things Lincoln said or wrote, most people remember best

his Gettysburg Address a speech given on November 19

1863 to dedicate part of the battlefield as a war cemetery the first part of which says, "Four score and seven years ago our fathers brought forth on this continent a new nation conceived in liberty and dedicated to the proposition that all men are created equal. Now we are engaged in a great civil war testing whether that nation or any nation so dedicated can long endure".

Mechanics

Mechanics are all those matters concerning the appearance of the written word. They are practices that have become conventions in all written formal English. Attention to small details—the placement of an apostrophe, the use or absence of a necessary hyphen, the spelling of words, and so on—is an important part of the way you present your writing. Errors in mechanics can ruin your message, directly by changing your meaning and indirectly by suggesting to readers that the words and ideas are carelessly presented. Proofread carefully to eliminate problems in mechanics. A mechanically clean paper reflects the care with which you prepare your written work.

34 APOSTROPHE

The apostrophe tells your readers how to interpret specific words, to show possession, to indicate contractions, and to form some plurals.

34a Use apostrophes correctly to show possession.

For singular nouns not ending in *s*, use *'s: the student's paper, the tiger's claws, the ambassador's mistake*

For singular indefinite pronouns, use *'s: anyone's problem, one's options, someone else's sweater*

For singular nouns ending in *s*, add just the apostrophe unless you want the possessive to be pronounced as a separate syllable. All of the following are correct: *Jones' house, Jones's house; the goddess' apple, the goddess's apple; Corliss' hair, Corliss's hair.*

To show joint possession, add *'s* to the last owner mentioned: *Joan and Dean's processor, the boy and the girl's bicycle, the woman and the man's house.*

To show individual ownership, add *'s* to each owner mentioned: *Joan's and Dean's processors, the boy's and the girl's bicycles, the woman's and the man's houses.* Notice the plurals *(processors, bicycles, houses.)*

For plural nouns that end in *s*, just add an apostrophe: *the animals' habitats, the sophomores' morale, the newspapers' headlines.*

For plural nouns that do not end in *s*, add *'s: women's responsibilities, children's toys, marksmen's targets.*

For abstract or inanimate nouns and familiar expressions, follow the normal rules: *a day's work, five dollars' worth, life's difficulties, today's news, 1984's Olympic games.*

34b Do not use apostrophes in possessive pronouns.

Do not use the apostrophe to show possession with personal pronouns: *its, hers, theirs, yours, whose,* and so on. Note carefully that there is no word *its'* in the language. See **34c** for *it's.*

34c Use apostrophes to show the omission of letters in contractions.

In contractions the apostrophe takes the place of a missing letter or letters. Contractions give a less formal tone to your writing, but they are generally acceptable except in the most formal writing situations.

Use an apostrophe to indicate that one or more letters have been omitted: *we're, he'll, I'm, you're, haven't, didn't, they're, who's, doesn't, it's (it is).*

34d Words referred to as words, abbreviations, and letters and numerals referred to as symbols form their plurals by adding *'s.*

p's and *q*'s	C.P.A.'s
rpm's	*if*'s, *and*'s, or *but*'s
M.A.'s	I used to think *3*'s were erased *8*'s.

⌄

Modern practice is often to drop the apostrophe when dates are treated as collective nouns:

1900s
1980s

ACTIVITY 1
Proofread the following sentences: insert apostrophes where appropriate.

1. The two mens car was in for repairs.
2. He doesnt have a nickels worth of sense.
3. Youre not serious, are you?
4. Liza rejected Sams offer.
5. James laughter echoed through the halls.
6. The cat scratched its ears negligently.
7. Freds and Mikes skis were stolen last night.
8. You have too many Is in your paper.
9. Its going to be a great summer if Kathy and Jims pool gets finished.
10. Everyones reputation is threatened by the tapes.

ACTIVITY 2
Edit the following paragraph to eliminate problems with apostrophes.

Dogs

Dog's have existed since at least 9000 B.C. Its not known exactly when or where the dog began it's relationship with humanity. Evidence found in the 1960's suggests Eurasia as the possible site. The dogs earliest ancestor may have been a wolf. Americas and Europes gray wolves are the most likely ancestors. Adding up all the +s and −s, it seems unlikely that dogs ancestors were jackals. The jackal isnt unrelated to dogs, but it's physiology and social behavior make it an unlikely candidate. <u>Canis</u> <u>familiaris</u> great grandfather was probably a small gray wolf howling in Indias forest.

35 HYPHEN

The hyphen indicates a break within a word. Some words are conventionally spelled with hyphens in them; in other cases writers supply hyphens as signals to the reader, explaining the relationship between words or parts of words.

35a Use correct forms for compound words.

Many compound words are spelled as two words, others as one word, and still others as hyphenated words. Look up in the dictionary any compound word you are unsure of.

handlebar mustache	dogtrot	hand-me-down
jigsaw puzzle	handwriting	Johnny-come-lately
kiss of death	happenstance	mother-in-law
pig in a poke	staircase	sergeant-at-arms
skull and cross bones	thingamajig	standard-bearer

Compound-word modifiers before a noun should be hyphenated. This guideline does not apply to *-ly* words, which are not hyphenated in American English:

UNHYPHENATED -LY COMPOUND	HYPHENATED COMPOUND
quickly dried material	quick-dried material
loosely packed fibers	loose-packed fibers
badly written essay	bad-tempered dog

Compound-word modifiers after a noun are not hyphenated. Modifiers that are hyphenated when they precede the noun do not need hyphens when they come after the noun.

This essay was *well written.*
Their dog was *bad tempered.*

Plurals of compound words may be irregular. The plural is formed on the most significant word in the compound: *mothers-in-*

hyph   law, *sergeants-at-arms*. In some cases you must use your own judgment: *Johnnies-come-lately* or *Johnny-come-latelies*.

Possessives of compound words are usually regular. The possessive of a compound word is usually formed at the end of the word: *pig in a poke's, mother-in-law's, standard-bearer's*.

35b Hyphenate words formed with certain prefixes and suffixes.

Words that use the prefixes *all-, cross-, ex-, half-, ill-, well-*, and *self-* and the suffix *-elect* are usually hyphenated.

all-knowing   ex-President
self-sacrifice   governor-elect

When *self* is a word's root rather than a prefix, it is not hyphenated.

selfhood   selfish.

The prefixes and suffixes listed below form words that are spelled as one word (*antiballistic, counterrevolution, nonfattening, twofold, underrated*):

anti-	intra-	pro-	super-
co-	like-	pseudo-	supra-
counter-	non-	re-	ultra-
extra-	over-	semi-	un-
-fold	post-	sub-	under-
infra-	pre-		

But use the hyphen when one of these is attached to a proper noun:

un-American   anti-Reagan   pseudo-Martian

Two-word numbers are hyphenated. Spelled-out numbers from twenty-one to ninety-nine are hyphenated, as are spelled-out fractions.

twenty-one   three-fifths
one-half   fifty-four
eighty-two   two-thirds

hyph

35c Use a hyphen to signal a common root for two or more words or prefixes.

Nineteenth- and twentieth-century art is on display.
We have to write a 10- to 20-page paper.
They behaved that way at both the pre- and post-game shows.

35d Use a hyphen to avoid ambiguity, confusion, or an awkward combination of letters.

He was excited about the re-creation.

The hyphen is needed to distinguish between *re-creation*, a reenactment, and *recreation*, a diversion of some kind.

The hill-like effect was created with globs of paint.

The hyphen is needed here to avoid running three *l*'s together.

35e Use a hyphen to divide a word at the end of a line.

Insert the hyphen only between syllables of two or more letters. Dictionaries show syllable division.

It was not a sound of his own superiority but an exclamation of surprise.

See also **3e** and the beginning of section **40**.

ACTIVITY 3
Proofread the following sentences: make the use of hyphens consistent with the guidelines in this section.

1. At the present time the plans for the eventual reorganiza
   tion of the league have been shelved.

2. The report was well received by the committee.
3. Lee's preoccupation with food was mere selfindulgence.
4. Eighteenth century novels were his specialty.
5. There were thirty three different wines on the restaurant's menu.
6. The flowers were cross pollinated to produce a new variety.
7. Manufacturers claimed the yoghurt was non-fattening.
8. Although well intentioned, the proposal could have disastrous results.
9. It was part of his off day routine to walk his cat.
10. Somebody ought to do something about my brother in law's car.

---

36 Underlining (italics)

Typesetters use italic type *(type that looks like this: slanted)* for any words that are underlined in manuscripts. Italic type is special treatment given by convention to most titles, some names, and certain categories of words.

Underlining takes the place of italics in typed and handwritten papers. Of course, if you have a typewriter or word processor that has both italic and roman (regular, unslanted) type, you may want to use italics rather than underlining.

36a Use underlining (italics) for the titles of long works.

Titles of books, booklets, magazines, newspapers, long poems, plays, record albums, operas, films, works of art, legal cases, radio and television series (the name of the series, not the title of individual segments), require underlining.

Have you read Shakespeare's <u>Titus Andronicus?</u>
<u>Masterpiece Theatre</u> is one of the most popular offerings on PBS.
<u>American Gothic</u> has been parodied more than any other painting except, perhaps, the <u>Mona Lisa</u>.

The titles of court cases are underlined in the text of your paper, but not in footnotes. The *v.*, for "versus," is not underlined in either case.

> In the 1830s, <u>Freelink</u> v. <u>Bishoff</u> created a precedent
> that is still cited.
> [3] See, for example, Freelink v. Bishoff.

36b Use underlining (italics) for the names of airplanes, trains, ships, and other vehicles.

> The <u>Orient Express</u>   The <u>Nina</u>, <u>Pinta</u>, and <u>Santa Maria</u>

Do not underline S.S., H.M.S., or similar abbreviations with names of ships.

36c Use underlining (italics) for emphasis.

> "What's <u>your</u> problem?" asked Bevins as I raised my hand.

In general, let your word choice and syntax carry the emphasis. Like a page peppered with exclamation marks, too much underlining for emphasis distracts readers and gives writing an informal look.

36d Use underlining (italics) to indicate words from other languages.

If a word or phrase from another language becomes widely used by and generally familiar to speakers of English, the special treatment is dropped. When in doubt, check your dictionary.

> The first part of the piece is played <u>vivace</u>, fast and
> light.

ital

"How are things going, amigo?" [No underlining; although <u>amigo</u> is Spanish, it has become so familiar to Americans that it is accepted as part of our language.]

36e Underlining (italics) may be used with words referred to as words and with letters and numerals referred to as symbols.

Our assignment is to trace the history of the word <u>aromatic</u>.
Professors complain when students make their <u>f</u>'s look like <u>t</u>'s.

See **29h** for use of quotation marks here. In very formal writing, underlining is preferred,

36f Use underlining (italics) for the scientific (genus and species) names for animals and plants.

The doctor announced that I had been in contact with <u>Rhus radicans</u>, poison ivy.

36g Use underlining (italics) to introduce key words and special or technical terms.

The <u>hypothalamus</u>, one of whose functions is to regulate body temperature, is a region in the forebrain.

ACTIVITY 4
Proofread the following sentences: underline where necessary.

1. Sports Illustrated features an article on the New York Islanders this week.

2. Steinbeck's book East of Eden was banned by the school board.   *cap*
3. The Hasslebergs had purchased tickets to sail on the Titanic but changed their plans just before departure time.
4. When I asked Julio where the fish were biting, he smiled and said, "Quien sabe?"
5. The jury in Maxwell v. Carmody deliberated for twelve days.
6. Two famous sixteenth-century comedies are Grammar Gurton's Needle and Ralph Roister Doister.
7. Trinitrotoluene is more commonly referred to as TNT.
8. Chaucer pronounced a word like bite as we would pronounce Rita: his long i sounded like e, and his final e sounded like a schwa (ə).
9. The dramatic technique of suddenly introducing a deity to solve a difficult problem is called deus ex machina.
10. The space shuttle Discovery first suffered a computer malfunction and then a fire while still on the launch pad.

---

37   CAPITALIZATION

Capitalization began with the need to mark the beginning of a new idea; later it was extended to set off important words from others. Through proper capitalization you help your reader to interpret your sentences. Proofread carefully for conventional use of capital letters.

37a Capitalize the first word of a sentence and first word of a direct quotation.

Looking out over the crowd, she said, "Let us pray for world peace."

Do not capitalize the first word of an incorporated quotation.

The government report cited "repeated violations of Health Code Regulation 145–G" as the reason for closing the factory.

Capitalize only the first word of an interrupted quotation.

"The country you know as Iran," she said, "was once known as the Persian Empire."

cap   **Capitalize the first word after a colon if it begins a quotation, a speech in dialogue, a formal statement, a question, or material of more than one sentence.**

Patrick Henry stated: "Give me liberty, or give me death."

In response to accusations of embezzlement,' Pembroke was emphatic: "I have never and will never misuse the company's funds."

We are faced with this question: Where are we going to get the money?

Capitalize the first word of a line of verse. (Some modern poets ignore this convention.)

Some say the world will end in fire,
Some say in ice.
From what I've tasted of desire
I hold with those who favor fire.

From Robert Frost's "Fire and Ice"

37b Capitalize names, nicknames, and descriptive names.

Clara   Virginia Woolf
Snooky   the Wizard of Menlo Park

Descriptive names following a given name are usually set off with quotation marks: *Babe Ruth, "the Sultan of Swat."*

Capitalize words formed from proper nouns.

Alaskan peninsula   American oil fields
Shakespearean sonnet   Victorian household

Do not capitalize derivatives of proper names used with a special meaning.

brazil nut   french dressing   panama hat
brussels sprouts   morocco leather   roman numerals
india ink

Capitalize names identifying nationalities and ethnic groups. *cap*

Irish   Indian

Black and *White* as racial designations may be capitalized or not; whichever practice you follow, use it for both words.

Capitalize the names of awards, brand names, structures, and historical, cultural, and other events.

Congressional Medal of Honor	the Fourth of July
the Heisman Trophy	(Independence Day)
the Tony Award	April Fool's Day
Izod shirt	Rosh Hashanah
Ace bandage	the Battle of Hastings
the Holland Tunnel	the Crusades
Hoover Dam	the French Revolution
the Sears Tower	the Depression
the USS *Arizona* Memorial	the Bronze Age
Thursday	the Nobel Prize
April	the Croix de Guerre

Do not capitalize popular names for or informal references to periods of history.

the seventeenth century	nuclear age
the classical period	information age

Capitalize the names of geographic features and places.

the Badlands	Detroit
Carlsbad Caverns	Maple Street
Great Bear Lake	Point Barrow, Alaska
the Mojave Desert	Yellowstone National Park
Mount St. Helens	the North
Niagara Falls	Moscow
South China Sea	Khartoum
City of Brotherly Love	Lakes Titicaca and Nicaragua

Do not capitalize the names of seasons.

autumn   fall   spring   summer   winter   **229**

cap   **Capitalize** *north, south, east, west* **and their derivitives only when they refer to specific geographical areas, not when they refer to directions.**

> From Canada we drove southeast to Bismarck.
> The United States cannot afford to mistake the motives of Western Europe's peace activists.

Do not capitalize terms like *city, county, state* when written without a name or when written before the name:

> Workers in the city often live in its suburbs.
> The village of Logansport has a population of ninety-seven.

Capitalize the names of military groups, battles, and wars.

the Battle of Bull Run	the Coldstream Guards
the Boer War	United States Air Force
the National Guard	U.S. Military Academy
Purple Heart	War of the Roses

Do not capitalize informal references to the armed services:

> Lester is going into the army, but I chose the marines.

Capitalize names of institutions and organizations.

Bureau of Indian Affairs	Exxon Corporation
Continental Congress	Federal Reserve Bank
Democratic Party	Parliament
Department of the Treasury	the Politburo
Environmental Protection Agency	United States Congress

Do not capitalize the words that are formed from names of political parties unless you are referring to the party or a member of a party.

> He said that *communism* was a failed experiment.
> They were promised *democratic* elections.
> He is a Libertarian [party member].

Capitalize the names of religious groups, books, deities, events, figures, holidays.

Hindu	the Exodus	Jehovah
Methodist	the Great Flood	St. Peter
Islam	the Resurrection	Mohammed
the Bible	God	Christmas
the Koran	Allah	Good Friday
the Torah	the Lord	Yom Kippur
Proverbs	Hera	Hanukkah
the Creation	He(God)	Ramadan

Do not capitalize the names of religious objects.

crucifix   mezuzah   rosary   stations of the cross

Capitalize such school-related terms as languages, specific courses, degrees (with names) and their abbreviations.

English	History 300
Latin	Business Education 205
M.A.	Karen Siegle, Ph.D.

Do not capitalize subjects other than languages:

chemistry   physical education   computer sciences

Do not capitalize school years:

freshman   sophomore   junior   senior

Do not capitalize academic degrees except after a name:

associate of arts   master of arts   bachelor's   doctorate

Capitalize scientific names of heavenly bodies.

Antares	Regulus
Tyrannosaurus rex [genus only]	Saturn
the Andromeda Constellation	Uranus
Orion	Earth

Do not capitalize the common names of most plants and animals:

maple tree	blue jay
rose	dachshund

cap Do not capitalize generic terms without names.

asteroid	moon
comet	sun
meteor	quasar

Do not capitalize the generic term when it comes before the name.

the comet Kohoutek   the asteroid Ceres

Do not capitalize the names of diseases or medical conditions:

arthritis	jaundice
multiple sclerosis	measles
rickets	pleurisy

Capitalize the names of ships, planes, and trains.

The Spirit of St. Louis	the *Titanic*
the *Merrimac*	the *Orient Express*
the *Super Chief*	*Viking II*

37c Capitalize titles of address, position, and rank.

Mr. and Mrs. Kester	the Pope
Ms. Kwan	Empress Josephine
Uncle Rex	President Truman
Her Excellency	the President

The title *President* is often capitalized even without a specific name.

Do not capitalize words signifying family members unless they are used as names or with names.

Both my mother and my uncle were physicians in Anchorage. [Compare *Both Mother and Uncle Chris were physicians in Anchorage.*]

Do not capitalize most titles without names or when the name precedes.

the lieutenant
a congressman
the judge
the senator
Martha L. Collins, governor of Kentucky

37d Capitalize significant words in the titles of publications.

In general, capitalize the first word and the last word and all significant words in between (excluding articles, coordinate conjunctions, and short prepositions). Capitalize the first word of a subtitle following a colon.

> *Great River: The Rio Grande in North American History*
> *Present at the Creation: My Years in the State Department*
> *The Dred Scott Case: Its Significance in Law and Politics*

Do not capitalize *the* as part of a newspaper title.:

Her interview was in the *Wall Street Journal*.

In footnote and bibliographic references, omit *The* as a first word in titles of newspapers and journals.

Capitalize both elements of a hyphenated word in a title.

> *The Ballad of the Harp-Weaver*
> *Hell-Bent Fer Heaven*
> *V-Letter and Other Poems*

Capitalize divisions of a book or paper.

Preface	Bibliography
Introduction	Appendix
Conclusion	Chapter Seven: Red Giants

Capitalize the important words in the titles of government documents, acts, and policy statements. Such documents do not require quotation marks or italics.

cap
the Constitution (of the United States of America)
the Declaration of Independence
the Emancipation Proclamation
the Lend-Lease Act
the League of Nations Covenant
the United Nations Charter
the Bill of Rights

37e Capitalize both the pronoun *I* and the exclamation *O*.

"Lurch on, lurch on, O skateboard of fools," I muttered.

37f Capitalize significant words in the greeting and the first word only in the closing of a letter.

Dear Mr. Chekzikksy: Respectfully,
My Dear Friend,   Sincerely yours,
Dear Alice and Tom,   Very truly yours,

ACTIVITY 5

Proofread the following sentences for capitalization.

1. each tuesday the visitors to the lincoln park zoo were treated to a fine display by bushman and the other gorillas.
2. using only a radio shack trs-80 and a simple random access program, two high school students tried to break into the computer at chase manhattan bank.
3. professor logan had been a rhodes scholar in the thirties and had written his dissertation, "extinction of the grizzly bear," while studying in a tibetan village high in the himalayas.
4. archbishop frankendorf turned and said, "mr. president, the prime minister will see us now."
5. After surveying homes on lakes superior and huron, we decided to move farther west.
6. Jane had a choice between majoring in history or english.
7. His study of the bible required him to study hebrew.
8. The Scotch Terrier chewed up chapter one of charlotte's new book.

9. the president will address the nation on the subject of the equal rights amendment.
10. While the north was suffering a bitter winter, most of the south was clear and warm.

38 ABBREVIATIONS AND NUMBERS

General rules are given in this section. However, you should also abbreviate and spell out numbers or use numerals according to the standards of the subject you are writing about: in chemistry papers, follow the conventions of chemistry, and so on. These conventions are usually given in the style manual of a given field or academic discipline.

38a Abbreviate titles and honorifics before and after names.

Dr. Carter   George M. Montgomery, D.D.
Ms. Piazza   Mark L. Donnaly, Jr.

38b Abbreviate institutions, companies, agencies, organizations.

Wellington Corp.   YMCA   CIA   UNESCO   CBS

38c Abbreviate time, dates, measures, etc., with specific numbers.

12:00 a.m.   1066 B.C.   12 qts.   9 mm.   **235**

sp

38d Abbreviate bibliographic references.

p. (for page, *pp.* for pages)   vol. (for volume);
ed. (for editor or edition)   no. (for number)

38e Use numerals for numbers that are expressed in more than two words.

1,568   7,120,000   3½

38f Spell out numbers expressed as one or two words.

twelve   seventy-seven   forty billion

38g Spell out numbers that start sentences.

One hundred and forty-three students graduated.

39 SPELLING

Most readers will forgive one spelling mistake, and many will forgive two. But readers who recognize more than two errors may begin to develop a prejudice against the writer. If you are a good speller, the chances are high that you will still miss some words or make some typing errors. If you have a spelling problem, you need to memorize the words that cause you difficulty. In either case, learn to proofread carefully.

39a Proofread thoroughly.

Proofread your work several times because your eyes are likely to miss errors. It is possible to stare at words and yet not see the mistakes. A quick reading does not work; force yourself to look at each word, one letter at a time. Some writers can proofread by reading aloud. Others use a card or sheet of paper, covering all but one line at a time. A number of writers read their sentences *backwards* to make sure they are truly spelling out the letters and not "sight reading" the words.

Seek help. Unless your instructor says otherwise, seek help in proofreading. Professional proofreaders charge by the page, but a friend may be willing to help you in trade for the same help from you. The more important the paper is, the more sense it makes to seek help in proofreading. (Check with your instructor for your school's proofreading policy.)

Create objective distance for more effective proofreading. Writers fail to see errors because they are "too close" to their work. They are carried along by what they *think* they have written. You need some objective distance on your writing—time enough to allow objectivity. Finish your paper at least a day before it's due. A day later you will have a more critical view of everything in your writing—including mistakes.

Memorize the correct spelling of words you habitually misspell. Though English is largely phonetic (spelled by sound), there are many exceptions to the sound system. Only memorization is foolproof. Some writers deliberately mispronounce or "overpronounce" words mentally to help them remember certain letters (like the *p* in *pneumonia* or the first *l* in *colonel*). Remembering things like the *iron* in *environment* and *a rat* in *separate* may help you.

39b Watch for troublesome letters and letter combinations.

The greatest difficulty is not obviously misspelled words, but words about which you are not quite sure. Many of these have built-in trouble spots, like the *-able/-ible* and the *ei/ie* combinations.

237

sp There are some general guidelines about these trouble spots, but few absolute rules. The best policy to follow when you use troublesome words is (1) to memorize them or (2) to look them up in the dictionary or a spelling list. Familiarize yourself with this list:

-able/-ible These two suffixes sound alike. More words end with *-able*, but *-ible* frequently follows an *s* sound: *forcible, plausible, visible.* (But note *kissable, passable.*)

-age/-edge/-ege/-idge These letter combinations all sound similar:

mileage	dredge	college	abridge
suffrage	knowledge	privilege	partridge
sewage	pledge		

-ant, -ance / -ent, -ence These endings are generally pronounced alike: *redundant, insistent; redundance, insistence.*

-ceed/-cede/-sede Most of the words with the sound of *eed* are spelled *-cede: accede, concede, precede, recede, secede.* Only *exceed, proceed,* and *succeed* end in *-ceed.* Only *supersede* ends in *-sede.*

Double consonants Many words double a final consonant before adding a suffix : *scar, scar r ing; bar, bar r ing.* Words containing a long-vowel sound before the final consonant *(scare, bare)* do not double the final consonant: *scar ing, bar ing.*

ei/ie Most cases are covered by

I before *e*
except after *c*
or when pronounced as *a*,
as in *neighbor* and *weigh.*

That is, the combination is usually *ie (believe, die, fiend, friend),* but after *c* the combination is *ei (ceiling, receive, deceive);* and it is also *ei* when the combination is pronounced with a long *a* sound (as in *freight* and *sleigh*). However, there are a few exceptions (*leisure, seize,* and so on).

-ery/-ary Most words end with *-ary;* only a few words end with *-ery: cemetery, stationery* (paper).

Final e Finale *e* is usually dropped before a suffix beginning with a vowel: *hop[e]ing, scrap[e]ing.* But in some cases it is kept: *changeable, peaceable.* And it is kept when the suffix begins with a consonant: *hopeful, boredom* (but note some common exceptions: *argument, judgment, truly*). Check any word you are not certain about; many words today are spelled either way (*livable, liveable*).

-ful Words formed with *-ful* always end with one *l: cupful, eyeful, handful, teaspoonful, thankful.*

-ly Add *-ly* to a word that already ends with an *l: accidental (ly), real (ly).* Words ending in double *l* add only the *-y: fully, hilly.*

-or/-er/-ar All these endings sound alike (*author, grammar, painter*). When in doubt, check your dictionary.

-o Words ending in *-o* usually become plural by adding *es: tomatoes, potatoes, mosquitoes, zeroes.* But words related to music add only *s: solos, sopranos, pianos, radios.* A few words can be spelled either way.

pre- / per -/ pro- Check words with these prefixes: (*perspiration, performance, prepare, protect*). Don't count on sound here. Many people pronounce them all alike; others interchange them ("prespiration," for "perspiration" or "pertect" for "protect").

Silent letters A number of words contain silent (unpronounced) letters: *clim(b), hon(e), Conne(c)ticut, (k)nife, (p)syc(h)ology.*

-y words Change *-y* to *i* before all suffixes (endings) except *-ing: beauty, beautiful; noisy, noisily; buy, buying.*

-y words Change *-y* to *i* and add *es* for the plural : *babies, families.* But note that proper names do not follow this rule: *Kennedys, Sheltys.* When the *y* follows a vowel (*monkey*) the plural is formed by adding *s* only (*monkeys*).

39c Distinguish between homonyms.

Many words, though spelled differently, sound alike or very similar. Homonyms are often hard to detect because they don't *look* misspelled.

LIST OF COMMON HOMONYMS

bare/bear
been/bin
board/bored
cite/site
complement/compliment
for/fore/four
groan/grown
hear/here
higher/hire
rain/reign
right/rite/write
rote/wrote

sail/sale
sea/see
stair/stare
stake/steak
steal/steel
tail/tale
their/there/they're
threw/through
to/too/two
wail/whale
weak/week
your/you're/yore

39d Learn the correct spelling of irregular plurals.

SINGULAR	PLURAL
alumna	alumnae (f)
alumnus	alumni (m)
analysis	analyses
appendix	appendixes, appendices
bacterium	bacteria
cactus	cactuses, cacti
crisis	crises
criterion	criteria
curriculum	curriculums, curricula
datum	data
die	dice
formula	formulas, formulae
index	indexes, indices
medium	media
memorandum	memoranda
nucleus	nuclei
octopus	octopuses, octopi
parenthesis	parentheses
stimulus	stimuli
stratum	strata
thesis	theses

ACTIVITY 6

Proofread these sentences and correct spelling errors you find.

1. The doctors hoped to releive the pain in her knee with a traction splint.
2. The sequel to the movie made a permenant impression on college students in the audiance.
3. The President's advisers refused to concede that thier policies concerning foriegn aid to Israel would be difficult to administer.
4. The nation's traitors had been arrested but not executed.
5. It wasn't long before the station began to fill with attendents and with perspective passengers, and, appropriatly, a train.
6. My instincts rallied together and introdused the thought that later led me to my decision of a drastic hairstyle change.
7. When I see you on the street or catcht a glimpse of you, I get the weirdest sensation inside, like falling through a pit with no bottom.
8. The biggest, burliest Marine sergent D. I. (drill instructor) has just turned away and clicked his heels.
9. We were lounging around the pool side of a local racket bal club, gazing up into the sky.
10. The morning went by quickly with the tempeture rising to a humid 96 degrees at noon.
11. Now the only lights noticable are ocasional cigerretes casting minute red sparks like fireflies blinking in the night.
12. Most people, being somewhat apprehensive about anything with more than four legs, do not appreciate spiders—much less taranchulas.
13. I realize there are problems and inconvenences in voting: the weather's bad, you have to work, your going out of town, you don't trust the government, you don't like the choice of candadates, and so on.
14. "From a public health perspective it is quite clear that this increase in the drinking age is in the interest of that (18–20–year old population," stated Richard Douglass, assistent research scientist at the University of Michigan's Highway Safety Reserch Institute.
15. Reserchers claim that by using a large number of animals per experiement, they are more certain of their results and can also predict the percentage of people who will be effected.

ACTIVITY 7

Proofread the following paragraph and correct any spelling errors you find.

sp

Chalenger's prime busness on her maiden voyage was
the deploying of the $100 million Tracking and Data
Relay Satelite (TDRS) into its position in space over
Brazil. Plans on this agenda had to be altared, however,
when the satelite developed orbiting problems due to one
of its thrusters being stuck closed. Engineers at NASA
studying the problem are confidant the orbit will be
back to normal after a series of manuvers in a two-week
period to boost the satelite into its projected orbit.
TDRS will bring future shuttles "in constant contact
with Mission Control instead of comunicating only when
passing within range of ground stations."

Diction

Diction refers to word choice. Effective word choice implies a writer's sensitivity to words, a feeling for language distinctions; and it depends on purpose, audience, subject, your stance as a writer. *Effective* means not just "good" but "having an effect on the reader," the effect you intend.

40 THE DICTIONARY

If you don't have one, buy a college dictionary now. These dictionaries, with *College* in the title or called *College Edition*, are indispensable. A college dictionary will provide you with the proper spelling, pronunciation, and meanings for words; the syllabic division; the part(s) of speech; the level of formality; synonyms, antonyms, origins; and more. Read your dictionary's introductory pages to see how to read its entries. Here is a sample entry from *Webster's New Collegiate Dictionary*:

> **im·bro·glio** \im-'brōl-(,)yō\ *n, pl* **-glios** [It, fr. *imbrogliare* to entangle, fr. MF *embrouiller* — more at EMBROIL] (1750) **1 :** a confused mass **2 a :** an intricate or complicated situation (as in a drama or novel) **b :** an acutely painful or embarrassing misunderstanding **c :** a violently confused or bitterly complicated altercation : EMBROILMENT

This entry shows the syllabication of the word (for word division in typing) and the pronunciation of the word; note that the syllables for pronunciation are slightly different from those for hyphenation. This dictionary gives a pronunciation guide at the bottom of the page, showing the pronunciation of an unmarked *i* and the long *o*. Note that the *g* is silent and there is an optional secondary accent on the last syllable. The dictionary shows the part of speech (noun), giving you a clue to its use.

The entry shows the historical origins of the word. Our word *imbroglio* comes from the Italian word *imbrogliare*, which itself came from the Medieval French word *embrouiller*. The dictionary directs you to the entry for *embroil* for more information about the history of the word; at *embroil* you would discover that the French word means, as you might suspect, *to broil.*

Imbroglio has three related meanings, as explained in the entry. And one of its synonyms is *embroilment*. If you look up *imbroglio* in a thesaurus you will find many other synonyms for it, like *disarray, hodgepodge, predicament, brawl, turmoil.*

ACTIVITY 1

Use a college dictionary to look up the following words. Write sentences using each word appropriately. In what kind of writing situations might you use these words?

brouhaha	penultimate	sesquipedalian
inchoate	obviate	turgid
infra dig	raze	venal

ACTIVITY 2

Revise the following sentences by replacing inexact words with precise diction.

1. We had decorated the house with little sprags of edelweiss.
2. From my hours of studying, I had found the history of the Punic Wars very edificing.
3. They had finally become lovelorn from kissing so often.
4. For Christmas we all chipped in to buy grandmother a ruby pedant.
5. "You must have your tonsures out," my doctor said—I think.

40a Use standard English and oral English appropriately.

Avoid oral English for any but the most informal writing situations. In conversation, rules governing social *situations* apply more than language rules. The opposite is true of writing, except for writ-

diction

ing meant to represent conversation. All native speakers of American English speak their own dialects, largely depending on what region of the country they live in—North, South, East, West—and whether they live in a city or in a rural area.

> I reckon y'all heard the news.
> We be back after a while.
> They ain't nobody here.

Many expressions that we all use and accept in oral English should be avoided in formal writing. Slang, regional words, "dialects," and other oral expressions are appropriate in formal writing only to create a special effect, such as realistic dialogue.

40b Understand the difference between denotations and connotations.

DENOTATION

The denotation of a word is its dictionary definition. A word has no inherent meaning but only that which is agreed upon by most people. Many words have several denotations, a fact that can sometimes cause problems. For example, the word *grave* means "burial site," but it also means "serious," and no writer can afford to use the word as if it meant only one thing and not the other. Many readers will "hear" the other meaning, despite the writer:

DENOTATION PROBLEM
Washington considers the death of the Russian ambassador a very grave matter.

REVISED
Washington considers the death of the Russian ambassador a very serious matter.

GENERAL CONNOTATIONS

Some dictionaries list not only a word's denotations but its general connotations. Connotations are clues to the way the word is actually used by speakers and writers. For example, *pretend* and *pretense* mean "fake or falsify." We can pretend to be sick, pretend to be someone else, make a pretense of doing homework. But we do not usually say, "The builders pretended the girders were steel." Nor are we likely to say, "The counterfeiter pretended his money was real." *Pretend* denotes "fake" or "false," but it generally connotes "fakery without serious consequences," the pretense of children. For more serious kinds of falsification we are likely to select more serious-sounding words: *allege, dissemble, simulate, fraud,* and so on.

SPECIAL CONNOTATIONS

In addition to general connotations, many words also have special connotations. These often suggest a positive or negative quality and evoke emotional responses from readers. They can also be private reactions: for example, different readers might respond differently to each of the following: *law-enforcement officer, police, cop, fuzz, smokey.* All the terms could identify the same individual, but each term carries a different emotional meaning.

People often try to change labels in order to get away from negative connotations. *Garbage dumps* become *sanitary landfills, janitors* become *maintenance engineers, toilets* become *lavatories or bathrooms, military attacks* become *preemptive strikes.* A person is *skinny* or *slim,* one a relatively negative term, the other positive. Another person is *determined* or *stubborn, eventempered* or *dull,* depending on whether our view is affirmative or negative. Knowing denotative meanings is not sufficient; you must also have an ear for connotations.

ACTIVITY 3

Read the following sentences carefully. Replace any words that interfere with the meaning of the sentence.

1. The host herself was a very cheerful party.
2. Her complexion bloomed with the ruddy glow of blemishes.
3. Ollie is a pig farmer and a terrible bore.
4. The directions said to force the spit through the mouth of the chicken.
5. Though he was a famous ventriloquist, the critics felt he had given a very wooden performance.

idiom

40c Use synonyms carefully.

The dictionary lists synonyms (equivalent or approximate words) for most terms. A special dictionary for this purpose is called a *the-saurus*. But care must be taken with synonyms. They too have con-notations; few synonyms are *exact* replacements for other words. Here you need a writer's ear; you must think about the context of the word before selecting a synonym: *wastebasket* and *trashcan* may be synonyms, but there are subtle differences between the words. Some words are different only because they have different language histories: while *ice box* and *refrigerator* both denote the same thing, *ice box* now sounds dated, old fashioned. You may make an unin-tended statement about yourself if you refer to your *ice box*.

ACTIVITY 4

Revise the following sentences so that their use of denotation and con-notation becomes more effective.

1. All the boys were laughing and clowning around and being as supercilious as they could to try to get her attention.
2. After the tests, the psychologist explained that because of a birth defect the child was ignorant.
3. We soon learned that VD was a very healthy disease, one not easily controlled.
4. Everyone had been working for ten hours without rest, and we were all suffering from fugue.
5. Of all those huge tomes on ancient history, the epitome was the biggest one of all.
6. Construction companies found guilty of rigging their bids were required to find a more constructive use of their resources.

40d Use idioms appropriately.

An idiom is an expression that has become conventional, despite its logic or grammar. Often idioms will mean something more than or different from a literal translation of the words they contain: the words function as a unit. When English speakers say they will "take a train," they do not mean that they will take it away with them.

Similarly, expressions like *catch fire, do a good turn, give someone a hand,* and so forth are idioms that mean something different from their literal interpretation.

Occasionally even native speakers have problems with idioms, particularly with the prepositions that accompany them:

abide by	differ with (a person)
abstain from	different from
acquiesce in (an injustice)	disappointed in (a performance)
adhere to	discuss with (someone)
agree to (a proposal)	divest of
agree with (a person)	identical with
alarmed at (the news)	in accordance with
aspire to	independent of
assent to	indifferent to
avail oneself of	oblivious of (warnings)
capable of	plan to
concur in (an opinion)	prevail on (or upon)
concur with (someone)	refrain from
confer about (a problem)	required of (people)
confer with (someone)	resolve on (an action)
conform to (specifications)	succeed in
contend for (a principle)	superior to
contend with (a person)	try to
die of	wait at (a place)
differ about (an issue)	wait for (a person)
differ from (in appearance)	wait on (a customer)

SLANG

Slang is street-English, the latest fad words, "in" words by which individuals establish their relationship to a group. Only those in the group ("in the know") know the slang until it begins to creep into the general language. As we write this, "grody to the max" and "gag me with a spoon" are recent slang terms.

The use of slang has to do with appropriateness. In most formal writing slang should be avoided. Imagine writing about a President's reaction to Congress' overriding a veto: "The President was really bummed, but he decided to cool it and go to his ranch and kick back for a while." Though such use of slang may be effective in less formal writing, particularly in dialogue, it is inappropriate in formal writing.

ACTIVITY 5
Revise for correct use of idiom and to eliminate slang.

1. The archeologist flew to Egypt to try and discover whether the dates of the pottery shards were different than those in Israel.
2. The efficiency expert began to scope out the copying procedures to see if they were in accordance to those he had suggested.
3. The concert was awesome and one that nobody could be indifferent about.

41 EFFECTIVE LANGUAGE

All writing is a combination of the general and the specific, the abstract and the concrete, the literal and the figurative. One of your major steps in revising should be to examine your language choices to insure that you have made the best possible selections.

41a Clarify general concepts with specific language.

General language identifies groups or classes of things; specific language identifies individual members of a class. *Games* is a general term, *football* is specific; *literature* is general, *novel* more specific, *The Grapes of Wrath* most specific. General statements without specific examples can produce dullness, ambiguity, fuzziness, and confusion. Readers need specific details in order to make precise meaning from generalities.

GENERAL
People say the economy is their biggest worry.

REVISED
On the news last night, four patrons of city soup kitchens said they wanted jobs, not charity.

GENERAL

He was a cute guy.

REVISED

He was 6' 1", built like John Travolta, had blond, curly hair, baby blue eyes, and a smile that made him look like a mischievous little boy.

The specific details here allow the reader to understand what you mean by *people, economy,* and *cute.*

Specific language is greatly preferred to general. It takes study, observation, and thought to produce the specific details that constitute real information.

GENERAL

Changing Places is a fine movie that lives up to the reputations of its stars. The acting is superior in this film, and the plot is very good. Those who see this interesting new film will have an enjoyable experience.

REVISED

The film *Changing Places* stars the comic actors Eddie Murphy and Dan Ackroyd. Together the two young comedians are first the victims and then the winners in a plot set in motion by aging actors Don Ameche and Ralph Bellamy, two evil stock brokers who set out to manipulate the younger men for the sake of a one-dollar bet. The bet is that a penniless, low-grade street shyster (Murphy pretends to be blind and legless) can successfully take over the job of a rising young Wall Street analyst and that the analyst, when reduced to poverty, will soon resort to crime.

Except for the title of the film, there is no information in the general paragraph; it offers only a set of unsupported and imprecise evaluations.

Writers cannot separate the general from the specific in a mechanical way. The two must work together so that readers have both facts and ideas. If you could only describe the fact that every time you put your hand near the saw you lost a finger, without drawing any conclusion from this, you would soon have no fingers. The *generalization* about saws and fingers, after all, is an idea. While everyone prefers specific language to concrete *most* of the time, there are times when general language will be appropriate. The purpose of *lang* your writing determines the level of specification you need. For example, if you were tracing the history of a study carried out by a cost-control group, you might say at one point:

EXCESSIVE SPECIFICATION
The energetic and intelligent committee, comprised of six men and two women (one of whom had just been divorced), accepted by a vote of five to three the report.

USEFUL GENERAL LANGUAGE
The committee accepted the report.

It is difficult to lay out information or sum up information without generalizations. If you want to indicate only that the report was accepted, details about the committee and the vote may not be relevant.

ACTIVITY 6
Imagine that you have been asked to describe the results of a poll taken on a college campus to determine how politically active and aware the students are. Revise the following paragraph to illustrate your understanding of the interplay between the general and the specific. Make any changes you wish; add appropriate details where necessary.

The pollsters surveyed a pretty fair number of students, freshmen through seniors, some males and more females. One woman had been president of her local chapter of the Young Democrats. Most students said they were aware of some of the more important national issues but had not voted in the last presidential campaign. Only a few, those whose families lived in the area, knew about local issues, like the proposed zoning changes that had failed on the last referendum by a vote of 2,564 to 2,389, one of the closest votes in the town's history. Millage for the local school district, one that had an excellent reputation for both vocational and college preparatory courses, was the one that some knew about and had voted on sometime in the fall. A good

percentage of those surveyed knew who was running for
student government and planned to vote. A lot of people
were concerned about tuition increases and planned to do
something about it.

41b Clarify abstract concepts with concrete language.

Tie intangible concepts to physical reality. Abstractions are qualities and ideas removed from physical reality. Many writers consider generalizations and abstractions to be the same. But, although generalizations may have physical referents, abstractions don't. For example, "beauty" is an abstraction; beauty does not exist in the environment; it is an idea. We can find people we think *have* beauty, but beauty itself exists only in the mind ("in the eye of the beholder" we usually say). We cannot show people *freedom,* nor can we touch *democracy, socialism, purity, perfection,* and other abstract concepts. Abstractions are intangible: not observable by the senses.

Writers must not mechanically separate abstract ideas from concrete language. The writer's challenge is to tie abstractions to reality, to illustrate the intangible idea with concrete examples. Since, by their very nature, abstractions evoke different interpretations, a writer must help the reader to understand the writer's intentions. You may have your own idea of what *communism* means, but if you compare your definition with those of the people of the USSR, the People's Republic of China, Albania, Cambodia, France, and so forth, you would discover many different concepts of what the word means. To assist your reader, you must supply concrete terms that will illustrate abstract concepts.

ABSTRACT
He lost the election because of accusations of dishonesty.

REVISED
He lost the election because he was accused of taking a $10,000 bribe.

253

lang   *Dishonesty* is a vague abstraction; the specific charge gives readers a much clearer sense of the accusations.

Concrete means physical. If you kick a concrete block, you will get sharp information from your foot. Something similar happens with concrete language; it gives the reader information at the physical level. The closer language comes to describing physical reality, the more concrete; and the farther away, the more *abstract*. When people say, "Give me an example," they are asking for concrete information. The more intangible or abstract writing becomes, the harder it is for readers to know what you are talking about. "Liquidating my assets to increase cash flow" can mean several things, one of which could be "selling my old Ford because I'm short of money."

While abstractions have their uses, readers need to visualize what you are writing about. Examples, illustrations, and details help sharpen pictures, and concrete words help to clarify the impression.

ABSTRACT

The presence of deciduous windbreaks may produce less effective results than similar establishment of conifers.

REVISED

Pines and spruces make better windbreaks than do trees that lose their leaves.

ACTIVITY 7

Revise each of the following sentences by replacing abstract language with concrete wherever possible.

1. Upon termination of normal chronological development, mortal remains are customarily interred in a sepulcher.
2. Individual liberties such as those governing oral communication are guaranteed by governmental documents.
3. Counterfeiting one's emotions may sometimes produce an inability to experience sincere relationships.
4. Law-enforcement officials announced the recovery of a cache of merchandise illegally sequestered by criminal accomplices.
5. Presidential advisors at the highest levels proffered recommendations that recently expounded commitments be jettisoned.

Use effective modifiers. Some modifiers carry only vague meanings, often just a hazy positive or negative suggestion. Use precise modifiers to gain clarity and effectiveness.

WEAK
It was an interesting film.

REVISED
The way the film created the effect of space ships speeding around the buildings of the city nearly brought me out of my seat.

Without effective modifiers, what does the sentence mean? Did you like the film? What was "interesting" about it? The acting? the plot? the camera work? the special effects? The word *interesting* carries only a shadowy meaning, that something about the film caught your attention. Most readers will not respond to such a sentence; they need more specific information.

EFFECTIVE ADJECTIVES AND ADVERBS
He had an *evil, reptilian* grin.
The ice creaked *ominously*.

EFFECTIVE PREPOSITIONAL AND PARTICIPIAL PHRASES
At the base of the eye, a small artery pulsed, *squeezing out a drop of blood with every beat.*

EFFECTIVE ADJECTIVE AND ADVERB CLAUSES
When the thick gray smoke cleared, we could see the rubble *that the bomb had flung outward.*

ACTIVITY 8
Add effective modifiers to these sentences. Imagine they are sentences for essays for your composition class.

1. The alligator is a fairly long and ugly creature.
2. The performnce of the symphony was nice.
3. A lot of work was involved in writing the program.
4. Sap came slowly out of the tap in the maple tree.
5. Because of its violence, the storm's effects were terrible.

Use effective nouns. Using the most specific, concrete nouns can add power to your writing and can also save you from excessive use of modifiers to describe more general nouns. Selecting accurate nouns will also make your writing more economical.

lang

WEAK
They planted a tree between the bushes and the flowers.

REVISED
They planted a red oak between the lilacs and the rose garden.

WEAK
Grandfather was very proud of his old car.

REVISED
Grandfather was very proud of his Model–A Ford.

WEAK
We were all gagging from the strong, disagreeable odor.

REVISED
We were all gagging from the stench.

The more specific choice packs more meaning into the individual word. It carries all the qualities of the more general term plus its own individual qualities. Revise your writing with the most appropriate, the most specific nouns.

Particularly important to effective writing is the noun in the subject position of any sentence. Well-chosen noun subjects will add strength to your writing and will help to eliminate the colorless verbs that often accompany general and abstract nouns. Avoid starting sentences with "empty" subjects like *It is* and *There are*.

WEAK
It is the belief of most Americans that their taxes are too high.

REVISED
Americans believe that taxes are too high.

WEAK
There are several areas of determination that need our attention.

REVISED
Several problems need our attention.

Other relatively empty nouns that often produce dull sentences are words like *situation*, *facet*, *aspect*, *factor*, and *elements*.

WEAK

A factor that should be taken into consideration is class attendance.

REVISED

Class attendance should be a consideration.

The professor should count class attendance as part of the grade.

WEAK

The aspect most in need of examination is the chemical reaction.

REVISED

The chemical reaction is most in need of examination.

We need to examine the chemical reaction most.

Empty or abstract subjects cannot *do* anything, so choosing them limits the verbs you can use. Often the verbs must be passive or a form of *to be*, both relatively weak choices.

ACTIVITY 9
Revise the following sentences by restructuring them or supplying specific nouns.

1. The factor that caused everyone to fail to sleep was Jones's dog bellowing at the moon all night.
2. A promise was made to her by the army concerning her becoming a soldier and learning the provisions of weaponry care.
3. We knew the aspect of greatest importance was the cost of medicine.
4. The guards were told to be on the alert for any conflict situations.
5. With the practiced eye of a determined shopper, he selected various foodstuffs and household supplies in quick succession.

Use effective verbs. Verbs move your writing and control its rhythm, give it life and vibrancy. Weak verbs sap its strength. Use the most specific verb appropriate to your context. In general, look for direct, one-word, active, concrete verbs. Avoid overusing the passive voice and forms of the verb *to be*.

The passive voice can be effective now and then, but overuse dulls your writing. The subject of a passive verb is acted upon rather than acting directly. (See **14.**)

lang

WEAK PASSIVE
The grapes were crushed by the peasants' feet.

REVISED
The peasants' feet crushed the grapes.

The peasants crushed the grapes with their feet.

WEAK PASSIVE
The novel was read by the class.

REVISED
The class read the novel.

In writing and revising, follow this general rule: most readers prefer active verbs.

Forms of the verb *to be* are central to our language, but since they merely tell the reader that something "is" or "was," they are not strong verbs. They do not indicate action. In revising, circle these forms and change them whenever possible to more effective verbs.

WEAK *TO BE*
The man *was* a scavenger; he was often seen picking through the trash left by the roadside.

REVISED
The scavenger often *picked* through the trash left by the roadside.

The man, a scavenger, often *rummaged* through the trash left by the roadside.

Precise verbs give your writing power, as do exact nouns; meaning is condensed and the writing becomes efficient. For example, read this simple sentence:

Jean went down the hall.

Maybe that is all you wish to say, but there is much you could reveal about Jean and the way she moved by selecting a more specific verb:

Jean tiptoed down the hall.
Jean staggered . . .
Jean marched . . .
Jean strutted . . .
Jean reeled . . .

Jean wandered . . .
Jean swaggered . . .
Jean crept . . .
Jean ambled . . .

There are many possibilities. Writing loses strength when writers fail to select the most effective verbs, but it loses both strength and interest when they select the most common, predictable and least informative. Verbs, like nouns and modifiers, can be general or specific. Decide what your purpose is and choose accordingly.

ACTIVITY 10
Revise the following paragraph to make verbs, nouns, and modifiers more effective. Imagine this paragraph begins an essay for your composition class.

```
    There are several places that make me feel good; one
of them is my bedroom. There are a great number of
things that have been with me for a lot of years. I have
this bear that is a little worn, but it reminds me of
some happy times when I was a kid. On the wall is this
really interesting poster I got when I was in
gradeschool. Then there is my baseball glove on the
shelf. That sure brings back memories. My bed is really
different; my grandfather slept on it when he was a boy.
It has a wild cover on it that I like a lot. There are
all kinds of family pictures hanging up near my
brother's bed. It's a great room.
```

41c Avoid archaic words and neologisms.

Archaic words are obsolete words that have passed out of common usage, but that may appear in older texts or in special contexts. The dictionary labels such words as *obsolete* or *obs*. Archaic words *jargon* should be avoided unless you have a specific purpose for using them. Examples are words like *erst* (formerly), *anent* (about), *anon* (soon), and *fain* (gladly).

Words that have been created too recently to come into common use are called *neologisms*. Some will become permanent parts of our language; some will not. *Brunch, fallout,* and *space shuttle* are examples of ones that have. Whether words like *palimony* and *computerese* will become generally accepted remains to be seen. Use new words only if you are sure your audience will understand them easily and accept them in a particular writing situation.

In coining your own words, exercise extreme caution. It is often better to use an existing word than to try to invent a new one.

41d Learn when jargon is appropriate and when it is not.

Jargon is the specialized vocabulary of a particular profession or discipline, but the word has come to mean the inappropriate use of such vocabulary with general audiences. Each profession has its own necessary language, its own terminology to identify concepts, objects, and events. Used within its own field, jargon is efficient and helpful. But when you are writing to an audience of nonexperts, the use of such language can be irritating, confusing, even incomprehensible. Technical terms might be fine for your physics professor, but for another audience, those same terms might be confusing.

If it is necessary to use technical terms in papers for general audiences, you should define those terms. Do not use technical vocabulary to impress your readers; they will become frustrated rather than impressed. Remember that clarity is your goal, and jargon is often not clear.

UNNECESSARY JARGON
From a military point of view, your destination does not seem logistically accessible.

REVISED
The army doesn't think you can get where you want to go from here.

41e Avoid inflated diction.

Students sometimes think their own language is inferior, that their vocabulary is insufficient, or that teachers will be impressed with long, obscure words. As a result, they turn to a thesaurus or dictionary and pick out impressive-sounding words. *Predict* turns into *prognosticate, use* becomes *utilization, rich* changes to *opulent, rank* is transformed into *prioritize.* In general, it is better to select the simple words. When you use unfamiliar words, you risk missing shades of meaning attached to those words, producing a meaning you did not intend. Pretentious words call attention to themselves. We do not suggest that you neglect adding to your vocabulary—just the opposite. But additions should become part of your working language, not just borrowed to impress an audience.

41f Avoid euphemism.

Euphemisms are inoffensive words substituted for offensive ones. In daily conversations we may wish to spare our own or others' feelings when discussing sensitive subjects like death, sex, or bodily functions. People *pass on* or *expire* instead of *die.* People *make love;* children *tinkle* or *have a bowel movement.* In writing, too, it may sometimes be necessary to use the politer terms in order not to offend readers. However, a problem arises when euphemisms are used to cloud the truth or mislead the reader. For example, during the Vietnam War government sources spoke of "pacification programs," which, in reality, meant the wholesale destruction of villages. Recently the MX missile was referred to as a "peace-keeper." We all use euphemisms to protect ourselves in one way or another, but in writing you have an obligation to your readers to deal directly and honestly with your topic.

41g Avoid wordiness.

Unnecessary words make your writing sound loose and weak. Avoid adding extra words to reach an assigned paper length. Most instructors would prefer a shorter, concise and economical paper:

wordy   padding is never a good idea. Condense expressions like the following:

WORDY	REVISED
at this point in time	now
for the reason that	because
due to the fact that	because
because of the fact that	because
in American society today	in America
has the ability to	can
during the same time that	when

Loosely written sentences can almost always be condensed. Much depends on your purpose, of course: in other contexts *the President of the United States* could be shortened to *the President,* but in some contexts that change might produce an unwanted effect. The rule is not to cut every possible word, but every unnecessary word. In general, loosely written sentences can be tightened with the following kinds of deletions:

LOOSE
Uncle Billy Bob was a man who liked to smoke cigars.

REVISED BY REDUCING A CLAUSE
Uncle Billy Bob was a cigar smoker.

Uncle Billy Bob smoked cigars.

LOOSE
We had a date for a movie at twelve o'clock A.M.

REVISED BY REDUCING PHRASES
We had a movie date at noon.

LOOSE
All of a sudden there was this great big explosion that scared the heck out of us.

REVISED WITH SINGLE-WORD SUBSTITUTES
Suddenly there was a huge, terrifying explosion.

REDUNDANCY

Redundancy is another kind of wordiness, stemming from the use of different words to say the same thing. It is redundant, for example, to write *past history,* since history is by definition "past." Other redundant expressions include

rectangular in shape	disappear from view
orange in color	disregard altogether
basic essentials	revert back
separate and distinct	advance planning
until such time as	

WORD REPETITION

Sometimes writers unnecessarily repeat words within a sentence or in adjoining sentences. Avoid unnecessary repetition by finding adequate synonyms, using pronouns, or combining sentences.

REPETITIOUS

Charmaine wanted to study ecology. Ecology is the study of the relationship between organisms and their environment.

REVISED

Charmaine wanted to learn about ecology, the study of the relationship between organisms and their environment.

UNNECESSARY PASSIVE

The passive voice contributes to wordiness. It often takes more words to write a passive sentence than an active one. (See **14**.)

PASSIVE

It was decided by the group to close shop. [9 words]

REVISED

The group decided to close shop. [6 words]

PASSIVE

The tenement was torn down by Haley's construction crew. [9 words]

REVISED

Haley's construction crew tore down the tenement. [7 words]

cliché

ACTIVITY 11

Revise to eliminate wordiness.

1. Due to the fact that hang gliding gave him a sense of freedom, Ralph escaped from the city every weekend to go hang gliding.
2. Until such time as it is deemed advisable by the officers, the certificates will not be issued by the company.
3. It was Professor Edwards who insisted that we stick to the basic essentials for the reason that the command which we had of more sophisticated material was less than expert.
4. The game of basketball is a game that is becoming more and more popular in Europe at this point in time.
5. The record was recorded by Michael Jackson, and it was a unique and different rendition of a song that had never been done before.

ACTIVITY 12

Write a quick rough-draft paragraph about a page long. Revise by deleting every word that can come out without losing your overall meaning.

41h Avoid clichés.

A cliché is a trite, overused expression that has lost its freshness and force, a ready-made phrase that requires little thought from you or your reader. Clichés are predictable: readers can usually complete the expression after hearing the first word or two. "Blind as a bat," "straight from the shoulder," "out of the blue"—these and other expressions like them ought to be "avoided like the plague." Your own voice, your own expressions will be more powerful, more direct, and will have a greater impression on your readers.

Here is a partial list of clichés:

a chip off the old block	crying shame
all walks of life	dire straits
as happy as a lark	easier said than done
at the crack of dawn	few and far between
better late than never	fine and dandy
burn the midnight oil	good time was had by all
conspicuous by its absence	goes without saying

last straw
like water off a duck's back
makes my blood boil
nipped in the bud
off the beaten track
proud owner
rude awakening

selling like hotcakes
sink or swim
sneaking suspicion
straight and narrow
strike while the iron is hot
truer words were never spoken
truth is stranger than fiction

42 FIGURATIVE LANGUAGE

Figurative language makes a "figure," an "image" for the reader. These "figures of speech" help writers make comparisons, either explicitly or implicitly. Literal language is direct: it means exactly what it says. Figurative language, on the other hand, uses the literal term but stretches its meaning to make a comparison between different things. For example, a translation of "That guy eats like a pig" would be something like "That guy eats sloppily." The comparison, "like a pig," does not literally mean that he sticks his snout into the food, roots around, and grunts while ingesting huge amounts; but the comparison does suggest that his eating habits are very sloppy, like those of a pig.

In conversation we tend to rely on familiar comparisons, that whole stock of well-used, often overused, expressions. But in writing you have time to create original, vivid figures that can clarify, expand meaning, and bring life and color to your writing. You should always consider audience, purpose, and occasion, but in many cases the inclusion of an effective figure of speech can enhance your paper and generate interest from your reader.

42a Create effective metaphors.

A metaphor is an implied comparison, containing the subject and the thing compared. If you said, "The meeting was a zoo," the subject is *meeting* and you are comparing that to a zoo. The comparison is implied: it does not say the meeting is *like* a zoo, but the meeting *is* a zoo.

*fig
lang*

EFFECTIVE METAPHORS
The parking meters, urban pelicans, gulp quarters instead of fish.
The television set, a drug that lulls and pacifies, sapped her vitality.

42b Create effective similes.

Like a metaphor, a simile expresses a comparison, but directly,
using the words *like* or *as*.

EFFECTIVE SIMILE
Aunt Mary's coffee pot, like a fountain of youth, brought movement
back to aged limbs, activity back to her tired mind.

Max was attracted to the gambling table like a lemming to the sea.

42c Use effective personification.

Personification is a kind of comparison in which human qualities
are attributed to animals, objects, or abstractions.

EFFECTIVE PERSONIFICATION
The video games called to him invitingly.

Don't fool with Mother Nature.

In general, make figurative language blend with your meaning;
avoid overused comparisons; exercise restraint. A simile or a metaphor should not call such attention to itself that it would distract the
reader from your purpose.

EXCESSIVE FIGURE
The pencil slipped from his hand just as a soul slips from a dead
body.

REVISED FOR RESTRAINT
The pencil slipped from his hand like a falling leaf.

42d Use overstatement carefully to make a strong impression on your reader.

Avoid overemphasis. Beware of writing in absolute terms, overemphasizing, and making dogmatic statements. Many readers are irritated by absolute statements and resist them. Words like *always, never, most, least, best, worst,* and so forth should be used with caution.

It was a day I'll never forget. [How do you know what you will remember thirty years from now?]

She was the best woman who ever lived. [Do you know all the women who ever lived?]

Create emphasis with understatement. Sometimes it is better to use understatement than to overstate the obvious.

OVERSTATED
Poor old Mr. Ditters was laid out stone cold dead as a mackerel in his coffin, stiff as a board and ready for the grave.

UNDERSTATED
Mr. Ditters lay unnaturally quiet and unresponsive, a manikin in a box.

Avoid overusing intensifiers. Intensifiers are modifiers indicating degree. Intensifiers like *very, really, certainly, rather,* and so on, should be used with care. Overuse can give your writing an excessive, insincere tone. Often they suggest you have a limited vocabulary.

UNNECESSARY INTENSIFIERS
I felt really alive.
Are you perfectly sure?

INTENSIFIERS DELETED
I felt vigorous.
Are you positive?

*fig
lang*

Intensifiers may be needed in some contexts. For example, if a statement is doubted, an intensifier may be used to insist on its truth: "Nelly *really* ate the frogs." In other cases the intensifier may be appropriate to indicate degree: "The kettle soon got *too* hot to handle." But in general, use intensifiers with care.

Avoid overly dramatic modifiers. Sometimes writers try to force an impression on their readers, not by effective writing, but by using excessively dramatic modifiers.

> He had *incredible* strength and a *terrific* personality.
> Her success was *fabulous* and her future *marvelous*.

Other words to avoid or use with care are *good, nice, wonderful, stupendous, fantastic, terrible, devastating, ghastly,* and the like. These overused words have been have been nearly drained of meaning; they indicate only positive or negative emotions.

WEAK
It was a terrible day.
She had this ghastly dress on.

REVISED WITH SPECIFIC MODIFIERS
The day was cold, rainy, bleak.
She was wearing an electric-green silk dress covered with little pink and yellow baby chicks.

ACTIVITY 13
Revise the overstatements and overused modifiers.

1. It was a fantastic book that I really liked a lot.
2. He's not real sure what to do with this perfectly terrible assignment.
3. Nothing will ever change my mind about nuclear power plants; they will always be a dreadful threat to our country.

42e Avoid unconscious echoes.

Sometimes, without realizing it, writers will produce rhymes and alliterations that become noticeable, and therefore distracting, to readers: *It made no sense; the album only cost ninety-nine cents;* ~~fig~~ *Sid's simple suggestion was certainly a sensible solution.* Read your *lang* paper aloud to find and revise unconscious echoes.

ACTIVITY 14

Revise the following paragraph for more effective use of language. Imagine this is a paragraph of an essay for your composition class.

> While the play was good, there were a few things that were bothersome. The man who played the lead didn't say his lines very well. Also, he was supposed to be playing an old man, but he moved around the stage like a youngster. The plot was interesting, but the solution to the murder seemed unbelievable given the clues presented. The only other shortcoming was that the scenery didn't seem to fit what was going on.

Paragraphs

43 EFFECTIVE PARAGRAPHS

A paragraph is a group of related sentences developing a single idea. Now and then paragraphs may consist of a single sentence; however, in formal writing, most contain at least several. A paragraph begins with an indented sentence: half an inch for handwritten paragraphs, five spaces on a typewriter or computer.

A paragraph may be a small composition by itself, a one-paragraph summary, report, description, and so on. But usually the paragraph serves as a division of a larger composition. Paragraphs can also serve a structural use as the introduction or conclusion of a composition, and they may be used on occasion as transitions between sections of a longer paper.

43a Recognize various paragraph structures.

A paragraph is a set of sentences related structurally; that is, the sentences fit together in a certain way: they have a relationship to one another. The "structure" of a paragraph is, like the structure of a skyscraper, an underlying set of components, an outline of the paragraph. Creating or revising a paragraph often means analyzing and improving its structure.

Use topic + development structure. One common structure is "topic + development." The most general statement (frequently a topic sentence) comes first, followed by specific details, specific examples, or other specifics. (See "General to Specific" under Coherence.) For example:

TOPIC (GENERALIZATION)
Every detail of the cell interested me.

DEVELOPMENT (SPECIFIC INSTANCES)
Sleep fled, and when the peephole was not in use I studied it all furtively.

¶/*no* ¶

Up there at the top of one wall was a small indentation the length of three bricks, covered by a dark-blue paper blind.

They had already told me it was a window.

Yes there was a window in the cell.

And the blind served as an air-raid blackout.

Tomorrow there would be weak daylight, and in the middle of the day they would turn off the glaring light bulb.

How much that meant—to have daylight in daytime!

> Aleksandr I. Solzhenitsyn, *The Gulag Archipelago, 1918–1956*

Use development + topic structure. It is possible to turn the common structure around so that the developmental sentences come first and the topic sentence comes last. (See "Specific to General" under Coherence.)

DEVELOPMENT (SPECIFIC INSTANCES)
The Chevy was wheezing and squealing and dipping alarmingly over its right front wheel on each revolution.

Every throaty roar from the muffler when Chingo pressed down on the pedal was followed by a sharp bang and a flash of blue fire out the tail pipe.

Raul's Firebird was hissing and spitting hot water and steam through the radiator and grinding and clanging with spine-jarring metal crunches through every gear.

TOPIC (GENERALIZATION)
Neither car was in any condition for a race.

Use coordinate structure. When the developmental sentences are merely added to the topic sentence (either before or after it), the paragraph has a coordinate structure; each of the developmental sentences is merely another illustration of the topic. To show that the developmental sentences are similar and have the same relationship to the topic, we have given each of them the same number in this example:

TOPIC (GENERALIZATION)

1 Dr. Howe devised a slate with type on which Laura could set up any word she wished to use, but shortly afterwards the manual alphabet was introduced.

DEVELOPMENT (SPECIFIC INSTANCES)

2 This alphabet consists of simple movements of the fingers of one person's hand upon the palm of another person's.

2 It was invented by a group of Spanish monks who had taken a vow of silence and used it to communicate without breaking the vow.

> Joseph P. Lash, *Helen and Teacher:*
> *The Story of Helen Keller and Anne Sullivan Macy*

ACTIVITY 1

Write a paragraph illustrating coordinate structure (either topic + development, or development + topic). Label your paragraph, like the one above, to show the structure.

Occasionally use an implied topic sentence. When the developmental sentences clearly imply the idea, it is sometimes possible to leave the topic sentence unstated. The readers are permitted to make the generalization themselves (after the writer has made it fairly obvious). For example:

2 In San Francisco, the police department began issuing plastic resuscitation devices and rubber gloves in reponse to officers' fears that they might be infected during the course of first aid work.

2 In Los Angeles, some medical personnel refused to care for infected patients, and laboratory technicians worried that they could contract the disease by handling blood samples and transfusions.

2 And in New York, employees at a major national shipping company refused to handle a shipment of blood and biopsy specimens when they noticed the return address was marked "AIDS Foundation"—an independent research group that is delving into the Acquired Immune Deficiency Syndrome, a deadly disease that has already claimed 520 lives and shows every sign of claiming untold more.

"The AIDS Hysteria," *Newsweek*, 30 May 1983, p. 42.

We have labeled these sentences 2 because they are all second level examples of an implied topic sentence ("There is a growing hysteria over AIDS"). Since the examples make the point almost too obvious, there is no need for a topic sentence here.

Use subordinate structure. In the subordinate pattern, each developmental sentence adds only to the sentence immediately above it. To show that each developmental sentence is of lower (or subordinate) level we have given each one a different number:

TOPIC (GENERALIZATION)
1 In Mexico roadrunner meat is sometimes eaten.

DEVELOPMENT (SPECIFIC INSTANCES)
2 It is prescribed as a medicine by curanderos, or folk healers, in recognition of the bird's formidable ability to digest poisonous animals.

3 In the town of Ojinaga in Chihuahua, Crispina Gonzales de Martinez, a 92-year-old curandera, told me that tuberculosis could be cured by eating a stew of roadrunner meat, onions, tomatoes, and garlic.

4 This elixir is also good for backaches, itches, boils, lung problems, and leprosy, she claimed.

Martha A. Whitson, "The Roadrunner, Clown of the Desert,"
National Geographic, May 1983, p. 702.

Note that each sentence refers to something in the sentence above it. Sentence 2 (an instance of the bird being eaten) comments on sentence 1, the topic sentence. Sentence 3 adds to sentence 2, describing a medicinal stew to be made with roadrunner meat; and sentence 4 adds other diseases the stew will cure.

ACTIVITY 2
Explain the subordinate structure of the following paragraph. How should its sentences be numbered? Why?

From behind a tree a trumpeter stepped to the edge of the ring. Blowing on a make-believe bugle he sounded a call and the bull rushed in—a boy with a plain serape over his shoulders, holding with both hands in front of his chest the bleached skull of a steer complete with horns. Between the horns a large, thick cactus leaf from which the thorns had been removed, was tied. It was at the cactus pad that the matadores and picadores aimed their wooden swords and bamboo spears.

Ernesto Galarza, *Barrio Boy*

ACTIVITY 3

Write a paragraph of your own illustrating subordinate structure, each sentence related to the one above it. Label your paragraph like the subordinate example above.

Use mixed coordinate-subordinate structure. The most common pattern is a mixture of coordinate and subordinate structures. In a mixed pattern, some of the sentences are similar and bear the same relationship to some sentence above them; other sentences are subordinate and add only to the sentence immediately above themselves. For example:

TOPIC (GENERALIZATION)
1 The tall grass of the Hill Country stretched as far as the eye could see, covering valleys and hillsides alike.

DEVELOPMENT (SPECIFIC INSTANCES)
  2 It was so high that a man couldn't see the roots or the bottoms of the big oaks;
    3 their dark trunks seemed to be rising out of the rippling, pale green sea.
1a There was almost no brush, and few small trees—only the big oaks and the grass, as if the Hill Country were a landscaped park.
  2 But a park wasn't what these men thought of when they saw the grass of the Hill Country.
    3 To these men the grass was proof that their dreams would come true.
      4 In country where grass grew like that, cotton would surely grow tall, and cattle fat—and men rich.
      4 In country where grass grew like that, they thought, *anything* would grow.

Robert A. Caro, *The Years of Lyndon Johnson: The Path to Power*

In this example by Caro, there are several levels of coordination and subordination. The third sentence ("their dark trunks seemed to be rising out of a rippling, pale green sea") was introduced with a semicolon. The fourth sentence we have labeled "1a" because it reintroduces the idea of the first sentence and includes the ideas in the second and third sentences. The whole paragraph has a subordinate structure, but the last two sentences, labeled 4, are coordinate.

TOPIC

1 I wear rotten shoes because you never know what is to be found in a brook.

DEVELOPMENT

2 Old tires, broken bottles, and old record albums have been a few of my discoveries.
1a Anyone who wears a pair of waders into a brook has got to be missing a few marbles.
2 A pair could be ruined in just minutes after stepping into a dirty, junky brook.
2 Hip waders are for sissies, anyway.

Don Johnson, "Brookie Fishing for Fun and Frustration"

ACTIVITY 4
Write and then label a paragraph of your own illustrating mixed subordinate and coordinate structure.

43b Make sure your paragraphs are coherent.

Make sure each sentence relates to the main idea in a paragraph and that the relationship between one sentence and another is clear. Coherence governs the entire composition. A paragraph (or composition) is incoherent at any point where the reader is unable to follow the progression of ideas.

Coherent paragraphs have a unified idea. A paragraph is a unit; it develops a single idea. Without a unifying idea, your paragraph becomes a series of unrelated sentences. There should be nothing irrelevant in your paragraph, and the unifying idea should be obvious to your readers.

¶/no ¶   INCOHERENT PARAGRAPH

The computer is a very useful device today. The future of technology is now upon us. Typical home computers have as much as 64K of memory. Even though you may not have much math aptitude, you will find that you can understand most computers today. Many companies are now offering machines at very low costs. One of the biggest and best known companies is IBM. The heart of the computer is the silicon chip, which makes it all possible.

The writer might claim that this paragraph is "about" computers, but it is really only a loose collection of sentences on the subject of computers; it has no *central* idea. Each of the sentences in this paragraph could start a separate paragraph. To revise a paragraph like this, you must reconsider the point you are trying to make; is the paragraph to be about uses of computers, about cost, about silicon chips? Revise your paragraphs until each one contains a single idea to which every sentence is related.

Use topic sentences to increase paragraph coherence. The topic sentence states what the paragraph is about. One of the simplest ways to show your readers that a paragraph is both unified and coherent is to write it with a topic sentence. Topic sentences can appear first, last, or in the middle of a paragraph. Not every paragraph needs a topic sentence, but obviously one way to help your readers follow the thread of your ideas is to use topic sentences.

In the following paragraph, we have italicized the topic sentence:

Animals that we do not use for food also act as carriers of radioactive particles. A study at the Hanford Reservation showed, for example, that jackrabbits had spread radioactivity over a wide area. They picked up the material by burrowing near trenches where radioactive waste was buried. They obviously ate or ingested some of this material, since traces of radioactive isotopes were found in their feces. Such traces were also found in the feces of coyotes and the bones of dead hawks—animals which had apparently eaten the radioactive jackrabbits.

Dr. Helen Caldicott, *Nuclear Madness*

ACTIVITY 5

Outline the paragraph above by Caldicott to show the relationship of the ideas.

ACTIVITY 6

Analyze for topic sentence. Where is the topic sentence in the following paragraph? How can you tell? Explain the relationship of the sentences in this paragraph. What is its structure?

As a businessman, I was surprised to learn that the handgun industry markets its products just like any other business, despite the fact that the product is potentially deadly. A typical handgun moves from the factory to the street almost as if it were toothpaste or chewing gum. By paying a modest license fee, a manufacturer buys the right to produce and sell handguns. There are no restrictions on quantity, quality, or size. Beyond minimal recording and reporting require-ments, little else is required to keep the license. The manufacturers sell the handguns to dealers, who pay only a $10 annual licensing fee to sell to the public.

Pete Shields with John Greenya, *Guns Don't Die—People Do*

ACTIVITY 7

Write a paragraph of your own, placing the topic sentence first. Write about some subject you know well.

Use transitional signals to help the reader follow your ideas. Not every sentence needs a transitional signal; the more closely re-lated your ideas are, the less you will need other signals. But the transitional signal is a good device to use any time you want to revise for greater coherence and readability. Remember, though, that transitional signals cannot add coherence if the sentences them-selves are not related. The signals are not substitutes for coherence. Note the use of time signals in the following paragraph:

Shortly after noon we arrived back at the smoking oven and dumped a truckload of corn into the hole. *Then* we covered it for the night. *Next day at dawn* Susanne and I met the three of them at the oven.

Jake Page and Susanne Page, "Inside the Sacred Hopi Homeland," *National Geographic*, 162 (Nov. 1982), 613.

STANDARD TRANSITIONAL SIGNALS

FOR ADDITION *again, also, and, and then, besides, finally, first, fur-ther, furthermore, in addition, lastly, moreover, next, second, sec-ondly, too*

FOR COMPARISON *also, as, by the same token, in comparison, likewise, similarly, then too*

FOR CONCESSION *after all, although it is true, at the same time, granted, I admit, I concede, naturally, of course, while it is true*

FOR CONTRAST *after all, although, and yet, but, by contrast, however, nevertheless, on the contrary, on the other hand, otherwise, still, yet*

FOR EXAMPLES AND ILLUSTRATIONS *by way of illustration, for example, for instance, incidentally, indeed, in fact, in other words, in particular, specifically, that is*

FOR RESULT *accordingly, as a result, consequently, hence, in short, then, thereafter, therefore, thus, truly*

FOR SUMMARY *as I have said, in brief, in conclusion, in other words, in short, on the whole, to conclude, to summarize, to sum up*

FOR TIME *afterwards, at last, at length, hence, immediately, in the meantime, lately, meanwhile, of late, presently, shortly, since, soon, temporarily, thereafter, thereupon, while*

Repeat key words and concepts to help the reader follow the development of your paragraphs. You can gain coherence within (and between) paragraphs by repeating key words, ideas, synonyms, and pronouns. In the following paragraph, we have marked several different kinds of repetitions. The italicized words indicate the subject of the paragraph, *the box*. The parentheses indicate the specific transitional signals for sequential order. And the chain of pronouns referring to the box is marked in bold print:

With his own hands he had made a *gift* for her at school, a small wooden *box*. At first glance **it** appeared somewhat crude. (First), **its** hand-sawn edges were not quite perfect, the bottom piece being the most uncertain. (Then too), one of the wire brads that held **it** together had gone in at an angle, leaving a sharp protrusion. (Secondly), the little brass hinges for the lid were slightly misaligned so that the lid didn't quite fit right. (And finally), the lacquer that covered **it** had gone on a little unevenly so that in spots **it** was still sticky. (But all things considered), she said, he had made a fine *box*.

Elaine Meyers, "The Gift"

ACTIVITY 8

What coherence techniques are used in the following paragraph? Mark the paragraph to highlight the techniques.

While it's true that a computer is a very complex piece of technology, it is a machine that really does only three very simple things; it adds, subtracts and moves numbers electronically from one place to another. Before it can do these things, though, it has to get the numbers from somewhere. It may also have to permanently store the numbers it will work on—or the results of its calculations—somewhere else. It must know what its user wants it to do, which means it must be able to understand instructions and sequences of instructions. Finally, it has to present its data to its user in a form the user can understand, which means the machine must have communications capability.

"Now about That Computer,"
Computer Buyer's Guide and Handbook, Guide No. 11, p. 9.

ACTIVITY 9

Write a paragraph of your own using several coherence techniques. Mark the techniques in your paragraph with underlining, parentheses, circles, and so on.

Use transitional sentences to increase coherence between paragraphs. One way to increase coherence between two paragraphs is to provide a transitional sentence, either at the end of one or the beginning of the next one. For example:

Until recently, the two dominant forces in the home videogame world were Atari and Mattel. If a consumer was looking for something inexpensive or simply wanted the most variety of games published, the Atari Video Computer System was the choice. If, on the other hand, a higher level of graphics was important or the enthusiast simply craved the best sports simulations available, Intellivision was the intelligent choice. *But, with the introduction of Coleco-Vision all this has changed.*

"The Game Machines Grow Up."
Computer Buyer's Guide and Handbook, p. 158.

Although the paragraph is a comparison of Atari and Mattel's Intellivision, it ends with a reference to ColecoVision. The last sentence

281

¶/*no* ¶   is a transition to the next paragraph (and the rest of the article), about Colecovision.

43c Develop each paragraph logically and fully.

A plan of development helps the reader follow the sequence of ideas. You must develop your paragraphs based on the overall purpose of your composition. There can be many variations on developmental plans; nearly anything is possible as long as the reader can follow what you are doing. The following plans are standard:

TIME ORDER (CHRONOLOGICAL/NARRATIVE)

Begin at the beginning and proceed to the end, or begin at the end and "flash back" to the beginning. Many stories begin *in medias res*, "in the middle of things." As long as the reader can follow the order of events, many different time orders are possible. Use transitional devices and other techniques to help the reader follow.

POSITION ORDER (SPATIAL/DESCRIPTIVE)

Much depends on the effect you are trying to achieve. For dreamlike or surrealistic images, random details may work. But for informative writing you need a plan the reader can understand. Select a point of reference and then move in an orderly fashion away from or toward the observer. That is, you might describe the farthest objects first and then describe those closer to the observer, or you might start with those closest to the observer and then move in a clockwise fashion.

ORDER OF IMPORTANCE (CLIMACTIC)

Only one plan really works for presenting ideas, examples, illustrations, or arguments. Since ideas, examples, and arguments have no "natural" order, beginning with the least important and ending with the most important imposes order. It is possible to write a paper with some other plan (ending with the weakest point, perhaps), but experience tells us that readers remember best what they read last, and most readers expect the most important point to come last.

GENERAL TO SPECIFIC (DEDUCTIVE)

¶/no ¶

In paragraphs with topic sentences, it is common to have the topic sentence first, followed by the specific examples or details that illustrate it.

SPECIFIC TO GENERAL (INDUCTIVE)

It is possible, though less common, to present the specific details first, leading up to the generalization at the end of the paragraph. Sentences about Agatha Christie, Helen MacInnes, and Marjorie Allingham, for example, might lead to a generalization about mystery writers.

ACTIVITY 10

Write a paragraph illustrating each of the plans of development above.

Specific details help to develop each paragraph fully. A difficult problem for writers concerns the amount of information in each paragraph. A paragraph is "underdeveloped" when the reader feels there is not enough information. It is not enough to make general statements; you must supply specific details for the reader, usually the more the better. Most of us have seen rocket launches, and therefore only a detailed description is likely to interest readers. For example:

Far in the distance, almost out of sight, like an all-but-transparent fish suddenly breaking into head and tail, the first stage at the rear of the rocket fell off from the rest, fell off and was now like a man, like a sky diver suddenly small. A new burst of motors started up, some far-off glimpse of newborn fires which looked pale as streams of water, pale were the flames in the far distance. Then the abandoned empty stage of the booster began to fall away, a relay runner, baton just passed, who slips back, slips back. Then it began to tumble, but with the slow tender dignity of a thin slice of soap slicing and wavering, dipping and gliding on its way to the floor of the tub. Then mighty Saturn of the first stage, empty, fuel-voided, burned out, gave a puff, a whiff and was lost to sight behind a cloud. And the rocket with Apollo 11 and the last two stages of Saturn V was finally out of sight and on its way to an orbit about the earth. Like the others he stayed and listened to the voices of the astronauts and the Capcom through the P. A. system.

Norman Mailer, *Of a Fire on the Moon*   **283**

¶/*no* ¶   How much detail is enough? How specific must the details be? Rough-draft paragraphs are more likely to be underdeveloped than overdeveloped. The amount of development depends on the impression you are trying to make. Mailer is trying to recreate his *impression* of the launch to help the reader experience the sensations of actually witnessing the launch. However, in a paper on the costs of the space program, a very different description might be written.

ACTIVITY 11
Write a paragraph in which you try for maximum specific details. Recreate a scene out of your own life so that the reader can experience it vicariously. Later, revise it for effectiveness, not just profusion, of detail.

43d Start an essay well with an effective introduction.

The introduction should raise the reader's interest, it should introduce the thesis or topic of your paper, and it should form a transition to the rest of your composition. If you have trouble getting started, you may find it easier to skip over the introduction until later, after you have completed a first draft. Never let agonizing over the introduction stop you from getting a first draft down on paper. But when you come back to work on the introduction, be generous with the care and thought and work you put into it.

INTRODUCTORY STRATEGIES

CONTRAST OR REVERSAL
Explain what people should *not* do, for example, in a paper on buying a home computer.

DEFINITION
Explain the legal defintion of *malpractice* in a paper on patients' rights.

DESCRIPTION
Describe the great damage of the mudslides of Utah in a paper on homeowners' insurance.

DRAMATIC INCIDENT

Describe the lift-off of the shuttle *Columbia* in a paper on space industries.

HISTORICAL BACKGROUND

Give the history of the various sightings of "Nessie," starting with A.D. 565, in a paper on the Loch Ness Monster.

QUESTION OR PROBLEM

Start immediately with the thesis question and expand on it, or ask some other relevant question. For example, ask whether arms reduction can be forced by arms increases in a paper on the arms race.

QUOTATION

Use a relevant quotation from your research or from a book of quotations or some well-known source like the Bible.

REFUTATION

Discuss the misconception that old age is a time of mental and physical decrepitude in a paper on age discrimination.

SETTING THE SCENE

Describe the effects of napalm attacks on the jungles of Vietnam in a paper on the ethics of warfare.

TELLING A STORY

Narrate a brief personal experience with a car wreck, for example, in a paper on highway safety.

UNUSUAL FACTS AND FIGURES

Give some figures on America's changing ethnic patterns in a paper on immigration policies.

FAULTY INTRODUCTORY STRATEGIES

Empty introductions. An introduction that seems to wander or only vaguely specifies the thesis is a mistake. If you draw a blank, go back over your prewriting notes. You may find an incident or detail there to develop into the introduction. The finished introduction should not give the appearance of a writer thinking out loud. The introduction has serious work to accomplish, and you must revise until it is as interesting and informative as you can make it.

One-sentence introductions. Almost as bad as the empty introduction, the one-sentence introduction also gives the impression of an author unable to find a beginning.

Lazy introductions. Some writers assume that the reader knows things, and therefore the writer can take shortcuts. Even though the subject may have been assigned by an instructor, your paper must stand on its own. There should be no references to "This assignment," or "An Assignment like this." The introduction should not be written with the assumption that the reader has read the title of the paper. The title is not part of the introduction, and there should be no implied references to information in the title: "*This* is an interesting subject " or "*These people* have a fascinating history."

Self-conscious introductions. It is a mistake to call attention to yourself as the writer: "I don't know how to begin this, so I"ll just start" or "I'm not really an expert on this subject, but I'll do my best." Such beginnings sound apologetic at best and start the paper on the wrong tone; at worst they sound immature.

Cute introductions. All too often, cute introductions don't seem cute to readers. Serious papers that start with inappropriately droll stories or highly imaginative beginnings ("Have you ever imagined what it might be like to have a long sticky tongue for catching flies?") usually produce a dour reaction.

43e End an essay with an effective conclusion.

The word *conclusion* has two meanings; one is simply "the end." It *is* necessary to find an effective way to end your composition. But *conclusion* also means "a deduction." Your paper must not only reach an end, it must come to some *conclusion*. The conclusion is never merely an ornament stuck on the end of a paper; it is the *point* of the paper. Save something for your conclusion. Conclusions that are too short or weak neither end nor deduce well enough.

CONCLUDING STRATEGIES

CALL FOR ACTION

End a paper on waste in government by urging readers to write to their congressmen about it.

CONTRAST OR REVERSAL

End a paper on fad diets by contrasting with medical advice on healthful dieting.

DRAW A DEDUCTION

After presenting data on the question of whether marijuana is harmful (for example), draw a deduction based on the facts. A deduction is not an opinion; it is a *necessary* conclusion, based on the data.

DISMISS OPPOSING IDEA

End a paper on rape by dismissing the myth that some victims enjoy it.

FINAL ILLUSTRATION

End with a good example, story, argument. It is sound advice to save something for the conclusion; don't use up all your good material in the body of the paper.

PREDICTION

End a paper on the competition between American and Japanese automobile manufacturers by predicting what may happen in the future.

QUOTE RELEVANT AUTHORITY OR SOURCE

End your paper on modern warfare with a relevant quotation from the Bible, for example.

RELEVANT QUESTION

End by asking (and answering) the thesis question or some other related question. For example, in a paper on the MX missile, end with the question—If we do gain a temporary nuclear superiority over the Russians, how long will it last?

REVIEW OF MAIN POINTS

A brief review of main points makes a good start for a conclusion that will analyze and evaluate the evidence in a paper.

RETURN TO THE BEGINNING

If a paper on the whaling industry (for example) starts with a description of blue whales peacefully swimming, the ending can bring back this peaceful scene as a hope for the future.

FAULTY CONCLUDING STRATEGIES

One-sentence conclusions. Especially in formal papers, one-sentence conclusions seldom sound effective. In personal experiences, occasionally the one-sentence ending may work for humor, irony, or mystery; but for reports, research papers, and other objective kinds of writing, the fully developed ending is almost always preferred.

¶/no ¶

Summaries. The summary ending is a cliché—so overworked that it amounts to a fault in many cases. A brief review of main points is always permissible, especially in a long or complex paper; but in shorter papers, the ending that does nothing more than restate what has already been said is likely to disappoint readers. The best use for the summary ending is to write it as part of a more fully developed ending.

Tacked-on moral or lesson. Obviously, nothing should appear "tacked-on" in an effective composition. Avoid telling the readers what they are supposed to "learn" from your composition. ("So you can see that it is very dangerous to go hunting with a borrowed gun.") Such endings give the appearance of forcing the obvious on the reader.

Contrived endings. "I woke suddenly; it had all been a dream!" Past a certain age, few readers care for sudden, implausible, "hokey" endings. Contrived endings are like cute beginnings: never as witty for the reader as they seem to the writer.

Self-conscious endings. "I guess I should end this. . . ." "Well, I can't think of anything else to say, so. . . ." References to yourself as writer sound immature. Readers give their attention to the subject matter of a well-written paper; the conclusion is not the place to turn them away from the subject matter of your composition toward you as author.

Introduction of new subjects. The function of the conclusion is to bring the paper to an end; this is not the place to introduce a new subject. For example, a paper on the dangers of nuclear waste should not end with the sudden introduction of "other dangers" like possible meltdowns or nuclear terrorists. If you decide that after all you really want to write about nuclear terrorism, you should start over with that as your thesis instead of appending it to a paper about nuclear waste.

Reasoning

44 Effective Evidence

Academic writing requires students to reason about various subjects. Reasoning is not the same as reporting. To reason about anything, you must analyze and interpret information. You must weigh evidence and reach conclusions. Conclusions should not be merely your personal opinions about the subject; if you use standard reasoning procedures, your readers should agree with your conclusions. The rules of reason are techniques for convincing readers that you are trustworthy.

44a Use sound reasoning to evaluate evidence.

In general, we reach conclusions and make judgments in one of two ways: inductively or deductively. Given a certain number of similar experiences, we make generalizations about those experiences. For example, if you begin to sneeze and itch every time you are around a cat, you eventually come to the conclusion that you are allergic to cats. This is called *inductive reasoning*, the process of moving from the specific instances to the general rule. However, once you have arrived at a general conclusion, that you are allergic to cats, you then apply it to new instances. You enter a room in which there is a cat, and you know that you must keep away from it if you are to avoid itching and sneezing. This is called *deductive reasoning*, the process of applying the general rule to particular instances.

These two processes represent the basic ways people reason. Notice that in the inductive method you can only arrive at various degrees of probability, not absolute truth, unless you are able to exhaust every specific incident. You have, in the example, experienced only a representative number, not all cats. The emphasis, therefore, in inductive reasoning is based on the nature, reliability, and the adequacy of the evidence and on the conclusions you draw from that evidence.

On the other hand, in deductive reasoning, the emphasis is on the truth of the generalization and on how that generalization is applied in certain circumstances. This method is based on the *syllogism*. A syllogism contains a major and a minor premise, which when properly stated, lead to a conclusion. For example, "All dogs like bones. Rover is a dog. Therefore Rover will like bones." The syllogism is often stated in abbreviated form: "Rover will like this bone, I am sure, because all dogs like bones." The syllogism is valid, even though one of the premises has been left unspoken (Rover is a dog). *Valid* means that the syllogism is properly constructed: the major premise makes a statement about all members of a group, and the minor premise identifies a member of the group. Therefore, whatever is true of the group must be true of its individual members. But the syllogism can be *valid* even if we use fantastic premises. For example, "All dogs can fly. Rover is a dog. Therefore Rover can fly." The syllogism is valid because the premises are properly stated. If it were true that all dogs could fly, we would have to conclude that Rover too can fly. Thus *valid* only means *logical*, stated according to the rules of logic. *True*, on the other hand, means *real*, agreeing with reality.

ACTIVITY 1

Identify the following statements as *inductive* or *deductive*.

1. Everyone I know likes Michael Jackson, so you probably will like him too.
2. I've had a dozen people cough or sneeze in my face today; the flu must be going around.
3. First Marjorie told me, then Larry told me, and now you are telling me: apparently everyone knows my secret!
4. Athletes need a special diet, so you better not eat that donut if you want to play basketball.
5. Students are forever complaining about their workloads, so it's no surprise that you feel overworked.

ACTIVITY 2

Identify the following statements as *valid* or *invalid*. Be prepared to explain any statements that you think may be valid but untrue.

1. Students enjoy time off from studies, and since you are a student, you will enjoy spring break.
2. Our dog hates cats, so you better keep your Siamese inside.
3. My magical powers will protect you from poison, so you can safely drink this strychnine.
4. All students are interested in education; you are interested in education; therefore you are a student.
5. All basketball players are quite short; you are quite short; therefore you are a basketball player.

44b Follow standard procedures for evaluating primary and secondary evidence.

Primary evidence is first-hand data. If you conduct experiments, collect answers to a questionnaire, or do other "hands on" research, you have primary evidence. If you read books and articles about other researchers' work, you have secondary evidence. Both kinds of evidence must be carefully evaluated.

Determine the distribution of evidence. In general, the more evidence there is, the more credible it becomes. In research questions and logical arguments in which there is good evidence on both sides of the question, the weight of the evidence becomes the determining factor. If there is more evidence on one side of the question than the other, most people will conclude that the "heavier" side is correct.

Evaluate the sources of evidence. Reliable sources written by experts and aimed at educated readers have more credibility than popular sources aimed at general audiences. Professional journals like *College English,* authoritative works like *The Oxford English Dictionary* and the *Encyclopaedia Britannica,* and highly respected newspapers such as the *New York Times* and magazines like *Time* and *Harpers* are credible sources. Other publications, such as small local newspapers and movie magazines, and encyclopedias designed for children, should generally be avoided in college work.

Experts and authorities with a history of excellent research and publications should be relied upon more often than less experienced researchers or celebrities with little expertise. Beware of researchers who may have some bias, some personal interest in the outcome of research: commercial interests, for example, sometimes hire researchers to prove products are harmless.

Some kinds of evidence are more reliable than others. Information gathered through questionnaires, for example, may not be reliable. Respondents frequently are self-selected and may not be typical of the general population. Respondents sometimes say whatever they believe the researcher wants to hear. Many respondents fail to understand the questions. Frequently only a small percentage of those asked respond.

Use timely data. Always use the most recent data. Research is cumulative; recent studies usually subsume older ones. In order to be sure your information is current and has not been outdated by more recent work, always make sure you have found the most recent data possible. Your research must begin where you are; work backwards from today's date when collecting information.

Determine the relevance of data. Objective papers have no room for side issues. Use only material that is clearly relevant to your thesis.

Distinguish between "probable" and "certain" data. Most investigations today, especially in secondary research, use only probable data and reach probable (versus indisputable) conclusions. It requires many repetitions of research experiments before you can determine whether any question is "proved." For most of the investigations undertaken in school, you can only hope for reasonable or probable results.

Use statistical data with care. Most general audiences cannot cope with complex mathematical data. You must translate statistical data into plain English. Avoid statistical generalizations ("most students prefer to wear blue jeans"); use the exact statistic instead ("75% of students in our sample were wearing blue jeans"). Follow standard procedures for collecting statistical data: make sure your sample population is representative of the entire population, and make sure the sample is large enough to support your conclusions. It is a good idea to present statistical data in charts (see **46g**).

Define the terms in your research. Research or argumentation cannot reach valid conclusions unless the terms are clearly understood. Define the key terms in your papers unless you know a general reader will understand the words as you mean them. (To find out, have someone unfamiliar with the subject read your paper and circle the words he or she doesn't understand.) When reading source material, make sure your sources all mean the same thing when they use similar terms.

Accept the simplest explanation. Researchers must remain skeptical of strange or bizarre assumptions. Occam's Razor, the rule of simplicity, requires that researchers accept the simplest explanation, the explanation that requires the fewest assumptions. Thus you should resist assumptions about monsters, ghosts, and supernatural phenomena, for example, until you have very convincing proof.

Remain impartial. Objective investigations require impartial investigators. Do not undertake research for the purpose of "proving" you are correct; researchers must be prepared to accept whatever conclusion the data indicate. Avoid research questions in which you have a personal interest or any biased research question or procedure: loaded questions have built-in assumptions that make objective conclusions impossible.

Evaluate "common knowledge" carefully. Common knowledge is information widely known among educated people. But students must not assume too much "common" knowledge. Any and all information you acquire from source material must be documented, whether it is common knowledge or not. Only information you know from your own experience to be well known by most educated people should be treated as "common knowledge."

Do not mistake assumptions, inferences, or premises for facts. Assumptions are basic, fundamental beliefs. We assume that animals will die if they consume enough toxic materials. Inferences are deductions or conclusions based on data. We infer (conclude) that the animals did die because they ate the toxic substance. If the animals did not die, we would not change our assumption; we would suspect our inferences about the toxic material were inaccurate (i.e., it wasn't really as poisonous as we thought, or the animals didn't eat as much of it as we thought). It takes much more evidence to change an underlying assumption than to change an inference.

Premises are the ideas or questions being tested in research; a premise is a *hypothesis*. In the rat experiment, the premise may be that given n quantities of toxic substance x, rats will die. None of these beliefs about toxic substances and animals is a *fact*.

Facts are objective data; we test facts by referring to reality. What was in the food? How much was present? Did the rats actually eat it? How much did they eat? Facutal data must be observable by the senses or testable by physical means—chemical analysis, observation of rat behavior, autopsies on dead rats.

ACTIVITY 3

Identify the possible error in each of the following statements as confusion between primary and secondary sources, faulty distribution of evidence, unreliable source, ambiguous terminology, outdated material, Occam's Razor, biased researcher, faulty assumption of common knowledge, irrelevant data, confusion of probability with certainty, improper use of statistical data, or mistaking assumptions, inferences, or premises for facts.

1. Based on an interview in *TV Guide*, we can conclude that the actor Tom Selleck is a heck of a guy.
2. Because I saw a bright light hovering above our house, heard a humming noise, and suddenly felt strange, I am convinced that what I saw was a UFO.
3. I have found some excellent articles written in 1980 about America's space shuttle, and since they are so good I shouldn't need any other information.
4. I plan to write a research paper proving that addictive drugs should be legalized for the good of society.
5. The basis of my research is the answers to a questionnaire I got from one hundred students.
6. Since you have had one car accident, you are not allowed to take the car, because you may have another.

---

45 VALID ARGUMENTS

In dealing with everyday matters, most people generalize freely and draw conclusions based more on intuition and experience than on facts and logic. Intellectually we may know that actions are not right just because many people accept them, but emotionally it is difficult to resist this kind of popular reasoning. However, you must be on guard against errors of this kind in the sources you read and in your own writing.

45a Avoid fallacies of insufficient evidence.

Avoid making large, unsupported generalizations. Many errors in reasoning arise from making generalizations based upon too little evidence. This problem, often called a *hasty generalization,* occurs when it is assumed that what is true of one person or in one situation is true of all people or all similar situations. The conclusion *may* be true, but you will not be convincing unless you can demonstrate that you have examined a truly representative sample of the evidence. Do not generalize from the few people you know to "people in general" or "most people" or "everyone." It is an overgeneralization to say that "most people prefer light entertainment to heavy drama." Even if you believe such a thing, there is no way to verify it. Limit your generalizations to what you actually know: "most of my friends prefer light entertainment to heavy drama"; "of ten students who were asked, nine said they preferred light entertainment."

Do not select only data that support your conclusion. Ignoring evidence that challenges or contradicts your opinion is "cardstacking." It means stacking the deck (stacking the evidence) so that only one conclusion is possible. If you start out to prove that cigarettes cause cancer, you must not disregard evidence about people who have smoked all their lives without cancer. You must account for *all* the evidence, not just that which supports your thesis.

Do not argue from negative premises. Avoid reasoning that something must be true if we cannot prove it false; nor should we reason that something must be false if we cannot prove it true. Reasoning on the basis of what we do not know is called *argumentum ad ignorantium.* The fact that we cannot prove whether extraterrestrials have or have not visited earth should not be the basis for any conclusion.

Avoid faulty cause and effect reasoning. Do not assume that one thing causes another just because one follows the other. Cause and effect is a very difficult and complex relationship; arguing that one event must have been caused by a preceding event solely on the basis that one happened after the other is called the *post hoc ergo propter hoc* fallacy (literally, "after this, therefore because of this"). One thing *may* cause another, but there is no *necessary* relation between events that follow each other in time.

45b Avoid fallacies of irrelevant information.

Avoid attacks on the source of an idea. Avoid suggesting that an idea is not good because the person who gave it is not good. It should be possible, for example, for criminals to have good ideas about law and crime prevention, despite their personal behavior. An attack on the person instead of on his or her ideas is called an *ad hominem* (literally, "to the person") argument.

A related error is called *guilt by association:* assuming that anyone who associates with those we dislike must be as bad as those we dislike. It should be possible for loyal, patriotic Americans to have friends who are communists without being suspected of being communists themselves.

Another related fallacy is called the *genetic* fallacy; it suggests that ideas coming from places we dislike or think inferior must be bad ideas. A good idea can be valid no matter where it comes from. You must judge the idea, not the source.

Use emotional appeals with restraint in objective writing. Appeals using descriptions or pictures of starving people, wounded soldiers, and sick children are among those that play on human emotions. Such an appeal is called an *ad misericordiam* (literally, "to pity") argument. There is nothing wrong in arguing that we should help the misfortunate; but using pathetic, emotional material to persuade people is an error. Such appeals often seem coercive and manipulative; they make people feel guilty. Raising guilt in people you are trying to persuade often backfires; they become angry instead.

Avoid sloganeering and other appeals to popular sentiment. Using traditional or popular slogans such as "my country right or wrong" forces people to respond to group identity. Appealing to popular sentiments or prejudices is called an *ad populum* (literally, "to the people") argument. It causes people to react as members of a group, instead of thinking for themselves. Politicians who campaign with slogans about the goodness and wisdom of the American people are using *ad populum* appeals.

A related fallacy is called *bandwagon,* arguing that an action or idea is good if many people approve of it (an appeal to group pressure). The idea is that if others like it, you will too. Some bandwagon appeals are described in *plain folks* language: plain, ordinary people eat hamburgers and pizza, not quiche. Other bandwagon appeals are described in *snob* language: if you want to be an important person, you must wear designer clothes.

Avoid citing inappropriate authorities. When you quote experts, be sure they are really experts. Celebrities are often quoted on subjects about which they have no real expertise. Frequently experts in one field are quoted as if they were authorities in some other field. Using inappropriate authority is called an *ad verecundiam* (literally, "to authority") argument.

Avoid arguing something other than the main point. A *straw man* argument is one in which you create some generalization to attack instead of the specific point of the argument. In an argument about the costs of education, for example, you may be tempted to create a straw man called "the modern student." Then you can attack this straw man, instead of the main question, the cost of education. ("The modern student is lazy and doesn't deserve education. The modern student doesn't use the education already available, so further costs are unnecessary.")

A related fallacy is the *red herring* argument. Instead of arguing the main point, writers may sometimes switch to a minor or secondary point. Focusing all their attention on the secondary issue, writers may soon cause the reader to forget the main point. Then when the writer proves or disproves the minor point, it looks as if the argument has been won.

Avoid excuses based on what others do. The fact that others may cheat on their income tax is no justification for your doing it. This argument is called *tu quoque* (literally, "you also"). Wrong behavior is wrong, regardless of how many people do it.

45c Avoid fallacies caused by ambiguity.

Avoid circular reasoning. In *circular* reasoning, the same idea appears in both subject and predicate: "The reason it is so hot today is that the temperature is so high." Circular reasoning is also called *begging the question,* meaning that instead of answering the question we have only restated it in different form. For example: "We know it is winter because it is no longer fall." Or, "Criminals should be punished because what they do is against the law."

Avoid misusing the definitions of words. Many words have several meanings, and most words have connotations that can easily be misused in argumentative or investigative writing. The word "religious," for example can refer to piety, the study of holy texts, membership in a congregation. But it can also mean "dedicated," "persevering," "conscientious," as in the sentence "We study our computer manuals religiously." The sentence means only that these computer users are serious about their work, working hard to learn; it does not mean that they "worship" the computer. Arguing over the meanings of words or misusing their meanings is *equivocation*.

Do not use false metaphors or false analogies. In objective writing, metaphors and analogies can cause trouble. The two things being compared in a metaphor or analogy often are not very similar. For example, "War in Central America would be like the war in Vietnam, an endless struggle that we could not win." Only if Central America and Vietnam are very similar in many aspects would this analogy be valid.

Avoid ambiguous language and data. Implications are not arguments. "Nine out of ten athletes prefer Gatorade" implies that ninety percent of all athletes have expressed an opinion, but that seems unlikely. Arguing an ambiguous proposition is *amphiboly*.

45d Avoid fallacies caused by faulty reasoning.

Avoid asking complex questions. Complex ("loaded") questions are worded so that they are not safe to answer: for example, "Do you still take drugs?" Even a "No" answer makes the responder appear to be a drug-user. Often such questions are worded as "complex issues": "The President's inability to make decisions has pushed us to the brink of war with Russia." Such loaded statements must be analyzed before anyone attempts to respond to them. It must first be determined whether the President is indecisive, then whether we are in fact on the brink of war, before we can attempt to connect the two ideas.

Avoid using either/or reasoning. There are usually more than two solutions for any problem. Arguing that we must *either* raise taxes *or* suffer an economic recession creates a *false dilemma*. A dilemma offers only two equally unattractive options. The dilemma is valid if there are truly only two possibilities.

Avoid conclusions that do not follow from your premises. Stating conclusions that do not necessarily follow from the premises is called *non sequitur* reasoning. The term is used any time the audience "cannot follow" or analyze how the speaker reached his or her conclusion. For example, "Since the window is open and letting in cold air, we may as well open the door too." Or, "Smith was seen going into the courthouse: he must have committed some crime."

Avoid making excuses or giving self-serving explanations. Excusing yourself by blaming others is called *rationalizing:* for example, "I could have done better on the test, but it was too hot in the testing room" or "It isn't my fault that the cup fell and broke; someone left it where I was bound to knock it to the floor."

ACTIVITY 4
Identify the fallacy in each of the following statements. In some cases there may be more than one possible answer.

1. I'm failing my earth science class, but it's only because the professor dislikes me personally.
2. This must be an excellent book since it was written by a famous professor at one of our greatest universities.
3. Our young soldiers have come home without arms and legs, blinded, suffering mental disorders; we owe them our charity.
4. Either you like modern art, or you hate it; there is no middle position.
5. All elephants are dangerous creatures.
6. Since we don't know who ate all the candy, we will punish everyone in the room.
7. How can ·you accuse me of reckless spending when your own spending is as wild as anyone's?
8. The senator must be a poor speaker, because after he had spoken all across the country, he lost the election.
9. Butter pecan is the most popular ice cream flavor; you'll like it.
10. Our cows kept injuring their tails on the boards in their stalls, but my father solved the problem by amputating their tails.
11. It's no use asking Alicia where to party; she's a total drip.
12. Because the President was unavailable, the reporters interviewed his wife about developments in our foreign policy.
13. If you love America, don't knock it.
14. Lloyd has been hanging around the computer nerds lately; I think he may be turning into one himself.
15. The reason smuggling is a crime is that it's illegal.

Writing
Assignments

46 RESEARCH PAPERS

Term paper, research paper, reference paper, library paper—these are all names for writing assignments designed to teach research skills and to test your ability to analyze, evaluate, and draw conclusions from evidence. Such assignments usually do not require you to come up with startling new insights nor to unearth never-before-discovered facts. However, by proceeding systematically and carefully, you can learn to become an independent researcher.

46a Begin your search for a specific, limited research question.

If your instructor has not given you a specific research question, you can use the assignment to study a field that interests you. Begin by thinking about broad areas that are generally familiar to you. You should not select totally unfamiliar subjects (if you know nothing about music, a comparison of jazz and rock is not a good project for you). But neither should you select "old hat" subjects you already know thoroughly. Start your search by listing general areas that you think might yield workable topics: the President, the economy, nuclear weapons control, human rights, education, history, religion, business, or other broad fields.

Narrow a general topic to a specific research question. You cannot write a paper "about" Israel; you must narrow your focus to some question that not only interests you but may interest your readers as well. *What* about Israel do you want your readers to understand? After you have decided on a general subject, begin to brainstorm. Ask yourself questions about the subject. You can ask the journalist's questions—*what, when, how, where, why?*—to get yourself started. If, for example, you are concerned about the environment and have in mind a general idea about pollution, the following are some preliminary questions you could ask yourself:

What is "pollution"?

What do my readers need to know about pollution?

What kind of pollution is most disturbing to me: air, water, chemical, nuclear, a combination?

What have I heard about pollution or read recently that made a particular impression on me? (Why pick this subject?)

What did it have to do with: dioxin? acid rain? PBB?

What do I know about each one of these?

What are the observable effects of each?

What are the intangible—moral, ethical, psychological—effects?

Can I discuss or find out about a particular geographical area where one of these pollutants has appeared?

What causes pollution?

Who causes pollution?

Who is supposed to monitor pollution problems?

What's being done about it?

What should be done about it?

How can I find out more?

From a general concern about pollution, you must narrow your focus to a specific problem—with dioxin in Midland, Michigan, or Times Beach, Missouri, for example. A good research paper must be thorough, a detailed analysis of a worthwhile question, and that is why you must find a very limited question—one you can investigate fully.

ACTIVITY 1

Select a general subject area you would like to research. Write out a list of every possible question you can think of related to your subject.

46b Use a search strategy to find materials in the library.

There are two kinds of research evidence: primary and secondary. *Primary evidence* is first-hand data, evidence collected in experiments, field work, "hands-on" data. *Secondary evidence* is published information about the research others have done. Most library material is secondary evidence, but the library does have some primary material. If you are writing about a novel, for example, the novel itself is the primary evidence; what critics have said about it is secondary evidence. If you are researching Louis, Mary, and Robert Leakey's anthropological work in Kenya's Olduvai Gorge, their writings are primary sources; anyone else's writings about them are secondary sources. (See **44b**.)

Start with general sources first. In order to use the library efficiently, plan a *search strategy*. Much depends on your topic, but the simplest search strategy usually starts with the most generalized sources and proceeds to more specialized ones. In general, this means (1) starting with the general encyclopedias, almanacs, and dictionaries for background material; (2) checking any specialized encyclopedias, bibliographies, or handbooks that may apply to your topic; (3) using first the general and then the specialized indexes for magazine, journal, and newspaper articles; (4) and finally, perhaps, using the card catalog to find books and other sources your library may have. It may be a good idea to leave books until later in your search, after you have built up some background familiarity with the subject. You can read many articles in the time it takes to read one book. This advice, of course, depends on your subject and on your own level of expertise. The point is to be systematic: plan your search strategy and then stick with it.

46c Use reference materials: almanacs, dictionaries, encyclopedias, periodical indexes, card catalog.

In addition to general encyclopedias like the *Americana, Britannica,* and *Collier's,* there are many special encyclopedias, dictionaries, and almanacs you should investigate. For example:

ALMANACS, DICTIONARIES, ENCYCLOPEDIAS

Current Biography, 1940—
Dictionary of American Biography, 1928–1937;
supplements 1944–1980
Dictionary of American History, 1976–1978
Dictionary of National Biography, 1885–1901
Encyclopedia of Philosophy, 1967
Encyclopedia of Religion and Ethics, 1908–1927

Encyclopedia of World Art, 1959–1968
Facts on File; a Weekly World News Digest, 1940–
Information Please Almanac, 1947—
The Mythology of All Races, 1916–1932
New Century Cyclopedia of Names, 1954
New Grove Dictionary of Music and Musicians, 1980
Oxford Classic Dictionary, 1970
Oxford English Dictionary, 1888–1933, and supplements
Statistical Abstract of the United States, 1878—
Webster's Third New International Dictionary, 1976
World Almanac and Book of Facts, 1868—

Use periodical indexes to find newspaper, magazine, and journal articles. Most journals, magazines, newspapers, and other "periodicals" (periodically published) are indexed and kept up to date with supplements. You can find recent magazine and newspaper articles by looking up subject headings in the index. Two of the most helpful general indexes are the *Readers' Guide to Periodical Literature* and the *New York Times Index.* The *Readers' Guide* lists articles from well over one hundred magazines; entries are by subject, author, title, and cross references that suggest other headings for related information. For example:

READERS' GUIDE ENTRY
TELEVISION stations, Black
TV first at Howard [first television station owned
and operated by a black university; WHMM] I. J. Poole. Black
Enterprise. 11: 22+ D '80.

This entry shows that under the heading "Television Stations, Black" there is an article, "TV First at Howard," described in brackets and written by I. J. Poole in volume 11 of the magazine *Black Enterprise;* the article starts on page 22 and has more than one page (+); it was published in December of 1980, (D '80).

The *New York Times Index* refers you to articles that have appeared in that newspaper from 1913 to the present. For example, in the *New York Times Index* for June 16 through June 30, 1981, you will find the following:

NEW YORK TIMES INDEX ENTRY
CABLE Cars
Dean Havron article recounts ride in cable car up rocky
summit of Pico Bolivar, Venezuela's highest peak; travel
tips; illustrations; map (L), Je 28, X, p.1.

This entry shows that under the heading "Cable cars" there is a listing for an article by Dean Havron. The entry gives a brief description of the article, indicates other information in the article, tells you (L) that it is a long article (over two columns), and that it appeared on June 28, section 10 (X), page 1.

Each index has its own system of symbols and abbreviations; check the front of the index for an explanation. In addition to the general indexes, there are many others. For example:

SPECIAL INDEXES

Applied Science and Technology Index, 1958—
    Previously titled *Industrial Arts Index,* 1913–57
Art Index, 1929—
Biography Index, 1946—
Biological and Agricultural Index, 1964—
    Previously titled Agricultural Index, 1919–1964
Book Review Digest, 1905—
Book Review Index, 1965—
Business Periodicals Index, 1958—
Current Index to Journals in Education, 1969—
Education Index, 1929—
Engineering Index, 1884—
Essay and General Literature Index, 1900—
General Science Index, 1978—
Humanities Index, 1974—
    Previously titled *Social Sciences and Humanities Index,* 1965–73,
    and *International Index,* 1907–65
Index to Legal Periodicals, 1908—
Music Index, 1949—
Nineteenth Century Readers' Guide to Periodical Literature, 1890–
    1899
New York Times Index, 1851—
Poole's Index to Periodical Literature, 1802–1906
Public Affairs Information Service Bulletin, 1915—
The Readers' Guide to Periodical Literature, 1900—
Social Sciences Index, 1974—
    Previously titled *Social Sciences and Humanities Index,* 1965–
    1973, and *International Index,* 1907–1965
United States Government Publications: Monthly Catalog, 1895—

SOCIAL SCIENCES INDEX ENTRY
Television and children
    See also
    Television advertising and children

> Television programs—Children's programs
> Lessons from videogames and media: effects on the young [symposium] bibl *J Commun* 34:72–167, Spr '84
> Sex-role differences in children's identification with counterstereotypical televised portrayals. B. Eisenstock. bibl *Sex Roles* 10:417–30 Mr '84

This entry suggests under the heading "Television and children" that the researcher might also look under two other headings in the index, "Television advertising and children" and "Television programs" under the subheading "Children's programs." Two articles are listed: one is in the *Journal of Communication* which appeared in volume 34 on pages 72 through 167 in the spring of 1984. The article was of corporate authorship (symposium), and it contains a bibliography (bibl). Full names of journals to which abbreviations refer can be found in a list at the front of the index. The second article was written by B. Eisenstock and appeared in volume 10 on pages 417 through 430 of the March 1984 publication of the journal *Sex Roles*. It also contains a bibliography.

ELECTRONIC INDEXES AND COMPUTERIZED DATA STORAGE

Your library may have a *"computerized"* card catalog. Operating the terminal usually requires nothing more than typing in an access number and the title or author of a book.

ERIC (Educational Resources Information Center) is a computerized data bank for teachers, and students studying to be teachers. Find ERIC documents in *Current Index to Journals in Education* and *Resources in Education*. ERIC documents can be ordered in hardcopy (print) or microfiche (explained below).

If you have ever spent time thumbing through the *Readers' Guide* or the *New York Times Index*, you will appreciate the great speed and ease with which you can use *microfilm indexes*. *The Magazine Index* covers many of the popular or general magazines; furthermore, many of the current issues covered in magazine articles have already been researched for you in "Hot Topics," a monthly bibliographical printout. *The National Newspaper Index* covers the *Christian Science Monitor*, the *New York Times*, and the *Wall Street Journal*. *The Business Index* covers several hundred magazines, journals, and newspapers. *The Legal Resource Index* covers law journals, law newspapers, and other publications relevant to law. Some libraries now offer computer searches to students. For a small fee you can get a computer-generated bibliography on nearly any subject.

Learn to use *microform readers*. Most libraries already have material in microform (microfilm on reels or spools and microfiche, microfilm in small sheets the size of an index card). Back issues of newspapers and magazines for example, are often kept in microform. If you discover, for example, in researching the problems of the American steel industry that an important article, "Big Steel's Winter of Woes," by Christopher Byron, which appeared in *Time* magazine on January 24, 1983, is in microfiche, it is easy to go to the microfiche catalog, locate *Time* (the entries are arranged alphabetically and by date), and read the article.

```
MICROFICHE CATALOG ENTRY
Time
New York, N.Y.      Vol. 121  Issue:4   Fiche: 1 of 2

January 24, 1983   Pages: 1-92         ISSN:0040-781X
```

The entry says that the microfiche contains pages 1 through 92 of the January 24, 1983, edition of *Time* magazine and that there is another fiche that contains the rest of that edition (1 of 2).

Use the card catalog to find books and other materials. The card catalog is the major guide to a library's books. In some libraries, the card catalog also includes other sources as well—printed, photographed, and recorded material—classified under three separate designations: subject, title, and author. Before using the catalog, you will save yourself much time and effort if you find out first how your subject is listed. Find the *Library of Congress: Subject Headings.* Go through the *Subject Guide,* looking under likely headings. For example:

```
Occultism in literature
     sa Mysticism in literature
        Supernatural in literature
      x Occultism
     xx Mysticism in literature
        Occult sciences
        Supernatural in literature
```

This entry shows that "Occultism in literature" is not found under "Occultism" (*x* in this case means error). The *Subject Guide* tells you to see also *(sa)* "Mysticism in literature" and "Supernatural in literature." It also shows you that there are other headings in the *Subject Guide* (marked *xx*) that are cross-referenced to this entry. Not only does the *Subject Guide* save you time and effort with the catalog, it can give you many ideas for research by showing you how to analyze various subjects.

Figure 46-1 shows a subject card from the card catalog.

FIGURE 46-1 Card catalog subject card

A — MYSTICISM IN LITERATURE.
B —
PS
595 Hunter, Irene Louise, 1885-1924. — H
.r4 American mystical verse : an — I
H8 anthology / selected by Irene Hunter ; — J
1975x preface by Zona Gale. -- Miami : Royale
House, 1975. — K
xxiii, 308 p. ; 21 cm. — L
"First published 1925." — M

1. Mysticism--United States.
2. Mysticism in literature. I. Title
II. Title: Mystical verse.

Mimpt 25 APR 77 2053053 EZCUsc

A Subject heading
B Author's name
C Library of Congress call numbers
D Number of front matter pages (title page, copyright page, table of contents, preface, etc.) and other pages
E Publishing history
F Other cards for this book
G Library information for ordering catalog cards

H Author's birth and death dates
I Title
J Publisher
K Place of publication
L Date of publication
M Height of book in centimeters (1 centimeter = .04 inch)

Cards in the Author and Title sections contain the same information except that the former is headed with the author's name and the latter with the title of the book.

As you examine the cards, be selective. Information on the card will often suggest whether the book may be useful. The title is not necessarily descriptive of the contents of the book. If chapter headings are listed, see how they relate to your topic. Look at the date of publication. The book may be too old for current information but may be useful as background or history. If the book looks promising, record its author, title, place and date of publication, and the call numbers on an index card.

46d Begin preliminary reading and begin compiling a bibliography.

Make an index card for each source that looks useful. This is your preliminary bibliography, to be revised as your research continues. The 3 × 5 index cards work best.

At the top of the card write full bibliographical information: author, title, place of publication, and publisher; if dealing with a magazine, appropriate volume number and date (Figure 46-2). See also bibliography forms on pages 326–329.

FIGURE 46-2 Bibliography cards for a book (Heng and Shapiro) and a magazine (Farrell)

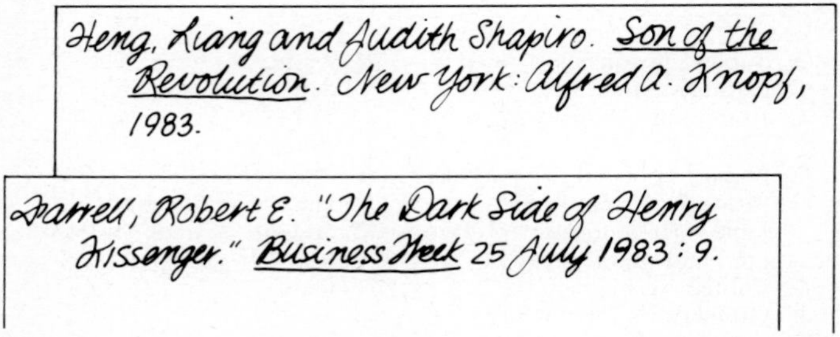

Heng, Liang and Judith Shapiro. *Son of the Revolution*. New York: Alfred A. Knopf, 1983.

Farrell, Robert E. "The Dark Side of Henry Kissenger." *Business Week* 25 July 1983: 9.

Follow the researchers' rule: find the most recently published material. Proceed from the most recent material backwards in a systematic fashion. Avoid hopping around in the research; some material may be unavailable when you go to the library, but you must make sure that in the end your references cover the time period from the most recent backwards.

ACTIVITY 2

Using the subject you chose for Activity 1, or another if you prefer, go to the library and conduct a thorough search. Write bibliography cards for at least a dozen sources, preferably more. See pp. 326–329 for model bibliography entries.

46e Take notes that summarize, paraphrase, or quote exactly.

Use a separate note card for each fact you find and write only on one side of it (see Figure 46-3). Cards are less awkward than whole sheets of paper; they are flexible and portable and can be stacked or shuffled into different arrangements as your research progresses. You may want to use slightly larger (5 × 7) cards for your notes, but learn to take selective notes. Code your note cards to correspond with your bibliography cards; that is, place the author's name in the upper right-hand corner to refer to the card containing the appropriate bibliographical information. If you have more than one work by the same author, you might want to create a number code that refers to author and work. In Figure 46-3, for example, the Farrell card is coded 5.1; the number 5 has been assigned to the author Farrell, and the number 1 indicates that the material comes from the first of two or more works by him.

Read source material critically. Be selective in reading your sources. Look at chapter headings and the index to find relevant material. The first time through, read quickly, looking for information, facts, opinions, examples that relate to your topic.

Record significant information on note cards. Limit your note-taking to material that is important in answering your research question. Use one card for each idea or fact, and give a page number for each idea, fact, or direct quote you put down. Use your time in the library to read and assimilate material. (Avoid copying long passages, even with the photocopy machine.) When you find useful material, write in your own words a shortened version of what it

Figure 46.3 Coding for note cards.

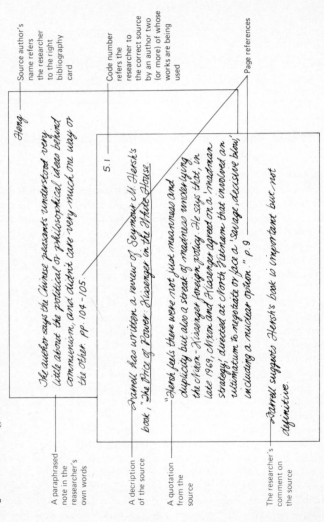

Source author's name refers the researcher to the right bibliography card

Code number refers the researcher to the correct source by an author two (or more) of whose works are being used

Page references

A paraphrased note in the researcher's own words

A description of the source

A quotation from the source

The researcher's comment on the source

Meng

The author says the Chinese peasant's understood very little about the political or philosophical ideas behind communism, and didn't care very much one way or the other. pp. 104-105.

5.1

Darnell has written a review of Seymour M. Hersh's book, "The Price of Power: Kissinger in the White House

"Hersh feels there were not just meanness and duplicity but also a streak of madness underlying the Nixon-Kissinger foreign policy. He says that, in late 1969, Nixon and Kissinger agreed on a 'madman strategy', directed at North Vietnam that involved an ultimatum to negotiate or face a 'savage, decisive blow,' including a nuclear option." p. 9

Darnell suggests Hersh's book is important but not definitive.

says. (See Paraphrases and Summaries below.) The less you copy, the more you will have to use your own words for your notes. The more you use your own words, the more you will have to think about what your sources are saying. That is how you assimilate material.

When you are taking notes, extract only the relevant data. Restate information and ideas as you understand them. Quote only when the information is important in its original form (for example, statistical data, the exact wording of a document, or an especially well-written statement or explanation). If you decide to quote from a source, copy the material *exactly* and make sure you indicate page numbers. Put the material in quotation marks so that there will be no doubt that the words are not yours. (See Section **29** for guidelines on quoting.)

PARAPHRASES AND SUMMARIES

A *paraphrase* restates the material of the original in approximately the same number of words. All the information contained in the original is included but in different language. When writing a paraphrase, you may need to use some of the key terms from the original, but in general, make sure you use your own words and sentence structures. Remember, too, that the source must be cited with a reference note.

A *summary* (or *précis*) differs from a paraphrase in that it condenses the original. Generally only the most important points are recorded; examples, digressions, and the like are not included. The same obligation to cite the source and to use your own words applies.

In general, use paraphrases for small pieces of material, for narrow issues. Use summaries for more complex, larger blocks of information, such as providing background or an overview.

ORIGINAL

A piece of liver is suspended from the top of a wire cage so that the liver rests on the floor inside the cage, loosely held by a thread. A hungry cat in the room with the cage, but outside it, sees the liver and walks over to the cage. It hesitates for a time and its head moves up and down as though studying the string. Then it jumps on top of the cage, catches the string in its mouth, raises the liver by joint use of mouth and paw, and leaps down with the meat at the end of the string in its mouth.

Arthur Koestler, The Act of Creation, p. 570

NOTE CARD SUMMARY

Koestler

a piece of liver hangs from a thread inside a wire cage. a cat outside the cage studies the string and then jumps on the cage and pulls up the liver with its mouth and paw. (570)

SUMMARIZED INFORMATION IN A PAPER

    Koestler indicates with a story about a cat that animals possess problem-solving intelligence. In the experiment, a cat quickly solves the puzzle of how to retrieve a piece of liver attached to a string inside a cage. After studying the problem briefly, the cat hops up on the cage and draws the meat up using its mouth and paw (570).

The idea must be documented with Koestler's name and the page reference, so that readers will know where the information came from. It must also have a reference (in a Works Cited list or other bibliography).

NOTE CARD PARAPHRASE

Koestler

Koestler uses a thread to suspend a bit of liver inside a cage. A cat entering the room sees the liver, approaches the cage and appears to think about the problem of how to get the meat. After a while, it jumps on the cage and pulls on the string with its mouth and paw, raising the liver. It retrieves the meat and jumps down with it in its mouth. (570)

The paraphrase may pick up some of the key terms, but essentially it must be in the note-taker's own words.

PARAPHRASED INFORMATION IN A PAPER

Faced with a puzzle in which liver is tied to a string inside a cage, Koestler's cat seems to look the situation over briefly, and then solves the problem by jumping onto the cage and pulling the string up with its mouth and paws (570).

ACTIVITY 3

Using a long paragraph or two or three short ones from a magazine, write a highly condensed summary of it in two or three sentences. Then write a paraphrase of the same material.

46f Conduct research to develop, and then answer, a thesis question.

Having read a number of sources and having moved from the more general to the more specific information about your topic, it is time to decide exactly what the paper will accomplish, what question it will answer. If you have examined a narrow, two-sided issue and looked at the material on both sides, evaluate that evidence and determine which, if either, side is the stronger. Sometimes issues are too complex or the evidence weighs equally on both sides; in such cases, the examination of the evidence and the presentation of the issues might be sufficient. The general rule is that when the thesis question can be discussed thoroughly and answered based on the data you have found, your central research has been completed.

46g After completing the central research, begin to put the paper together.

Research can be as enticing as an armchair detective's search for clues to a crime. But, since students are limited by time and resources, there must come a time to stop (or do less) researching and start putting the paper together. While writing the paper, you may need to research small, specific subpoints; but that does not mean you should delay beginning to put the paper together.

Organize your material: make a working outline. Gather together notes on the same topic or subtopic, grouping the cards into coherent sections. Organize your points in order of importance, from least to most important. Construct a preliminary outline based on the organization of your notes. List the major divisions along with their subdivisions to establish what ideas you will be dealing with and what supporting material you have. Your research may have altered your focus; there may have been some shifting, maybe even a complete turnaround in your thinking. Incorporate any shifts or changes of focus into your outline.

Formal research papers usually require outlines (check with your instructor). There are several styles of outline, but the roman outline is standard (see section **2d**). Your outline will help you decide whether you have enough research to support your conclusion.

Evaluate the evidence. You must evaluate your sources, examine contradictions, examples, conflicting statements, and the logic in your data. Be critical and hard on your sources, just as your instructor will be. Ask yourself, for example:

1. Is there enough material on each point? Will this amount of information seem credible, convincing?
2. What are the assumptions and implications in the research?
3. How old is this information? Are these the most recent data?
4. Who are the authorities? Has the information come from recognized experts writing in respected publications?
5. Are the terms defined clearly; are all the sources using the terms the same way? (If not, you may have to clarify for the reader.)
6. Is all the information relevant? There is no room for digressions in a limited research paper.
7. If there are statistical data, do you understand what they mean? How they were gathered?
8. What are the relative merits of the arguments: which are stronger, which less significant?

Your job is not just to present evidence but to explain it. You are the one who has spent time studying the subject and thinking about the material in your paper; your readers will need your help to understand the evidence (see sections **44** and **45**).

Write a descriptive title. The title of a research paper should appear on the title page (if there is one), on the outline, and on the first page of the paper itself. Research titles should be descriptive and informative; often the research thesis or question is the title. Avoid vague, inaccurate, or amusing titles.

Write an effective introduction. The introduction should appeal to reader interest and make clear what the paper is about. (See section **43d** for introductory strategies.) In the introduction, state the thesis or ask the thesis question. The question can come first, thus informing the reader immediately of the purpose of your paper; or the question can come last, forming a transition to the body of your paper. The introduction sets the tone for the rest of the paper.

Present the evidence. Organize the information in order of importance—ending with the most important. Present concessions to the opposing view first. Making concessions establishes that you have researched the issue thoroughly, not just hunted for material that supports your thesis. Conceding worthwhile opposing positions also establishes your credibility: a researcher must be impartial, pointing out strengths and weaknesses on both sides of an issue.

Link paragraphs and sentences together with transitional signals. Don't assume that the reader will follow you, inferring the relationships between ideas. As you move from one thing to another, give the reader a signal: *then too, however, on the other hand, nevertheless.* (See section **43b** for other transitions.)

The heart of any research paper is the evidence, facts, details. Unlike an essay, a research paper is usually a compilation of others' material, and there is no need to hide that fact. There is no bias against documentation in a research paper; you cannot have too much documentation (references). It is possible to have too many direct *quotations,* but you can reduce this number by using more summarizing, more paraphrasing, more extracting of data from sources—as long as you give references. But you cannot present the reader with unassimilated data. You must tell the reader what the data mean, show the reader how to weigh the evidence. You are not required to "prove" anything: your job is to discover, analyze, and evaluate information for the reader. Though it may all seem obvious to you, you must not assume the reader can understand.

Write an effective conclusion. The conclusion of a research paper is the culmination of everything that precedes it. In the conclusion you must answer the thesis question, and you must help the reader understand *why* you reach your conclusion. It is not enough, for example, to say, "This evidence shows that it was unwise to give the Panama Canal to Panama." You must help the reader understand why this is the correct conclusion. Write the conclusion as if the reader will skip the rest of the paper: review the main points. Save something for the conclusion—a final example, or quote, or something else that will give strength to the end of the paper. (See section **44e**.)

46h Use illustrations, drawings, tables.

Use drawings, charts, or tables, but keep them simple. (See Figure **46-4**.) If they are small, they can be inserted into the paper where you mention them. If they will not fit (you must not have part of an illustration on one page and part of it on the next) or if there are several of them, put them at the end of the paper, after the conclusion, in an appendix.

Draw figures in ink, using a ruler and compass for straight lines and curves. Type in any words. Tables of numbers should be done on the typewriter. All figures should be self-explanatory, but explain them anyway, and make sure to position them after, not before, the explanations. Figures need a descriptive label underneath: *Fig. 1 Diagram of Stress Patterns in Steel.* Tables of numbers should have a label (caption) above: *TABLE II Numbers of Athletes Earning High Salaries.*

If the drawing or table is based on one in a source, or if it is one you create using figures from a source, you must use a footnote (not endnote) directly below it. Mark the note with an asterisk after the caption.

Figure 46–4 Sample of a figure with footnote

```
Number of
Drinks
                        BODY WEIGHT 160

8
7
6
5                                                    X
4                              X                     .
3               X             .                      .
2               .             .                      .
1               .             .                      .
Blood          Mildly      Impaired          Intoxicated
Alcohol        Impaired
Content        BAC 0.05%   BAC 0.05--.09%   BAC .10% or more


          Fig. 1 ALCOHOL IMPAIRS DRIVING*


*Figures from Consumer's Report, Aug. 1983: 353.
```

46i Avoid plagiarism: document all evidence.

Documenting a paper—telling your readers where you obtained your information—is both a courtesy and a way of distinguishing between your language and ideas and those of someone else. It is careful use of documentation that separates research from mere opinion.

The best rule for students is to document everything: paraphrases, borrowed words, even ideas need a reference. The only exception to this rule concerns so-called common knowledge. Common knowledge is information most educated people should know or could easily verify with general reference materials. For example, if you wrote that Sally Ride was the first American woman in space, that might not require a note. If, however, you paraphrase her views on the evolution of the stars, you must show where you found the information. Experts talking to other experts may assume a great deal of "common knowledge," but students writing for a general audience must be careful. When in doubt, give a reference.

Do not document whole paragraphs of paraphrased material. It is better for every sentence to have a reference, regardless of the clutter, than to mislead the reader. If the last sentence of your paragraph requires a reference, write the sentence so that the reference falls within the sentence. If you must use a whole paragraph or more of source material, signal that fact to your reader with an introductory comment. It may be better to *copy* the material in an indented quote (see **29e**).

Supply clarifying information in content notes. A content note contains explanatory information. Usually such notes are not essential (and therefore you should not have many of them) but can be helpful if they clarify small points for your reader. Treat content notes as endnotes. Mark the information in your paper with a superscript (a raised note number) and put the note itself on a separate "Notes" page at the end of your paper. (See an example of a content note on p. 342.)

Provide a bibliography. Two widely used documentation styles—those of the Modern Language Association (MLA) and the American Psychological Association (APA)—use the limited bibliography. That is, the bibliography contains only those sources actually cited in the paper. Anything and everything referred to in a paper must appear in the bibliography, and anything not actually used in that paper must be excluded from the bibliography. The bibliography appears at the end of the paper and is called *Works Cited* in MLA style and *Reference List* in APA. (There are significant differences between the two styles; both styles are discussed in this section.)

Some instructors prefer that the bibliography contain all the works consulted during the research phase, whether or not each one is cited in the discussion. Find out which type your instructor expects for any given research project.

Do not plagiarize. Plagiarism is the use of someone else's ideas or words without giving credit. It is primarily a mistake in documentation. You are free to copy, paraphrase, summarize, and use source material as long as you document it. There is no rule in research that says you should not quote much or you should not use source material much. The source material is the evidence, and you cannot have too much evidence, as long as it is fully documented. The following uses, however, are not acceptable:

1. Copied material *without quotation marks* is plagiarized.
2. Summarized or paraphrased material *without documentation* is plagiarized.
3. Borrowed ideas *without documentation* are plagiarized.
4. Paraphrased material that is *too close to the original* is plagiarized.

Plagiarism violates the operating principle of research: the only way researchers can use secondary materials is to keep clear at all times which are the words found in the source material and which are the words of the researcher who is writing the report.

ORIGINAL

Writing a program amounts to making a listing of very exact instructions in a language "understood" by your computer. The fundamental language understood by any computer is called "machine language." This is not a good language for people, however, so higher level languages like BASIC have been invented.

Thomas Dwyer and Margot Critchfield,
A Bit of Basic, p. 14.

PARAPHRASE TOO CLOSE (PLAGIARISM)

```
To write a program you must make a list of very exact
instructions in a language your computer understands.
The fundamental language understood by your computer is
its machine language. But machine languages are not good
languages for people, and therefore higher level
languages like BASIC have been devised (Dwyer &
Critchfield 14).
```

The more terms and concepts taken from the original, the more the paraphrase looks like copying. Here the paraphrase is very close to the original, but without quotation marks it looks like the writer is claiming most of this for his or her own, even though a reference has been given. The writer should have quoted Dwyer and Critchfield directly here.

There is no prejudice against quoting or paraphrasing in a research paper. It is typical for research papers (unlike essays) to be made up almost entirely of material from sources, and therefore there is no point in trying to disguise the fact that you make use of source material. Researchers must, of course, avoid stringing quotation after quotation together with little or no intervening discussion, like a string of pearls. But more than one reference at any point in a research paper is permissible as long as the material has been properly assimilated and presented effectively for the reader.

46j Understand how to use the new MLA in-text documentation.

TEXT REFERENCES

The documentation style introduced by the Modern Language Association in 1984 replaces footnotes or endnotes with in-text references. Enough information is given in the text (the research report itself) so that a reader can find the source in the Works Cited list. Thus, much documentation can be reduced to an author's name:

```
In a recent study, Bellmont found no occurrences of
anorexia.
```

Direct quotations can be identified with a parenthetic reference to name and page number:

```
Certainly no one can favor "the imposition of a foreign
policy backed with the threat of warfare" (Masters 97).
```

This in-text style does away with notes (except for content notes to the reader), and it is meant to keep documentation conveniently close but unobtrusive. Learn how to incorporate documented information smoothly into your writing just as you learn to incorporate the words and ideas of your sources. The next few sections give some guidelines.

Use author's name. Most of your references should give the author's name in your text instead of in a note.

```
According to Adolph Kline, the world's oil reserves
cannot last another century. This assumption is sharply
rejected by Richardson, who insists there is enough oil
to last forever.
```

Give all authors' names unless there are more than three authors of a book.

```
That we can never be too critical of public figures is
the point made by Anderson and Boyd in Confessions of a
Muckraker.
```

```
The idea of "resource wars" was first suggested in 1945
(Horton, Peters, and Rigby).
```

For more than three authors, give only the first name followed by "et al."

```
A good source for the student is Literary History of the
United States (Spiller et al.).
```

For authors with the same last name, give full names in your text, or give the authors' initials in a reference note.

```
According to Alan Withers, the new non-fiction amounts
to a journalistic art.
```

```
In the opinion of at least one writer, the new non-
fiction is a journalistic art (Withers, A.).
```

For authors with the same last name and the same initial, give full names.

```
But Adrian Withers asserts that the problem of art in
journalism raises serious questions about objectivity
and the nature of truth in reporting.
```

Use name and title. If there is more than one book by the same author in your bibliography, you must include the titles in your references.

```
In World Resources, Burford suggests that wars over the
world's dwindling resources will begin early in the next
century, an idea he repeats in The Approaching Global
Holocaust.
```

Use page numbers. When making reference to a specific part of a source, you must give a page number in the reference. When the page number comes at the end of your sentence, the sentence period should be placed after the parenthesis. Note that page numbers are not identified with *p.* or other markers. If additional references are made to the same source, you need only the page number. Do not precede page numbers with a comma.

```
Mrs. Ellson's letter alleges that her husband was "a
brute, a savage brute" (Horton 57). Later (78) she
accuses him of having an affair with her sister. The
sister, Elvira Clay, says of Mrs. Ellson, "Nell was so
jealous of him, she imagined he had affairs all the
time" (Denning 102).
```

Use shortened titles. To keep references as brief as possible, shorten titles, but make them unambiguous so that the reader can recognize that title in the Works Cited. For example, additional references to Burford's work could use shortened forms:

```
We will run out of oil first, he says (Resources 81).
And, since we view oil as a military resource, the
United States may be first to resort to warfare
(Holocaust 213).
```

For references to books of the Bible, use standard abbreviations.

```
"He that hath an ear, let him hear what the Spirit saith
unto the churches . . . " (Rev. 3.11).
```

For references to plays, poetry, or other works with numbered sections or lines, give all the relevant numbers that would help a reader find the source: section, part, act, scene, line. Do not use *l.* or *ll.* for *line*.

```
"O, what a rogue and peasant slave am I!" (Hamlet
II.ii.534).
```

The line is from the play, *Hamlet,* act two, scene two, line 534. You may use arabic numerals if you prefer: 2.2.534.

```
"An aged man is but a paltry thing, / A tattered coat
upon a stick . . . " ("Byzantium" 9-10).
```

The lines are from Yeats' "Sailing to Byzantium," lines 9 to 10.

WORKS CITED LIST

The Works Cited list is the source for reference notes, and should therefore be compiled before the paper is written. Works Cited entries present an alphabetical listing, the first line of each entry starting at the left margin, the second (and all subsequent) lines indented five spaces. Main elements of each entry are separated with periods.

For most works alphabetize authors' names by last name first.

```
Tobias, Andrew. The Invisible Bankers. New York: Pocket,
    1982.
```

For works whose author is a group or organization, give the name in normal order. Do not include articles with group names: *The Society of International Rogerians* should be listed as *Society of International Rogerians*.

For unsigned or anonymous works, begin with the title. Do not drop articles from titles, but disregard them in alphabetizing. An anonymous work called *The Earliest Indians* should be alphabetized as if it started with *Earliest*. Do not label such works as *Anonymous* or *Anon*.

BOOKS

BOOK, ONE AUTHOR
```
Adolph, Robert. The Rise of Modern Prose Style. Cambridge,
    Mass.: MIT UP, 1968.
```

University Press is abbreviated UP.

BOOK, MORE THAN ONE BY SAME AUTHOR
```
Booth, Wayne C. Modern Dogma and the Rhetoric of Assent.
    Notre Dame: U of Notre Dame P, 1974.
---. The Rhetoric of Fiction. Chicago: U of Chicago P,
    1961.
```

Subsequent books by the same author use three hyphens in place of author's name. Disregard articles *A*, *An*, and *The* when alphabetizing.

BOOK, MORE THAN ONE AUTHOR
```
Anderson, Jack, and James Boyd. Confessions of a
    Muckraker: The Inside Story of Life in Washington
    During the Truman, Eisenhower, Kennedy and Johnson
    Years. New York: Random, 1979.
```

Only the first author's name is presented in reverse order. The name of the publisher (Random House) may be shortened.

BOOK, MORE THAN THREE AUTHORS

Spiller, Robert E., et al. <u>Literary History of the United States: History</u>. 3rd ed. New York: Macmillan, 1963.

Note the edition number.

BOOK, PART OF SERIES

Hatfield, Henry, ed. <u>Thomas Mann: A Collection of Critical Essays</u>. Twentieth Century Views Critical Series. Englewood Cliffs: Prentice, 1964.

BOOK WITH EDITOR

Adams, Hazard, ed. <u>Critical Theory Since Plato</u>. New York: Harcourt, 1971.

BOOK WITH TRANSLATOR

Perelman, Chaim and L. Olbrechts-Tyteca. <u>The New Rhetoric: A Treatise on Argumentation</u>. Trans. John Wilkinson and Purcell Weaver. Notre Dame: U of Notre Dame P, 1969.

BOOK IN MULTIVOLUME WORK

Wiener, Philip P., ed. <u>Psychological Ideas in Antiquity to Zeitgeist</u>. Vol. 4 of <u>Dictionary of the History of Ideas: Studies of Pivotal Ideas</u>. 4 vols. New York: Scribner, 1973.

BOOK, REPRINT

Clarke, Arthur C. <u>The Challenge of the Sea</u>. 1960. New York: Dell, 1966.

ESSAY IN BOOK

Young, Richard. "Invention: A Topographical Survey." In <u>Teaching Composition: 10 Bibliographic Essays</u>, Ed. Gary Tate. Fort Worth: Texas Christian, 1976. 1-43.

BOOK, INTRODUCTION

Grommon, Alfred H. Foreword. <u>A Long Way Together: A</u>
<u>Personal View of NCTE's First Sixty-Seven Years</u>. By J.
N. Hook. Urbana; NCTE, 1979.

ARTICLES AND OTHER SOURCES

POPULAR MAGAZINE, WEEKLY

Quinn, Jane Bryant. "The Real-Estate Exchange." <u>Newsweek</u>
11 July 1983: 12-13.

Page numbers always follow the colon.

MAGAZINE, MONTHLY

Schiller, Andrew. "The Coming Revolution in Teaching
English." <u>Harper's</u> Oct. 1964: 82-84.

Abbreviate months except May, June, July.

MAGAZINE, NO AUTHOR

"The Upheaval in Health Care." <u>BusinessWeek</u> 25 July 1983:
44-48+.

The plus sign indicates additional, nonconsecutive pages.

JOURNAL, TECHNICAL OR SPECIALTY MAGAZINE PAGED BY VOLUME

Putman, John J. "China's Opening Door." <u>National</u>
<u>Geographic</u> 164 (1983): 64-83.

Richard M. Collier, "The Word Processor and Revision
Strategies," <u>College Composition and Communication</u> 34
(1983): 149-55.

Some periodicals begin each issue where the last one ended. If the
first issue ends with page 175, the next issue will begin with page
176. Because a bound volume of such periodicals may contain several issues, and because there may be more than one volume for a
given year, it is necessary to provide the reader with the volume
number, *34*, the year, *(1983)*, and the page numbers, *149–55*.
Pages 149 to 155 are given as 149–55.

JOURNAL, TECHNICAL OR SPECIALTY MAGAZINE PAGED BY ISSUE

Howitt, Doran. "Whither Electronic Mail?" <u>InfoWorld</u> 6.27
    (1984): 28–29.

When each issue of a periodical begins with page 1, it is necessary
to know both the volume, *6*, and the issue number, *27*, since every
issue is likely to have pages 28–29.

ENCYCLOPEDIA ARTICLE

Fraser, Francis Charles. "Whale." <u>Encyclopaedia</u>
    <u>Britannica</u>, 1974 ed.

"Chickamauga Dam." <u>Encyclopedia</u> <u>Americana</u>, 1976 ed.

Because encyclopedias (and many other general references) arrange
entries alphabetically, no page numbers are necessary.

NEWSPAPER ARTICLE

Granat, Diane. "Parent–Power Groups Demand Bigger Voice
    in School Policies." <u>New</u> <u>York</u> <u>Times</u> 11 Nov. 1979, sec.
    12: 4.

Do not use *The* in newspaper titles in the Works Cited list.

DISSERTATION

Hazen, C. L. "The Relative Effectiveness of Two
    Methodologies in the Development of Composition Skills
    in College Freshman English." Diss. North Texas State,
    1972.

DISSERTATION ABSTRACTS INTERNATIONAL

Moore, M. L. E. "A Descriptive Survey of Secondary English
    Teachers' Attitudes Toward Language Norms &
    Variations." <u>DAI</u>, 39 (1979): 6052–53A

BIBLE VERSES

<u>The</u> <u>New</u> <u>English</u> <u>Bible</u> <u>with</u> <u>Apocrypha</u>. Oxford UP; Cambridge
    UP, 1970.

Only editions other than the King James edition of the Bible require a bibliographic entry.

BULLETIN OR PAMPHLET

Thorp, Margaret Farrand. <u>Sarah</u> <u>Orne</u> <u>Jewett</u>. University of
    Minnesota Pamphlets on American Writers, No. 61.
    Minneapolis: U of Minnesota P, 1966.

GOVERNMENT PUBLICATIONS

U.S. Central Intelligence Agency. <u>National</u> <u>Basic</u>
    <u>Intelligence</u> <u>Factbook</u>. Washington: GPO, 1980.

GPO stands for Government Printing Office.

U. S. Cong. House. Committee on House Administration.
    <u>National</u> <u>Publication</u> <u>Act</u> <u>of</u> <u>1980</u>, 96th Cong., 2nd sess.
    H. Rept. 836. Washington: GPO, 1980.

LEGAL REFERENCES

United States v. Whitmire, 595 F. 2d 1303 (5th Cir. 1979).

Use the following research paper as a format model. The writer
has researched a worthwhile topic and presented the evidence well.

Optional title page, information
centered on page

Space Shuttle: Worth the Cost?

by

Chuck Kristofek

English Composition
Professor Miller
April 28, 1984

Outline

Space Shuttle: Worth the Cost?

I. The shuttle in America's space program

    A. Description of shuttle

    B. Thesis question: Is the space shuttle worth the cost?

II. Arguments against shuttle

    A. The arguments

        1. Cost overrun

        2. Reasons for cost overrun

        3. Comparison with Howard Hughes' "Spruce Goose"

        4. Expendable rocket cheaper

        5. Turnaround time long

          a. Reduced number of missions

          b. Increased cost per mission

        6. Shuttle budget taking money from other space and science programs

    B. Evaluation

III. Arguments for shuttle

    A. The arguments

        1. Compared to first railroad

        2. Creating jobs

        3. Versatile

          a. Can carry cargo like any cargo transport

          b. Can carry spacelab

          c. Mini-labs in storage lockers

          d. Can double payload volume with adaptation

        4. Manufacturing

          a. Pharmaceutical

          b. Glass products

        c. New alloys

        d. High—purity electronic crystals

     5. Satellites

        a. Money maker for shuttle in mid—1980s

        b. Communication

          (1) Improved t.v. reception

          (2) Wireless telephones

        c. Earth observation

        d. Accurate weather forecasting

     6. Defense

        a. Satellites

        b. Lasers

     7. May provide way to dump nuclear waste in space

     8. Survey in favor of shuttle

  B. Evaluation of arguments

IV. The shuttle's potential

 V. Notes

VI. Works Cited

Space Shuttle: Worth the Cost?

Introductory strategy
The new space age began, by coincidence, exactly twenty years after the first got under way with the one-orbit trip of Soviet cosmonaut Uri Gagarin on April 12, 1961.

Indented, quote
> A little chipped on the outside but dead on course, the space shuttle Columbia hurled itself into orbit early Sunday morning atop the most powerful rocket engines ever fired. . . . It was the first manned American spaceflight since 1975, and the first flight ever of a space vehicle designed to be flown again after it returns to earth ("Shuttle Blasts Off" 44).

The space shuttle Columbia looks like a short, fat, commercial jet with small wings. Its appearance is rugged and rightfully so, since it can deliver up to 65,000 pounds of payload to space and then return to earth as if it had just taken a little vacation trip. The shuttle is 122.3 feet long and has a 78 foot wingspan (''Space Shuttle System'' 116). When joined to its external tank and solid rocket boosters it is a towering 184 feet long.

A typical shuttle mission could be described as follows: after a few moments into takeoff, the burned solid rocket boosters, which push the shuttle to medium altitude and speed so the engines can do their best work, are jettisoned to the ocean below. The boosters are retrieved, towed back to Kennedy Space Center, and refurbished to be used again on future flights. Moments after the solid rocket boosters are jettisoned, the main external tank, the only part of the shuttle not reused, is jettisoned and falls to its grave in the ocean below. Now, the shuttle is on its own and has enough speed to lock into orbit until payload is deployed or mission is

completed. Landing is just a gliding back down to earth,
where technicians wait to prepare the shuttle for the
next mission. The space shuttle may well be the weapon
used to conquer space. But it is a costly venture, and
we must ask the question, Is the space shuttle worth the
cost?

Thesis question

Presentation of opposing data

Anything as sophisticated and complex as the shuttle
has many problems. But the fact that problems are still
arising with the first manned, orbital shuttle,
<u>Columbia</u>,[1] makes people question the building of a fleet
of shuttles. One shuttle alone costs $9.9 billion, a 30—
percent cost overrun (Golden 17). NASA argues that that
is close to the original $5.5 billion plus another $1
billion as technical and inflation insurance.

The rising cost of the shuttle has increased the cost
of launching. The cost for a full payload will be around
$40 million by 1985; after that, commercial users can
expect to pay $90 million per launch (Banks 33). The
real moneymaker for the shuttle in the mid—1980s is
supposed to be satellite launching. But if the price
keeps rising, the shuttle will not be able to compete
with expendable rockets that can deploy satellites, such
as the French—led <u>Ariene</u>, the most promising of the
conventional, expendable rockets. Its launch price will
be perhaps around $25 million to $30 million a
satellite, roughly 20 to 25 percent less than the price
per satellite quoted by NASA (34) after the 1986
increase in prices.

Price is a key factor, but not the only factor of
concern to users. Original estimates were that
turnaround time would get down to two weeks; now,
however, "most space officials privately concede that
one month is probably the minimum turnaround period that
can be expected with the current shuttles" (Gwynne 73).
If that proves to be the case, the shuttle's expected

economic advantages over one-shot rockets will be less
pronounced.

The schedule of flights over the next 10-year period
has been sharply reduced from 487 to 312 (Waldrop 35).

> Reduction in the number of space shuttle missions
> has increased the price of external tanks used to
> carry propellants for the main engines. Martin
> Marietta believes the cost will settle between $10
> million and $15 million. ("Price of Tanks" 65)

This 85 percent rise in the cost of external tanks makes
the expendable rocket seem more competitive with the
shuttle.

NASA estimates that in 1983 the space shuttle will
need $300 million to $500 million more than earlier
anticipated ("Shuttle Costs" 16). Many space exploration
projects are now hurting or have been shelved because
money for these projects has been diverted to the
shuttle. The 1983 space budget contains a total of
$3.468 billion for space transportation systems (Dooling
and Danid 4). Over half that will go toward shuttle
production.

NASA's budget gloom has turned into panic at the
report that the Reagan administration would call for not
just cutbacks but a complete end to planetary
exploration. As one scientist said, "It would be like
Direct quote requires note
locking the door on the solar system" (Greenburg 260).
David Stockman planned to cut $357 million from the 1981
budget and $1 billion off each 1982 and 1983. Stockman
reportedly told his staff, "We'll have NASA out of
planetary exploration by 1984" (260). These severe
cutbacks in planetary exploration are largely caused by
the ever-expanding shuttle budget.

Evaluation, discussion of opposing view

The main problems of the shuttle are time and money. Everything seems to function as planned, but when it functions and how much it costs to operate may never be as planned. If these problems cannot be resolved with the present shuttles, perhaps the building of more shuttles should be postponed. According to Harvard professor Richard Garvin, the space shuttle is "a technological marvel but an economic disaster" ("Shuttle: Space Boost" 4).

The expendable rockets seem to be the greatest threat to the success of the shuttle. Present shuttles already exceed the costs of expendable rockets, and the shuttle costs show no sign of declining. Without more competitive prices, the shuttle will face economic disaster, loss of the satellite deployment market. The only way to reduce costs is to reduce the turnaround time to the two weeks originally planned, thus allowing for more trips at reduced rates.

Transition to favorable view

Despite the many problems with the shuttle, there are also many benefits and technological developments associated with it. Right now, the development of the shuttle program is providing many jobs, not only in the actual building of the shuttle but also in research. Researchers are developing more economical processes for the shuttle. Eventually, much of this research will be discontinued, reducing the overall expense of the shuttle.

The shuttle will be a versatile craft. It will be a large cargo transport, able to carry anything imaginable weighing up to 65,000 pounds that will fit within a cylinder 60 feet long and 15 feet wide (Dooling, "Space Shuttle" 15). This has given the shuttle the name "space truck" and gives it an advantage over expendable rockets because it can not only take its load, such as Spacelab, up and care for it while there, it can also bring a load back down.

One of the options being considered in shuttle research is that of increasing payload volume. If this can be done, it will reduce price per item on the shuttle. Martin Marietta has determined that it is technically feasible to more than double the payload volume of the space shuttle by adding a cargo compartment to the left end of the external tank (Kolcum 62).

New space materials will be manufactured inside Spacelab and inside factories the shuttle will put into orbit. Products like interferon and urokinase are essential in the fight against virus or cancer and stroke or heart attack. The current price tag per treatment with urokinase is $3,500 to $4,000 (Hanauer 128). But in space, under zero-gravity conditions, great quantities of these drugs could be produced at half the price. "In fact, the field of pharmaceutical processing alone . . . could result in a ton of new vaccines worth a total of more than $1 billion every year. . . ." (129).

Ellipsis for omitted material

There will also be an industry for glass products. In space, a process called levitation can be used to produce absolutely pure glass made from totally new materials. These products can be used in fiber optics and laser products. Without the interference of gravity, many new products will be possible: new metals, mixtures of metallic and nonmetallic substances, foam metals (which will float), high purity electronic crystals, and many others (129). None of these products would be possible without the shuttle to retrieve finished products and replenish base materials. Sometime this year an interferon factory prototype will be taken up in the shuttle.

This April, the shuttle took up its first

nonexperimental payload, a communications satellite.
This satellite will allow NASA to communicate almost
constantly with the shuttle. Though the satellite had
some difficulties in orbiting properly, this was not the
fault of the shuttle. The shuttle performed perfectly;
the satellite's own boosters did not work.

Satellites will be the big money maker for the
shuttle in the mid-1980s. The use of communication
satellites improves reception of anything that is
broadcast from space, including television. Telephones
too will be more efficient. "Under development are
wireless telephones that could be carried anywhere, and
some engineers predict they will become routine options
on new cars" ("Space Shuttle: Dividends" 29). Some
military satellites will be used to observe the Earth
and to monitor unfriendly countries. This kind of
surveillance will allow us to make serious arms
reductions. Furthermore, there are military weapons
potentials for the shuttle. The Air Force has spent $1.3
billion and is budgeting $250 million more for the
research and development of laser defense ("Space
Shuttle: Dividends" 31). Laser satellites offer the
chance to change our defense policy from one of mass
destruction to one of mass protection.

The shuttle may help us solve one of our most
serious, urgent problems. There are more than 38,000
tons of lethal radioactive waste in the United States
with no place to put them. Scientists are suggesting the
banishing of nuclear-age garbage to far off space, using
NASA's shuttle as a kind of celestial dump truck
("Nuclear Dump" 72). All approaches to nuclear waste are
beset with severe problems, but the government has
awarded the Boeing Company a $296,000 contract to start
up a four-year study (72) on the possibilities of using
the shuttle for waste disposal.

Avoid ending paragraph with a note

Does the American taxpayer object to the cost of the shuttle? A national survey conducted by Louis Harris & Associates shows that 63 percent of those surveyed believe the United States should spend the several billion dollars necessary to develop full potential of the space shuttle over the next ten years ("Poll" 33). The Harris survey said the results are within three percentage points of what they would be if the entire adult U.S. population had been polled (33). According to those surveyed, the most important reasons for the shuttle are that it will allow experiments with new pharmaceutical products that can help cure disease and that it may have military uses.

Evaluation, discussion of favorable view

Many of the arguments for the shuttle are not actualities just yet. Wrist telephones made possible by communications satellites may or may not be developed. The <u>potential</u> to develop the wrist telephone or the celestial dump truck creates much excitement among scientists and enthusiasts at this time. The communication satellites are the most concrete project for the shuttle and give the shuttle an immediate reason for existence. The fact that the American public backs the spending for the shuttle does not indicate anything concrete, but public attitude certainly has a bearing. Whether the shuttle is "worth" its cost must finally be decided by the taxpayer.

Truly, the shuttle is very costly, and such costs remind us of Howard Hughes' giant wooden troop-carrying seaplane, sarcastically nicknamed the "Spruce Goose." Its estimated cost was $9.8 million for the first plane; yet $6 million had already been spent when the project was scarcely one-third complete (Barlett 188). The "Goose" project ended forever after the test ship flew only a few hundred feet. But to say that the shuttle is in the same category as the "Spruce Goose" would be to ignore the shuttle's recent accomplishments. The rising price of launch because of increased turnaround time is a major problem. But the shuttle's prices can't be compared to the expendable rockets for long. The range of jobs the shuttle can do gives it unmatched versatility. Spacelab would not be possible with any expendable rocket. Then too, because the shuttle will be a commercial vehicle, its missions will usually be joint ventures, with everyone sharing the cost.

Conclusion

The shuttle is a business gamble with such high promise of success that its risks are well worth taking. Within a decade, zero-gravity manufacturing could mushroom into a multibillion dollar enterprise and provide revolutionary innovations for pharmaceutical products, electronic components, and building materials. Even if it doesn't turn out that way, the shuttle already has an occupation of deploying satellites, which will help it to pay for itself. The potential the shuttle has in developing a laser defense system is itself almost worth the gamble.

Answer to thesis question

The evidence in this report indicates that the shuttle is worth its cost. It is exciting to think of the things that the shuttle can do for this country. In addition to its practical applications, the shuttle has very attractive intangible values. The shuttle can help us reach the stars. Even if it did not have so many potential economic benefits, its promise of a way to the frontiers of space would make it worth any cost for many people. The shuttle arouses that thirst for adventure that humanity has always known. The line used to be "Go west, young man!" That is still a good idea, but it is time to change the words a bit: "Go up, young man!"

Notes

[1]*Columbia* is actually the second U. S. shuttle. The first, named *Enterprise* after the "star ship" in television's *Star Trek*, is used for training astronauts.

Works Cited

Banks, Howard. "Overload Shuttle." Forbes, 19 July 1982: 33.

Barlett, Donald L. Empire. New York: W. W. Norton & Company, 1979.

Dooling, Dave. "Space Shuttle Opens New Range of Missions." Space World, June/July 1981: 15–19.

Dooling, Dave, and Leonard Danid. "The 1983 Space Budget." Space World, Apr. 1982: 4–7.

Golden, Frederic. "Touch Down Columbia." Time, 27 Apr. 1981: 16–23.

Greenburg, Joel. "The NASA Budget: Planetary Panic." Science News, 24 Oct. 1981: 260.

Gwynne, Peter. "Shuttle Woes Raise Doubts of Cost Effective Turnaround." Industrial Research, Jan. 1982: 69–72.

Hanauer, Gary. "Gold Rush to the Stars." Penthouse, Mar. 1982: 29–32.

Kolcum, Edward H. "Martin Studies Shuttle Aft Cargo Unit." Aviation Week, 12 July 1982: 62.

"Nuclear Dump in the Heavens." Time, 2 June 1980: 72.

"Poll Finds 63% of Surveyed Back Full Spending on Shuttle." Aviation Week, 15 June 1981: 33.

"Price of External Tanks Increasing." Aviation Week, 12 July 1982: 65.

"The Shuttle: A Space Boost for the U. S. Spirit." Senior Scholastics, 18 Sept. 1981: 4–6.

"Shuttle Costs Threatening Science Programs." Aviation Week, 6 July 1981: 16–19.

"Space Shuttle System Operations." Space World, Jan. 1981: 16–19.

"Space Shuttle: The Dividends It Will Pay." U.S. News & World Reports, 27 Apr. 1981: 29–32.

"The Shuttle Blasts Off." Newsweek, 20 Apr. 1981: 44–45.

Waldrop, Mitchell. "NASA Cuts Flights, Sets New Shuttle Price." Science, 2 July 1982: 35.

46k Understand how to use other documentation styles.

APA STYLE

Another method of documentation, adapted from the *Publication Manual of the American Psychological Association* (1983), Is sometimes used in business, education, and various sciences.

Follow APA guidelines for text references. This style uses in-text (parenthetical) citations of author and date of publication enclosed. If the author's name has been mentioned, only the date appears in parentheses.

```
Howard Hughes' giant wooden troop-carrying seaplane,
sarcastically nicknamed the "Spruce Goose," also had an
estimated cost, $9.8 million for the first plane
(Barlett, 1979, p. 118).
```

or

```
Barlett (1979, p. 118) states that Howard Hughes' giant
wooden troop-carrying seaplane, sarcastically nicknamed
the "Spruce Goose," also had an estimated cost of $9.8
million for the first plane.
```

These text citations guide the reader to full publication information in a References list at the end of the paper.

For parenthetical references, supply the author's last name followed by a comma, the date of publication followed by a comma, and the page number or numbers if necessary. Quoted material, paraphrases, and references to specific pages all require page numbers. If the source has two authors, give both last names (Jones and Eckdahl, 1985, p. 317). If there are more than two, supply all authors' names in the first reference, but only the first author's name and *et al.* in subsequent references (Thrall, et al., 1960, p. 12). If no author is given, use a recognizable abbreviation, usually the first word or two of the title, and its date of publication ("Implications," 1981). If there is more than one source in a reference, list the authors in alphabetical order (Hanauer, 1982; Kolcum, 1982).

Follow APA guidelines for the reference list. The sources cited in the text are gathered in the References. Each work mentioned in the text must appear in References and the citations and references must clearly correspond. The list itself is arranged in alphabetical order by authors' last names.

Here are typical entries, the first for a book, the second for an article in a journal. Notice the order of information, punctuation, and capitalization:

BOOK
Roth, P. (1983). <u>The anatomy lesson</u>. New York: Fawcett.

Use only the initial, even if the author's full name is given on the title page. For titles of books, essays, articles in magazines and newspapers, capitalize only the first word, the first word of a subtitle, and any proper names.

JOURNAL ARTICLE
Bell, A. H. (1982). The trouble with software: An English
    teacher's lament. <u>Curriculum Review</u>, <u>21</u>, 497—99.

Capitalize all signficant words in the title of a journal or magazine. Do not put quotation marks around the title of an article. Underline the volume number. Do not add *p.* or *pp.* or other labels to page numbers.

Underline the titles of books, magazines, journals, newspapers, and journal volume numbers. Articles, essays, and chapter titles *are not* put into quotation marks:

Bean, J. C. (1983). Computerized word—processing as an aid
    to revision. <u>College Composition and Communication</u>, <u>34</u>,
    146—48.

Roman numerals that appear as volume numbers of books and journals should be changed to arabic numerals (volume 7, not VII). But do not change roman numerals that are part of a title:

Auten, A. (1982). Computer literacy, part III: CRT
    graphics. <u>The Reading Teacher</u>, <u>35</u>, 966—69.

Here are sample References entries in APA style. Compare them to the entries for the MLA Works Cited.

BOOKS

BOOK, ONE AUTHOR

```
Adolph, R. (1968). Rise of modern prose style. Cambridge,
    MA: MIT Press.
```

Give state names when cities may not be well known or may be mistaken for other cities with similar names. Use official two-letter postal abbreviations for state names.

BOOK, MORE THAN ONE BY SAME AUTHOR

```
Booth, W. C. Modern dogma and the rhetoric of assent.
    Notre Dame: University of Notre Dame Press, 1974
Booth, W. C. The rhetoric of fiction. Chicago: University
    of Chicago Press, 1961.
```

Repeat the author's name for subsequent books. Disregard the articles *A*, *An*, and *The* when alphabetizing.

BOOK, MORE THAN ONE AUTHOR

```
Anderson, J., & Boyd, J. (1979). Confessions of a
    muckraker: The inside story of life in Washington
    during the Truman, Eisenhower, Kennedy and Johnson
    years. New York: Random House.
```

Use the ampersand (&) in the References list, but not in your paper. Note the inverted order of authors' names and the capitalization in the title (first letter of title, first letter of subtitle, and proper nouns). Give the names of all authors of a work in the References list.

BOOK, PART OF SERIES

```
Hatfield, H. (Ed.). (1964). Thomas Mann: A collection of
    critical essays. (Twentieth Century Views Critical
    Series). Englewood Cliffs, NJ: Prentice-Hall.
```

Note the designation of editor.

BOOK, LATER EDITION

```
Leggett, G., Mead, C. D., & Charvat, W. (1978). Prentice-
    Hall handbook for writers (7th ed). Englewood Cliffs,
    NJ: Prentice-Hall.
```

Shortened forms for publishers are preferred except for university presses.

BOOK WITH TRANSLATOR

Perelman, C., & Olbrechts-Tyteca, L. (1969). <u>The new rhetoric: A treatise on argumentation</u> (J. Wilkinson & P. Weaver, Trans.). Notre Dame: University of Notre Dame Press.

This reference assumes you used the English translation. If you used the non-English (original) source, give the original title, followed by the English title in brackets. Note the translators' names in normal order.

BOOK IN MULTI-VOLUME WORK

Wiener, P. P. (Ed.). (1973). <u>Psychological ideas in antiquity to Zeitgeist</u> (Vol. 4 of <u>Dictionary of the history of ideas: Studies of pivotal ideas</u>). New York: Charles Scribner's.

BOOK, REPRINT

Clarke, A. C. (1966). <u>The challenge of the sea</u>. New York: Dell. (Originally published 1960.)

In-text references to a reprinted work should give the dates for each printing: (Clarke, 1960/1966).

BOOK, INTRODUCTION

Grommon, A. H. (1979). Foreword. In J. N. Hook, <u>A long way together: A personal view of NCTE's first sixty-seven years</u>. Urbana, IL: NCTE.

ARTICLES AND OTHER SOURCES

POPULAR MAGAZINE, WEEKLY

Quinn, J. B. (1983, July 11). The real-estate exchange. <u>Newsweek</u>, pp. 12-13.

For popular (nontechnical) sources, use *p.* and *pp.* for *page* and *pages.*

POPULAR MAGAZINE, MONTHLY

Schiller, A. (1964, October). The coming revolution in
teaching English. <u>Harper's</u>, pp. 82–84.

Do not abbreviate months.

POPULAR MAGAZINE, NO AUTHOR

The upheaval in health care. (1983, July 25).
<u>BusinessWeek</u>, July 25, 1983, pp. 44–48, 56.

Discontinuous pages are set off with commas.

JOURNAL, TECHNICAL OR SPECIALTY MAGAZINE PAGED BY VOLUME

Putman, J. J. (1983). China's opening door. <u>National
Geographic</u>, <u>164</u>, 64–83.

The page numbers run continuously through such periodicals, each
new issue beginning where the previous one ended.

JOURNAL, TECHNICAL OR SPECIALTY MAGAZINE PAGED BY ISSUE

Howitt, D. (1984). Whither electronic mail? <u>InfoWorld</u>, <u>6</u>
(27), 28–29.

It is necessary to know the issue number (27), since every issue is
likely to have pages 28–29.

ESSAY IN BOOK

Young, R. (1976). Invention: A topographical survey. In G.
Tate (Ed.), <u>Teaching composition: 10 bibliographic
essays</u> (pp. 1–43). Fort Worth: Texas Christian
University.

ENCYCLOPEDIA ARTICLES

Fraser, F. C. (1974). Whale. <u>Encyclopaedia Britannica</u>.
Chickamauga Dam. (1976). <u>Encyclopedia Americana</u>.

NEWSPAPER ARTICLE

Granat, D. (1979, November 11). Parent-power groups demand
bigger voice in school policies. <u>New York Times</u>, sec.
12, p. 4.

DISSERTATION

Hazen, C. L. (1973). The relative effectiveness of two
    methodologies in the development of composition skills
    in college freshman English. Unpublished doctoral
    dissertation. North Texas State University.

DISSERTATION ABSTRACTS, INTERNATIONAL

Moore, M. L. E. (1979). A descriptive survey of secondary
    English teachers' attitudes toward language norms &
    variations. Dissertations Abstracts International, 39,
    6052A–6053A.

BULLETIN OR PAMPHLET

Thorp, M. F. (1966). Sarah Orne Jewett (University of
    Minnesota Pamphlets on American Writers, No. 61).
    Minneapolis: University of Minnesota Press.

GOVERNMENT PUBLICATIONS

U. S. Central Intelligence Agency. (1980). National basic
    intelligence factbook. Washington, DC: U.S. Government
    Printing Office, 1980.

Committee on House Administration. (1980). National
    publication act of 1980 (96th Cong., 2nd sess. House
    Report 836. Washington, DC: U.S. Government Printing
    Office.

LEGAL REFERENCES

U. S. v. Whitmire, 595 F. 2d 1303 (5th Cir. 1979).

The excerpts on page 350 show the APA style of documentation.

Space Shuttle: Worth the Cost?

The new space age began, by coincidence, exactly twenty years after the first got under way with the one-orbit trip of Soviet cosmonaut Uri Gagarin on April 12, 1961.

> A little chipped on the outside but dead on course, the space shuttle <u>Columbia</u> hurled itself into orbit early Sunday morning atop the most powerful rocket engines ever fired. . . . It was the first manned American spaceflight since 1975, and the first flight ever of a space vehicle designed to be flown again after it returns to Earth ("Shuttle Blasts Off," 1981, p. 44).

The space shuttle <u>Columbia</u> looks like a short, fat, commercial jet with small wings. Its appearance is

References

Banks, H. (1982, July 19). Overloaded shuttle. <u>Forbes</u>, p. 33.

Barlett, D. L. (1979). <u>Empire</u>. New York: W. W. Norton & Company.

Dooling, D. (1981, June/July). Estimates vary on cost of space shuttle. <u>Space</u> <u>World</u>, p. 19.

Dooling, D. (1981, June/July). Space shuttle opens new range of missions. <u>Space</u> <u>World</u>, pp. 15–19.

Dooling, D., & David, L. (1982, April) The 1983 space budget. <u>Space</u> <u>World</u>, pp. 4–7.

Golden, F. Touch down Columbia. (1981, April 27). <u>Time</u>, pp. 16–23.

FOOTNOTE OR ENDNOTE STYLE

Often called *traditional,* another documentation style uses foot-notes or endnotes numbered consecutively throughout the paper. Each reference appears in a note, and all notes are keyed to an alphabetically arranged bibliography. Note numbers are raised half a line, after (never before) the material to which you refer.

Unless your instructor says otherwise, use *endnotes* in this style. Put all endnotes on a separate page at the end of the paper. Avoid Latin notes *(Ibid., op. cit.)* Instead of *Ibid.* repeat the author's last name with a page number: Heng, p. 107; Farrell, p. 9. If you do use the Latin notes (only in the traditional style), be sure to follow conventional usage. *Ibid.* always refers to the note immediately pre-ceding it and always requires a page number: *Ibid.,* p. 97. *Loc. cit.* refers to exactly the same place as in a previous note. It never needs a page number, but does need a name, unless referring to the im-mediately preceding note: Harvey, *Loc. cit. Op. cit.* refers to a work mentioned earlier but not the same page reference: Henry, *op. cit.,* p. 55.

The following excerpts show documentation with endnotes and bibliography. For more specific details about this system of docu-mentation, see the *MLA Handbook* (1977).

ENDNOTE DOCUMENTATION SYTLE

```
        Space Shuttle: Worth the Cost?
    The new space age began, by coincidence, exactly
twenty years after the first got under way with the one-
orbit trip of Soviet cosmonaut Uri Gagarin on April 12,
1961.

        A little chipped on the outside but dead on
    course, the space shuttle Columbia hurled itself
    into orbit early Sunday morning atop the most
    powerful rocket engines ever fired. . . . It was
    the first manned American spaceflight since 1975,
    and the first flight ever of a space vehicle
    designed to be flown again after it returns to
    Earth.[1]
```

ENDNOTE DOCUMENTATION STYLE

Notes

[1]"The Shuttle Blasts Off," <u>Newsweek</u>, 20 Apr. 1981, p. 44.

[2]"Space Shuttle System Operations," <u>Space World</u>, Jan. 1981, p. 16.

[3]Frederic Golden, "Touchdown Columbia," <u>Time</u>, 27 Apr. 1981, p. 17.

[4]Howard Banks, "Overload Shuttle," <u>Forbes</u>, 19 July 1982, p. 33.

[5]Banks, p. 34.

[6]Peter Gwynne, "Shuttle Woes Raise Doubts of Cost Effective Turnaround," <u>Industrial Research</u>, Jan. 1982, p. 73.

Bibliography

Banks, Howard. "Overloaded Shuttle." <u>Forbes</u>, 19 July 1982, p. 33.

Barlett, Donald L. <u>Empire</u>. New York: W. W. Norton & Company, 1979.

Dooling, Dave. "Space Shuttle Opens New Range of Missions." <u>Space World</u>, June/July 1981, pp. 15—19.

——————. "Space Shuttle Opens New Range of Missions." <u>Space World</u>, June/July 1981, pp. 15—19.

Dooling, Dave and Leonard David. "The 1983 Space Budget." <u>Space World</u>, Apr. 1982, pp. 4—7.

Golden, Frederic. "Touch Down Columbia." <u>Time</u>, 27 Apr. 1981, pp. 16—23.

Greenburg, Joel. "The NASA Budget: Planetary Panic." <u>Science News</u>, 24 Oct. 1981, p. 260.

Gwynne, Peter. "Shuttle Woes Raise Doubts of Cost Effective Turnaround." <u>Industrial Research</u>, Jan. 1982, pp. 69—72.

47 WRITING ABOUT LITERATURE

Writing about literature is one way to help yourself understand and appreciate creative works. Ideas, patterns, images, the emotional power of a work of literature may not be clear until you try to express your thoughts about these things in writing.

You can assume your reader loves literature and appreciates good writing. But does your reader expect from you astonishing critical insights? unique ideas no one else ever thought of? Not really. What most readers want is a well-written composition in which your ideas are fully explained and supported with examples from your reading. A good paper shows your reader that you have read and thought carefully about the literature.

47a Begin by reading closely and analyzing the assignment.

The first step in writing about literature is to read the work closely, more than once if time permits. Make sure you understand the plain sense of each sentence before you begin to search for deeper meanings. Look up words you do not know; identify people and places. Be sure you understand any figures of speech in the work. To read closely means to make sure you understand exactly what each word means. Be sure you know who the characters are and what each is doing, what the relationships among characters are. In the end you must be able to say in considerable detail what is going on in the work of literature and why. Don't skip over the hard parts or parts that have less appeal for you personally. Each element in a work of literature is there for a purpose, and close reading means reading carefully enough to discover what that purpose is.

Next consider the nature of the assignment. Are you free to select your own topic, to develop your own focus? Or have you been provided a topic?. If the assignment has been left open, look for something that particularly impresses you, either positively or negatively: a character, a scene, the setting, the use of language, a particular pattern of images or a symbol. Think of a question that seems especially relevant to the work you are reading. For example, "What is the significance of the image patterns of light and darkness in the play *Macbeth*?" or "What is the structure in John Irving's *Hotel New Hampshire*?" Your paper will be more effective if you write about something to which you have a strong reaction.

47b Analyze characters in a work of literature.

You gain information about characters in literature by what they say, what they do, what others say about them, and, in the case of fiction, what they think and what the narrator says about them. Generally characters are people, but they can also be animals, robots, inanimate objects, or even sometimes forces of nature. The characters set the story in motion; they cause the action to happen.

In many literary works, someone tells the reader what is going on. Such works are said to have a *narrator*. The narrator is sometimes actually one of the characters, like Huckleberry Finn, who tells the story; in other cases, the narrator is simply an unidentified voice that comments on the characters and action. Do not assume that the narrator is simply the author, providing needed explanations and transitions for the reader. The narrator is as much a part of the story as the other characters, and many interesting insights about the work of literature can be reached by analyzing the narrator's function. Some narrators seem to be omniscient, knowing everything, even what is going on inside the heads of other characters or what has happened in the past before the action of the story or what will happen in the future. Other narrators are much more objective, telling the reader only what a real observer could actually know.

If you decide to write about a character, ask yourself the following questions:

1. What does the character you are analyzing look like? Is the character's appearance significant?
2. What kind of language does the character use? What does he or she sound like?
3. Does the character fit into a category? Is it a type or a stereotype?

4. Is there anything about the character that makes it unique?
5. How does the character relate to other characters in the work?
6. Does the character share similar qualities with other characters? Does the character contrast with other characters?
7. What does the character think about him- or herself?
8. What do others think about the character? Do these two views conflict in any way? How?
9. Is the character you are analyzing a major one?
10. Does the character change during the course of the work? How? If so, what causes the change?
11. Does the character's view or others' opinion change?
12. What is the character's motivation?
13. How do you relate to the character? Is the character appealing, memorable? Do you care about the character?
14. How does the author reveal the character to you?
15. How does the character fit into the plot? The meaning?
16. Is the character a minor one? If so, what is the character's function in the work? Would the work be the same if this minor character were omitted?
17. What is the personality of the character? What values does he or she hold?
18. Does the character have any flaws, any poor personality traits, habits, or behaviors?

47c Analyze setting in a work of literature.

Setting refers to the time and place in which an action occurs and also to the prevailing political, moral, and social attitudes of the society in which the characters live. Setting can be a major element in a piece of literature and can affect the actions of the characters. For example, it is crucial to the story that the children in William Golding's *Lord of the Flies* are on an island, cut off from civilization. Setting is important in drama and fiction and long narrative poems such as Homer's *Iliad* and also in shorter works such as Sandburg's "Fog" or Sylvia Plath's "The Colossus." Following are some questions you might ask about setting:

1. What is the setting—time, place, atmosphere?
2. Does the setting change? Why?
3. What effect does the change have on the characters, on the plot, on the mood or tone?
4. How important is the setting to the characters? To the action?

5. Does the setting influence how the characters act? How? Why?
6. Is the setting realistic?
7. If not, why not? What effect does a non-realistic setting have?
8. How do you get your sense of the setting? From the author? From the characters?
9. How does the setting reinforce the meaning?
10. How do the characters react to the setting?
11. Does it control them, or vice versa?
12. Does the setting conflict with the motives of the characters? How?
13. If not located in the present or in a world with which you are familiar, what comparisons and contrasts can you make with your own world?
14. What atmosphere is created by the setting?

47d Analyze actions and structure in a work of literature.

In a general way, *action* can be defined as the events that occur in a work of literature and *structure* as the order of events, how they are organized. To illustrate, in Shakespeare's *Henry IV, Part 1,* there are serious scenes about the king and his son in conflict, both verbal and physical, with a group of rebels who are trying to take over the throne. Within this same play, there are a number of comic scenes, laid in a tavern or in the countryside, that deal with Falstaff and his criminal cronies. Particularly in the first half of the play, Shakespeare alternated between the serious and the comic. The individual scenes make up the play's action; the alternation of comic and serious scenes has to do with structure. A legitimate question is "Why?" What effect is achieved? How does that kind of structure add to the meaning of the play? The same kinds of questions can be asked about action and structure in fiction or poetry. Why, for example, does an author of a piece of fiction choose a particular sequence of actions? Does he or she depart from chronological development, go back in time or jump forward? Why does a poet select a particular sequence of images or ideas? How do they relate? What is the progression?

In some works of literature, the action seems to have no particular purpose. One thing happens after another, and the reader is drawn along wondering what will happen next. Such works are called *episodic;* episode follows episode with no particular reason or with only the thinnest excuse as in some adventure stories or comedies. This kind of structure of actions can be very entertaining, although only loosely controlled by any overriding purpose.

More tightly structured stories are said to have a *plot*. The plot is a sequence of cause and effect events, the overriding purpose of the actions. In many stories, the characters face some kind of problem or complication they must deal with. In a mystery tale, for example, the plot is usually the development and solution of the mystery. Plots can be very simple or they can be quite complex, with many twists and turns and unexpected developments. The traditional structure of a plot has three stages of development: the *exposition*, which tells the reader essential information for understanding the story, setting forth the situation as the story begins; the *conflict* or climax, which introduces some problem or complication the characters must deal with; and the *denouément* or resolution, in which the problem is solved, the plot conflict resolved. The climax is the high point of the story, the point of greatest intensity; action leading up to this point is called rising action, and action leading away from this point toward the resolution is called falling action. Not all plots are this neat, but in a well-written story, you should be able to say not only what happens but why it happens and how the actions of the characters lead to the ending.

Related to plot is *theme*. Most works of literature have a point beyond simply the resolution of the plot. The theme is an overriding meaning the reader deduces from the story: that war is brutal, perhaps, or that love makes life endurable, or some other meaning. The theme is not simply the lesson to be learned from the story, like the moral at the end of a fable. Different readers will find different themes in the same story. Although it may seem that the story is written for the purpose of portraying the theme, it usually is not. The theme is more like the author's underlying vision. The theme is the controlling idea that lets the author select and exclude characters, actions, details. It is the set of values, the ideas about life and human affairs that the author brings to the story. Sometimes the theme can seem to arise despite the plot, almost in contradiction to it, as when a powerfully moving tragedy leaves the reader with a sense of hope and the possibility of a better world.

Don't rely solely on summarizing the actions or the plot. Instead, focus on the elements and the order of the action and the way they contribute to understanding the work. Here are questions on structure:

1. What is the structure? What are the main parts and how are they arranged?
2. Are there separate series of actions?
3. How do the actions relate? How do they come together?
4. Is the work episodic? That is, is it simply a series of incidents with no strong connection among them?
5. Does the author stick to a chronological development? Does the author go back or ahead in time? Why? What effect does this have?
6. Does the story have a plot? Is the plot plausible, the actions arise naturally from the motives of the characters? Is it believeable, given the premises of the story?
7. What is the structure of the plot? Is the plot simple or complex? Does it have a traditional exposition, conflict, denouement?
8. What is the theme of the story? How are the characters and the plot related to the theme?
9. If a poem, what form has the author chosen?
10. How does this form fit the content?
11. Are there particular patterns of images, meter, rhyme scheme, grammar? What effect is made by these patterns?
12. What are the divisions of the poem? What effect is achieved by dividing the work this way?

47e Analyze the use of language in a work of literature.

Words and word choice are the business of writers, who select words and arrange them to convey precise meanings and elicit specific kinds of responses. We learn about characters through their use of language. We learn about action, setting, atmosphere and meaning through the words and word patterns that writers have chosen to fulfill their purposes. Sometimes an author's intentions are clear and easy to grasp; other times you must work hard to decipher a consistent meaning. In any case, you should be aware of the author's choices and the patterns into which they fall.

The language of literature is both denotative and connotative: some words mean exactly what the dictionary says they mean; others suggest more, or even different, meanings. Connotative language may evoke mental pictures colored by emotions of our own experience. For example, a writer might describe a graveyard at midnight, using literal language about the darkness, the stillness, the sound of a dog howling, the open grave. If you read actively, participating in the literature, your own mind will add fearful emotions, thoughts of the undead, loneliness, and isolation because of your own experiences or because of what you have heard or read.

In a similar way authors use words as *symbols*. Roughly defined, a symbol is that which stands for itself and also suggests or means something else, as the flag is a symbol of a country, which in turn might suggest patriotism or hate, the stars and stripes or a swastika. The writer's use of *metaphoric language* is somewhat similar: the metaphor identifies one thing with another and transfers qualities of the second to the first. For example, Macbeth says, "I have fallen into the sear, the yellow leaf." He identifies himself with the leaf, and one of the qualities of a yellow leaf is old age, which he ascribes to himself.

Here are questions on language:

1. Is there anything remarkable about the language, anything that catches your attention?
2. What tone is achieved by word choice? Personal, distant, angry, sympathetic, bitter, and so forth?
3. Does the tone change?
4. Are characters differentiated by their use of language?
5. Are there specific images that are particularly effective?
6. Is there a discernible pattern of images?
7. How do the images add to the meaning?
8. Is there a controlling symbol in the work?
9. How does the author use it?
10. What is the author trying to accomplish with its use?
11. Are there specific metaphors that are especially effective?
12. Do any seem contrived, forced, artificial?
13. Is the language clear and simple? Difficult? Complex?

47f Interpret the meanings in a work of literature.

Meaning cannot be isolated from character, structure, language, and the other elements that comprise a work of literature; all must be taken into account when you attempt to discuss an overall meaning. It is usually not possible to reduce a book, story, poem, or play to a single meaning. The work itself is its own meaning, and your interpretations are influenced by your own experience, knowledge, and biases; the meaning of literature is really your meaning. But you can analyze what you think the author is trying to accomplish, and you can try to assess what a work means to you. Here are questions that help in thinking about and discussing meaning:

1. What basic issues are dealt with?
2. What are the conflicts, either within a character, among characters, or between characters and outside forces?
3. Are there resolutions to these issues or conflicts? What are they?
4. Does the author offer no resolution but simply observe?
5. Is a consistent philosophy presented? What is it?
6. Are there dominating ideas or concerns? What?
7. Does the work have broad-reaching implications, or is it limited in time or situation?
8. What is the historical background of the work?
9. Is there biographical information about the author that would influence the meaning of the work?
10. Is the work self-contained, or are outside sources needed to understand it?
11. What is your personal overall response? How and why do you react as you do?

47g Decide what approach to take in an essay about a work of literature.

The discussion so far has been intended to help you develop a focus, to assist you in finding something to write about. Once you have discovered an element that you think you might want to pursue and develop, even if the decision is tentative, you need an approach, a way to organize your thinking and ultimately your writing.

THE ANALYTICAL PAPER

Analysis means dividing a whole into its parts, and it helps you understand both the parts and how the parts work together to produce the whole. Analysis can be narrow or broad. For example, in a drama you could analyze an individual scene to discuss its movement, its actions, its language, its characters, its function, and how it relates to the rest of the play. On the other hand, you could analyze the structure of the whole play, demonstrating how each act or scene contributes to the overall impression. Similarly, you could analyze an individual character's personality, motivation, conflict, actions, or relationship with other characters. Or all the characters of a work could be classified into categories and analyzed as to their functions in the work. Poetry often lends itself to different kinds of analysis: structural, linguistic, imagistic, metrical, and others.

THE INTERPRETIVE PAPER

In an interpretive paper, you must decide on the meaning, not only of the whole work but also of the individual elements in the work. You might focus on what you think a poet means by a certain image or series of images, you might discuss various ambiguities of language; or you might concern yourself with how a poem's form serves the poet's purpose. In drama and fiction the use of character, action, setting, structure, and language all lend themselves to interpretation; you can write about what they mean in themselves and how they contribute to the sense of the whole work. Critical interpretation, then, asks you to discover meaning within the text and to demonstrate how the author accomplishes that meaning.

THE PAPER OF PERSONAL REACTION

It is sometimes difficult to draw the line between an interpretation and a personal reaction. Your interpretations are, after all, subjective simply because they *are* yours. But they are objective in the sense that they are based on evidence you find in the literature, which others can verify. However, if your instructor asks you what the work meant to you, or if, in an open assignment, you wish to respond personally to the literature, the emphasis shifts from the objective to the subjective. That is, the focus is on your personal relationship to the text. For example, you might write on how the work relates to your experience, your value system, your views of life. You might compare similar emotional experiences in your life to those expressed in a poem. Perhaps you know characters like those developed in a book or play. Maybe your sense of reality is much different from that of a story, and you would want to explore that difference. The text does not disappear in a personal reaction paper, but the focus is on how the text relates to you.

THE EVALUATION PAPER

Evaluation requires judgment: something is good, mediocre, or bad; it works or it does not work. In evaluating literature, the first question to ask is, What are the criteria for judging the work or the elements it contains? To answer this question, think about the author's purpose and your reaction to what was written. Although your judgments about the quality of a literary work are your opinions, there is a difference between a personal opinon and a judgement based on criteria and evidence others can verify. For example, a book might explore the love relationship between a man and a woman, probing their innermost thoughts about each other, the way they respond, their physical contacts, and so forth, as the author demonstrates how close two people can become. An evaluation of such a book must determine how well the author succeeds—not whether you "like" the book. You may attempt to explain where a book you dislike fails, but you must distinguish between your personal taste and the relative success of the book.

Literature can be judged in terms of character, action, setting, structure, language, meaning. The important things to take into account when making critical judgments are the context of the work, when and where it was written, and its purpose. When these have been established, you can apply specific criteria in making an evaluation. Again remember that any judgment, positive or negative, must be well-supported by quotes and paraphrases from the text.

THE COMPARISON PAPER

Comparisons within a given work or of one work to another can be worthwhile. The key here is to find a controlling reason for making the comparison—a specific purpose, a point you want to make. For example, the point of comparing a character's behavior in a crisis at the beginning of a novel and in another crisis later might be to show growth or change in that character. The possibilities with this approach are numerous and wide-ranging, from comparing one book with another to comparing syntax in two lines of poetry. Another possibility is to compare your interpretation of a literary work to that of a critic or to that of your instructor.

THE PAPER COMBINING APPROACHES

No single element of literature or approach to developing a topic is unrelated to the others. For example, it would be difficult to discuss character without considering the language that the character uses or to consider structure without reference to meaning. In practical terms, all papers on literary topics must blend both the elements and the approaches to development. The *dominant* concept is the one you have chosen to analyze; it becomes the focal point of your paper. Your paper will contain a mixture of components and relationships, but as long as you have a controlling idea and a purpose, and as long as you adhere to an observable pattern of organization, there should be no problem with a mixture of elements or approaches.

The following paper should be read as a model of how to use and document material from a work of literature to substantiate a thesis. The paper is essentially a study of character, particularly the relationship between two characters. This relationship is compared to a similar relationship between other characters. Read the paper to see how the character study develops a theme in the play.

```
                                    Mary Lou Dibaldi
                                    English Literature
                                    May 1, 1983



                    The Servant/Master Bond
        The evil, suffering, and injustice shown throughout
    King Lear made the play very depressing to read.
    However, there were some positive elements. One of these
    was the bond that existed between servant and a master
    as demonstrated by Kent, the Fool, and several other
    servants.
        Kent offers not only the service required of a
    servant but also love and commitment:
```

> Royal Lear,
> Whom I have ever honored as my King,
> Loved as my father, as my master followed,
> As my great patron thought on in my prayers—
>
> (1.1.139—42)

At first I thought Kent was laying it on rather thick
(like Goneril and Regan), but soon I realized that he
spoke with truthful devotion. Kent was willing to risk
his life to offer his king sound advice.

> Answer my life my judgment,
> Thy youngest daughter does not love thee least,
> Nor are those empty-hearted whose low sound
> Reverb no hollowness.
>
> (1.1.151—53)

And a line later,

> My life I never held but as a pawn
> To wage against thy enemies, nor fear to lose it,
> Thy safety being the motive.
>
> (1.1.155—157)

Of all the people present, Kent was the only one to
speak out against Lear's rash judgments. He was more
concerned with Lear's future than the consequences to
himself.

Even after Kent is banished, he returns under
disguise to serve his master.

> Now, banished Kent.
> If thou can serve where thou dost stand condemned,
> So it may come, thy master whom thou lovest
> Shall find thee full of labor.
>
> (1.1.4—7)

When the disguised Kent comes upon Lear, he offers
service to Lear's authority, "to serve him truly that
will put me in trust" (1.4.14–15). Kent stays in Lear's
service, first as a messenger and later as a companion
during Lear's madness and the storm. Kent finally
reveals his identity to his king and explains how he has
been with him from the first (5.3.289–90).

The Fool offers similar service to his master by
acting as Lear's counsel and conscience; his images and
riddles are an attempt to get Lear to face up to
responsibility and to look beyond himself.

> Why, after I have cut the egg i' the middle and
> eat up the meat, the two crowns of the egg. When
> thou clovest thy crown i' the middle and gav'st
> away both parts, thou bor'st thine ass on thy back
> o'er the dirt.
>
> (1.4.160–3)

The Fool describes the faithfulness of a true
servant as he contrasts his service with that of a
knave.

> That sir which serves and seeks for gain,
> And follows but for form,
> Will pack, when it begins to rain,
> And leave thee in the storm.
> But I will tarry; the Fool will stay,
> And let the wise man fly,
> The knave turns Fool that runs away,
> The Fool no knave, perdy.
>
> (2.4.76–83)

The Fool stays with Lear during the outside storm, and the inside storm of Lear's on-coming madness. The Fool only leaves when his job is done, when he has gotten Lear to look beyond self-pity.

Finally, the servants in Gloucester's castle speak out against the injustice to Gloucester. Cornwall's own servant rebukes his master when Cornwall is blinding Gloucester.

> Hold your hand, my lord!
> I have served you ever since I was a child;
> But better service have I never done you
> Than now to bid you hold.
>
> (3.7.74-7)

Cornwall responds with his sword, and both the servant and Cornwall eventually die. It may seem contradictory that I have added this example when stressing the bond between master and servant. However, Cornwall's servant did risk his life by giving Cornwall good advice, just as Kent had earlier. The servant's sense of morality and justice prompts him to try to prevent his master from committing a terrible crime. But the bond between him and Cornwall is shattered by the latter's evil.

The second and third servants show true service as they follow Gloucester, at some risk to themselves, to offer him some help. "Go thou. I'll fetch some flax and whites of eggs / To apply to his bleeding face" (3.7.108-9).

Service, truth, duty, and honor are displayed in the bond between master and servant. In the midst of the turmoil and the overwhelming demonstration of man's wickedness, these positive elements offer some hope.

48 SUMMARIES AND REPORTS

48a Write summaries to condense information.

A summary condenses information; it preserves the tone, purpose, major ideas, organizational pattern, and emphasis of the original. The writing of a summary should draw you into the original, making you aware of its structure, its most important points, and the method the author uses to make those points.

Read the work carefully. Read once to get a general understanding of the purpose and direction of the work. Look up any words and investigate any allusions you do not understand. Once you have an overall sense of the original, read again to identify the thesis. Then do the same with the major divisions of the work: look for topic sentences and controlling ideas that are developed in paragraphs or sections. Make an informal topic outline to get a clear idea of how the work is organized and, therefore, how your summary will be structured.

Write a preliminary draft. Here are four principles to follow:

1. Summarize: summaries can be very loose condensations or, especially in school, they can be very carefully written.

The *précis* is a formal summary that does not ask for any personal reaction; put yourself in place of the author and pretend that he or she is writing the summary. Do not refer to the author or yourself. Expressions such as, "I think that . . ." or "The author says that . . ." are not appropriate in this kind of summary.

2. Stick to the essentials: for the most part, examples and illustrations should be skipped. Though the author may be repetitive, you should not be. Do include major ideas and any details that are important to the author's point.

3. Be brief: it is difficult to generalize about length because some works are already condensed in thought and word and others are rambling and digressive. But a rule of thumb is that the summary should be roughly one quarter to one third the length of the original.

4. Use your own words: a summary is not just a list of topic sentences. As much as possible, recast the author's language into your own, rewording, condensing, and clarifying. Put quotation marks around any words you copy.

Revise the draft. Revising a draft of a summary presents some unique problems; for you cannot permit yourself to change the ideas, only the way you've stated them. First, read your draft to see that you have preserved the essential meaning and tone of the original. If, for example, the author has been ironic or humorous, preserve this tone in your summary. Second, check the outline you made to ensure that you have not rearranged the structure of the original. Avoid writing a series of very short paragraphs, each devoted to a single point made by the author. Review your first draft to see where you might combine paragraphs under more general controlling ideas. Remember, too, that your final draft should read and flow like other compositions—use appropriate transitions. Third, read your draft to eliminate any personal reactions to the material, either positive or negative. Finally, see if the draft can be further condensed without oversimplifying or distorting the meaning of the original.

Here is a passage from Jonathan Swift's "A Modest Proposal," followed by a summary.

ORIGINAL

It is a melancholy object to those who walk through this great town or travel in the country, when they see the streets, the roads, and cabin doors, crowded with beggars of the female sex, followed by three, four, or six children, all in rags, and importuning every passenger for an alms. These mothers, instead of being able to work for their honest livelihood, are forced to employ all their time in strolling to beg sustenance for their helpless infants, who, as they grow up, either turn thieves for want of work, or leave their dear native country, to fight for the Pretender in Spain, or sell themselves to the Barbadoes.

I think it is agreed by all parties that this prodigious number of children in the arms, or on the backs, or at least at the heels of their mothers, and frequently of their fathers, is in the present deplorable state of the kingdom a very great additional grievance: and therefore whoever could find out a fair, cheap, and easy method of making these children sound and useful members of the commonwealth, would deserve so well of the public as to have its statue up for a preserver of the nation.

But my intention is very far from being confined to provide only for the children of professed beggars; it is of much greater extent, and shall take in the whole number of infants at a certain age, who are born of parents in effect as little able to support them, as those who demand charity in the streets.

SUMMARY (PRÉCIS)

It is upsetting to see so many women, who could be working, begging for food for their children, who will just end up being thieves or selling themselves overseas. These children represent a burden on the country, and whoever finds a solution to this problem deserves our praise. I have a plan that will not only provide for beggar children but also all children whose parents find it difficult to support them.

ACTIVITY 4

Read the model research paper, "Space Shuttle: Worth the Cost?" on pages 334–341. Write a précis no longer than two pages for this paper.

48b Write reports to convey information.

Effective reports show an awareness of audience; contain an orderly structure; use language that is clear, precise, and economical; and try to be as accurate as possible. Although there are several types of reports, one thing is common to all reports: they are all based on facts, information, data. The purpose of a report is to convey information about something you have read, observed, or experienced in some other way. The report is an answer to a question: What is supply-side economics? How can microcomputers be used in a small business? Reports require you to find information, and to say where the information came from.

OBJECTIVE REPORTS

Objective reports require you to compile data only. *Objective* means that two or more observers would give similar reports. The information is outside of the observer (in external reality) versus "subjective" information (inside the observer, like opinions and attitudes). To write an objective report means that you give information only, without offering your opinions or expressing judgments.

ANALYTICAL REPORTS

The analytical report is a popular assignment: analyze the causes of the Civil War; analyze the communications problems in a large corporation; analyze the process of programming a computer. To analyze means to take apart, to break into components, to divide into steps. Analysis is an excellent technique for explaining the workings of physical objects and events, such as cars, computers, and weddings. Analysis is more difficult with abstractions and intangibles, such as the economy, democracy, culture.

INTERPRETIVE REPORTS

Another kind of report asks you to interpret data. To interpret is to say what something means, to identify values, motives, assumptions. In 1983 the Supreme Court ruled that Congressional vetoes are unconstitutional—what does that mean for the various laws Congress had already acted upon with the veto?

OTHER REPORTS

It would be impossible to list all the forms reports can assume, since they range from things like filling out a financial statement for a scholarship application to lab reports in a biology class to long, formal reports prepared by a President's commission on, say, the unemployment problem among teenagers. You could be asked to write a report in almost any class you take in school and in almost any career you pursue after school. In fact, much of the writing you will do in the technical, professional, or business world will be some type of report writing. The report is the essential method of furnishing information to those with whom you work and to clients and customers.

Use an effective style in reports. As in other types of writing, audience determines what you say in a report and how you say it. Identify your readers, and then make choices of material, explanations, level of technicality, and words that are best suited to those readers. If, for example, your readers are experts in the field about which you are reporting, technical language might be acceptable, even preferred to the less technical terms that would be required for a more general audience. The tone of the report should be impersonal, objective, distanced from both the reader and the writer (as opposed to personal, subjective, and intimate). A report is not the place for emotionalism, humorous anecdotes, personal opinions or figurative language. Keep it simple, precise, direct, economical.

Use a clear, effective structure for your report. Since there are so many different kinds of reports, it would be difficult to show all the structural variations. Find out from your instructor exactly what form is required and examine other reports to see how they have been put together. Many reports require an explanation of what was studied, the background necessary to understand the problem, a statement of the problem. If your project involved first-hand research, it is customary to give the reason for the study and the methods and materials employed in carrying out the study. Some reports require a table of contents; lists of figures, tables, and exhibits; and an abstract (a brief statement of the contents of the report).

Title: The title of a report should be descriptive, clearly and objectively identifying the report.

Introduction: The introduction must identify the subject of the report. Do not rely on the title as part of the introduction; write your introduction as if there were no title. (See Lazy Introductions, p. 286.)

Middle: The body of the report includes all the information you are presenting to your reader. In research reports, the body may state how the study was carried out and an account of the findings (the data the study generated).

End: The final section of the paper is the point of the report. In formal reports, the conclusion must discuss the significance of the findings, what the results mean, conclusions drawn from the collected data, and, perhaps, recommendations.

How the individual sections are organized will depend on your topic, purpose, and the specific requirements of the assignment. Here are some sample organizational patterns from three different areas.

LAB REPORT IN THE NATURAL SCIENCES
Title: precisely what was tested
Abstract: a brief summary of the experiment
Introduction: background and description of the problem addressed
Method and materials: how the experiment was conducted, what was used
Results: an organized account of the data generated

Conclusions: description and significance of the results; an explanation of discrepancies from predicted results
References cited: documentation of all written material consulted

SOCIAL SCIENCES

Introduction: an account of what led to the study and an evaluation of the study's significance
Methods: how the study was conducted
Results: what was discovered
Conclusions: significance of the results

BUSINESS

Abstract
Background
Statement of the problem
Purpose of the study
Description of the method
Description of how the study was carried out
Explanation of findings
Summary of results

Note the major divisions of the following report: the introduction of the problem, the presentation of data, and the conclusion, in which the meaning and significance of the findings are discussed. Because full bibliographic information is given in the notes (numbers 1, 2, and 5), and because the number of sources is small, this report does not have a separate bibliography.

Richard Barnhart
English Composition

A Report on Drunk Driving

The public attitude toward drinking and driving has traditionally wavered between regret and disgust in this country. But in recent years, various groups and individuals have sought to change those attitudes. The mass media have increasingly featured sensational coverage of the problem. With increased public awareness of the numbers and severity of drunk driving incidents,

it is not surprising to find public sentiment changing
to outrage over drunk driving. This report illustrates
the severity of the problem and offers suggestions for
its solution.

The statistics on drunk-driving at the national level
suggest a problem of extraordinary dimensions: "Someone
is killed in a drunk driving accident in the U.S. every
23 minutes, an annual toll of more than 26,000."[1] That
is more than half of all traffic deaths. Furthermore,
eighty percent of fatal accidents involve youths; drunk
drivers are a clear threat to the future of the nation.[2]

While the overall statistics are impressive, the
impact of specific cases may be more revealing of the
public's new attitude:

> One day last summer Tommy Sexton, 15, of Bowie,
> Md., and some neighbors were driving home . . .
> when a car driven by David Watkins swerved into
> their lane and hit them. Sexton was killed.
> Watkins, who was drunk, received a two-year
> probationary sentence and had to pay $200.[3]

Similar cases are not difficult to find. At age five
months, Laura Lamb and her mother were on their way to a
grocery store when a drunk driver, with 37 previous
convictions, hit them head—on doing 70 m.p.h. Laura
became the youngest quadraplegic in the U.S.[4]

Public reaction to cases of this sort has been to
call for greater punishment for offenders. "Stiffer
penalties for those convicted of drunk driving are being
considered in legislative chambers from coast to coast.
In Maryland alone, 80 measures aimed at reducing, if not
eliminating, the drinking and driving problem have been
filed."[5] Other states, including Michigan, are currently
debating the issue of mandatory jail sentences for first

offenders. "Washington State now has single day sentences for first offenders, but this has resulted in overcrowding of jails and a back log of jury trials."[6]

Outraged citizens, particularly the parents of children killed or injured by drunk drivers, have begun a campaign to stir greater legislative activity on this problem. Much of the energy of these individuals and groups is directed at what is seen as the failure of our laws to appreciate the severity of the problem in human terms: "Last year each drunk driver in New York paid, on the average, a $12 fine, while those who killed deer out of season had to pay $1,500."[7]

Among those seeking to change the lack of equity in the laws is Candy Lightner of Fair Oaks, California. Shortly after a drunk driver killed one of her three children walking in a bicycle lane, Lightner quit her job to found Mothers Against Drunk Drivers (MADD). The organization now has 25 chapters in five states and "has become the catalyst for a wave of legislation to crack down on motorists under the influence of alcohol."[8]

This report shows that drunk driving in this country has reached unprecedented heights: "Every year as many people are killed on the nation's roads as there were U.S. military personnel killed during the Vietnam War."[9] Public outrage is now causing a reevaluation of America's traditional permissive attitude toward the drunk driver. The trend is toward ever greater public awareness brought about largely through the efforts of citizen groups such as MADD. The solution to the problem so far, as indicated by the data in this report, appears to be to give heavy fines and take away the licenses of those convicted of drunk driving. Public sentiment has turned sharply against drunk drivers, and legislators will be sure to introduce tough new laws. The significance of this development is that injuries and deaths attributable to alcohol are no longer seen as regrettable accidents but willful acts of irresponsible drivers tantamount to manslaughter or murder, acts which should be punished accordingly. Drunk driving is no longer being seen as a misdemeanor to be handled in traffic court but as a capital crime to be treated under criminal law.

Notes

[1] "They're MADD As Hell," _Time_, 3 Aug. 1981, p. 79.

[2] Peggy Mann, "Death on the 'High'-Way," _Saturday Evening Post_, Sept. 1981, p. 54–57.

[3] "They're MADD As Hell," p. 79.

[4] Mann, p. 55.

[5] George B. Merry, "Coast to Coast, There's a New Campaign against the Drunken Driver," _Christian Science Monitor_, 4 Mar. 1981, p. 4, col. 1.

[6] Merry, p. 4.

[7] "They're MADD As Hell," p. 79.

[8] Merry, p. 79.

[9] Mann, p. 54.

ACTIVITY 11

Select an issue currently in the news. Using at least three periodical sources (newspapers, news magazines), write an objective report on the topic you have selected.

49 ESSAY EXAMS

The essay exam calls for an *essay*. It gives you an opportunity to show that you are an educated person, able to discuss an academic question. The higher you go in education, the more you will encounter this kind of examination. Unfortunately, essay exams allow for very little prewriting or rewriting. Such exams are, after all, tests; you are expected to produce a finished essay in a limited time. The exam tests two things: (1) your knowledge of the subject being tested, and (2) your ability to write educated English. If you really do not know the subject or cannot write under pressure, discuss these problems with your instructor.

Prepare yourself for the exam. Last-minute cramming is the least productive method of preparing for an exam. As a serious student, get ready for the test all term. First, read carefully all the assigned material, make summaries of your reading, make marginal notes, and underline significant matter in your text. Ideally, you should read more than the assigned material. In addition, take notes in class. Periodically review your notes and summaries to keep the information fresh.

When the test is announced, review your notes and reread any sections of the text in which you need additional study. Be sure you understand all major concepts and technical terms, and learn how to spell both significant terms and the names of significant people. When you feel you know the material, try to put yourself in the instructor's place: What would you ask if you were giving the exam? Look at the text and your class notes for clues. Recall what the instructor stressed in the lectures, the important ideas and movements in the reading. Practice writing answers about these ideas.

49a Read the test questions carefully.

Scan the whole test. Familiarize yourself with the range of the exam if there are several questions. Allot yourself time to answer questions depending on difficulty, relative value, and so on. Decide the order in which you will answer questions.

Make sure you understand the questions. If you don't understand, ask for clarification; never try to answer a question you don't completely understand. It is possible you don't understand because you have not studied thoroughly, but it is also possible that the instructor can and will clarify the wording of the question for you.

No matter what question is asked, all essay answers have in common a requirement for information, facts, details, examples. Imagine how the essay question might be worded on a multiple-choice or fill-in-the-blank test: the same information is required in the essay exam, except that you are meant to express it in full sentences and to make connections among the information. For example, imagine an exam question that asks you to describe the origins of OPEC:

A RAMBLING, GENERAL ANSWER

OPEC means Organization of Petroleum Exporting Countries, and is a cartel of Middle Eastern nations that produce oil. Some of these nations are Saudi Arabia, Iran, and Kuwait. Together they form a cartel, a monopoly, by which they can control the price of oil. When OPEC says a barrel of oil will cost $40, then that's the price of oil because they control all the oil production and can just cut back production until they get what they want. The Western nations need oil and must pay whatever the cartel says. During the 1950's oil was so cheap

---

because there was an oil glut, but then the OPEC countries got together and formed a cartel in 1960.

A BETTER ANSWER

OPEC was created in 1960 at a meeting between Saudi Arabia, Iran, Iraq, Kuwait, and Venezuela. Up to then, oil prices were set by the ~~buyers~~ of oil at less than $2 a barrel. The world had an oil glut, and the "seven sisters" -- a cartel of big oil companies -- kept prices low by refusing to buy from any country that tried to raise them. Venezuela had only 7 percent of the world market, but oil minister Juan Perez Alfonso had studied the policy of the Texas Railroad (and Oil) Commission, from which he learned the principle -- cut back on production to keep prices up. This idea was the heart of Alfonso's plan to unite the oil producers. The plan was well received by Saudi Arabia, but getting some other Middle Eastern States to cooperate was difficult. The world oil glut made any price increases seem impossible. But then, in 1960, without conferring with anyone, Exxon announced a cut in the price of crude, and the other companies quickly followed. This action outraged the oil countries, who overcame their long standing difficulties and sent ministers to the meeting in September of 1960 and announced the birth of OPEC.

By contrast, the better answer has more specific (and accurate) information in it; and, more important, it does what the exam question asks: it "describes the origins"—tells how OPEC originated. The first answer has the key date correct, 1960, but it misses the important role of Venezuela in the formation of OPEC. It is possible that the first student did not *know* all the necessary information, but it is also possible that if the student had thought more about what the question required, his or her answer might not have seemed so loose, rambling, and unresponsive.

49b Understand what kind of response the exam question requires.

Analyze carefully the kind of information the question requires. We cannot guarantee what all professors mean when they word exam questions, but in general the following questions are possible:

When the exam says *analyze* or *explain*, the answer requires an analysis of actions, events, or elements. "Explain why" calls for an analysis of both causes and effects; "explain how" calls for an analysis of process. "Explain the difference between a word processor and a computer" requires you to discuss the components and processes of each and the difference between data processing and information processing.

When the exam says *compare*, the answer requires a description of similarities and differences. A comparison requires you to give contrasts, whether the question uses that term or not. "Compare the 1985 Corvette with the 1965 Corvette" requires you to show how they are similar and how they are different. It is not enough to use vague general terms like "faster," "bigger," "more stylish," and so on; give specific details.

When the exam says *describe*, the answer requires details that support a general idea. "Describe Ronald Reagan's Presidential style" requires that you formulate a thesis and then give specific examples of what the President did and said that illustrate your thesis.

When the exam says *discuss*, the answer requires a controlling idea and a wealth of detail. Often the instructor has in mind a discussion similar to one in the text or one given in class. "Discuss Hamlet's character" requires you to state a thesis about Hamlet's character. You must refer to things that Hamlet says or does that support your view of his character. Almost never does a "discussion" question invite you simply to give your own opinion or to ramble on.

When the exam says *evaluate*, the answer requires you to express (and support) a value judgment. "Evaluate Joyce Kilmer's poem 'Trees'" requires you to judge whether the poem is good or bad. You must state what criteria you are using—structural or technical criteria, philosophical or moral criteria, and so on—and you must support what you say by quoting from the poem. You must either have memorized it or have a copy of it in front of you.

When the exam says *illustrate*, the answer requires detailed examples. "Illustrate Faulkner's theme of Southern decadence" requires you to describe the plots, themes, or scenes from several of Faulkner's novels as examples of "Southern decadence."

When the exam says *review*, the answer usually calls for a detailed chronology. "Review the events leading up to the Declaration of Independence" requires you to select and describe in as much detail as there is time for, in chronological order, things like the Stamp Act, the Boston Tea Party, and so on.

When the exam says *show that*, the answer requires substantiation of a particular point of view. "Show that the government's decision to go ahead with the MX missile is or is not correct" requires you to describe the details of the MX missile and give reasons why it should be called a mistake or a success. The more specific details you give, the better your answer.

49c Follow a strategy for writing an essay-exam answer.

1. Plan your answer. Though your time is limited, spend a few minutes planning your answer. Reread the question carefully and jot down any ideas that come to mind. Plan your answer just as you would plan any essay: arrange your ideas into a rough outline to provide a structure for your response. Chronological and descriptive questions imply the order you should use. For anything else, use order of importance: save the most important reasons and examples for last.

2. Create a controlling idea. An essay is not a loose collection of ideas; there must be a controlling idea. If you have been asked to explain the cause of the Great Depression, you are not free to describe instead its effects. The answer requires a thesis statement. A thesis is a statement requiring proof: for example, "The cause of the Great Depression was manipulation of the stock market by large banks."

3. Provide details, quotes, examples, specific information to support general ideas.

4. Do not write summaries unless asked to do so. Even when discussing the plot of a novel or a play, the plot summary is seldom the point of the question. A question asking you to evaluate the plot of a film requires you to say whether the plot is good or bad; if you merely summarize what happens in the film, your answer will be unresponsive.

5. Don't pad your answer. The instructor knows the answer to the question and is looking for specific information. If you don't know the answer, there is no way to fake it. If your answer is short or light on details, you must either supply more information or leave the answer as it is.

6. Don't try to switch the question or modify the wording. Don't create a "red herring," an answer that leads away from the exam question. If the question asks you to describe the level of readiness of the American armed forces, it is a bad idea to say that American readiness is not so good as Russian and then spend the rest of your time describing Russian readiness. Even if what you say is true, it does not answer the question.

7. Think of your reader; put variety, emphasis, and well-chosen language into your sentences. Remember that the writing too is part of the test—information alone will not bring a good grade if it is not well expressed.

8. Allow enough time to get to every question and to proofread your responses. Neat (readable) corrections are permitted on exams.

9. Leave space at the end of each question. You can then add material that occurs to you later.

10. When you reach the end of your answer, stop. Exam answers do not need formal conclusions.

50 BUSINESS WRITING

50a Write effective business letters.

Cover letters for job applications, letters of request or of refusal, of complaint, of gratitude, of inquiry, and follow-up letters are all business letters you may have to write at any time. The person to whom you are writing will form an image of you based on the letter you write, and this impression often affects that person's response to your letter.

Consider your audience. Most recipients of business correspondence are, like you, busy people. Get to the point as quickly as possible. (The one-page letter is standard.) Usually short sentences and short paragraphs are most effective. Select language appropriate to your purpose and audience. Be courteous, even in a letter of complaint.

The sample letter on p. 383 shows a useful format for a business letter. It is also a good example of a letter asking for a solution to a problem.

50b Write an effective resumé.

A resumé is a list of information about a job applicant: personal history, academic credentials, work experience, and so on. There are no standard requirements for resumés, except that they ought to be accurate and provide information relevant to the application. Like the business letter, the resumé should be kept concise, one or two pages at most. The resumé will not win a job for you, so there is no point in trying to make it seem long and impressive. It is meant instead to get you to an interview. Keep it neat and businesslike, and have it show your qualifications fit the job requirements. The resumé on p. 384 shows a useful format.

MODEL BUSINESS LETTER

```
              Lawrence Masterson
            907 High Road, Apt. 12
            Emmy, Michigan 48902


                        January 9, 1986

Mr. Clay Torrence
Emtor Sports, Inc.
134 159th Avenue
New York, New York  10112

Dear Mr. Torrence:

For Christmas I received from a distant relative a "Home
Tension-Stress Meter," model number 18956, made by Emtor
Sports, Inc.

The meter worked only once, when I first tried it.  Since
then, it has become erratic: the needle spins around,
reverses itself, pauses, and spins again, measuring 10, 80,
50, 100, or 20 pounds of tension on one pull.  It continues
to spin as long as I hold the pull, so that it never gives
a final reading.

The box says the meter is guaranteed, but since I don't
have a sales receipt, and we don't have an Emtor distribu-
tor here, I am writing to you for assistance.  Should the
meter be sent to you, or is there a customer service center
where I could send it for repair or replacement?

                   Yours,

                   Lawrence Masterson

                   Lawrence Masterson
```

MODEL RESUMÉ

ANNE MARIE CUNNINGHAM
10 Chauncey Street
Boston, MA 59380
617:555-0218

PERSONAL: Born in Los Angeles, CA; living in Boston since
1975. Age 23

EDUCATION: St. Christopher's High School, class salutatorian,
graduated 1979
Lawter's Business School, 1979-1980
Massachusetts Institute of Technology, B.S.; major in
petroengineering, minor in chemistry; graduated 1984

EXTRACURRICULAR ACTIVITIES: High School Orchestra, violin;
College Chemistry Club, Foreign Language Club, Vice-
president Young Engineers Club; annual participant
Boston Marathon

WORK HISTORY: Paper route 1973-1975
General office work, Cunningham Tool Co., 1975-1979
File clerk, computer familiarity (Lotus, IBM 55-20),
Levitt Industries, 1979-1980
Library assistant, Student Work Program, MIT, 1980-
1982
Lab assistant, running chemical analyses and maintain-
ing computer logs, Phillips International, Boston,
1982-present

SKILLS: Speak and write fluent Spanish and French; speak
and read passable German and Arabic
Data processing, some programming, advanced chem
lab skills, can do geologic surveys, field work

CAREER GOALS: Petroengineer with large oil company or
geologic survey company; possibly government work in
energy conservation or environmental protection

PLACEMENT FILE: Grade transcripts, recommendations, and
other information will be forwarded from Placement
Office, MIT, on request

REFERENCES:
Professor Lars Johannesen
Department of Geology
Massachusetts Institute
of Technology
Cambridge, MA 02139

Ms. Adel Halstein
Director of Field evalua-
tion
Phillips International
Boston, MA 02116

Glossaries

GLOSSARY OF GRAMMATICAL TERMS

absolute phrase A clause-modifying phrase. See 5h. Other names for the absolute are *adverbial phrase, nominative absolute, sentence modifier.*

abstract noun See 4a.

active voice A construction in which the subject is the actor in the sentence: *The girl **sang** the aria. Our army **fought** the enemy.* See *passive voice.*

adjective See 4d.

adjective clause See 5i.

adjective phrase A group of adjectives describing a noun or a pronoun: ***The old, grey, crumbling*** house was scheduled for destruction. See also *prepositional phrase* and *participial phrase.* See 5h.

adverb See 4e.

adverb clause See 5i.

agreement See 9.

antecedent See 10e.

appositive A word (usually a title or descriptive phrase) that identifies a following or preceding noun: *My wife, **a surgeon**, cooks our breakfast every morning. **A surgeon**, my wife cooks our breakfast every morning.*

article A noun modifier. The indefinite articles are *a* and *an.* The definite article is *the.*

auxiliary verbs See 4c.

case The form of a noun or a pronoun based on its use in a sentence. Nouns and pronouns may be subjects *(subjective case,* also called *nominative)* or objects *(objective case),* or they may show possession *(possessive case).* For example: *he* (subjective case), *his* (possessive case), *him* (objective case).

clause See 5i.

collective noun A group noun: *company, congregation, group, crowd.*

comma splice See pp 85–86, 114–175

common noun See 4a.

comparative degree In degrees of comparison *(quick, quicker, quickest)* the middle degree *(quicker)* is the comparative.

comparison The degrees of modification of adjectives and adverbs are positive *(heavy; noisily)*, comparative *(heavier; more noisily)*, and superlative *(heaviest; most noisily)*. A few modifiers have no comparison in formal writing (for example, *dead, unique*).

complement See 5c.

complete predicate See 5b.

complete subject See 5a.

complex sentence See 6b.

compound Two or more items forming a sentence element, such as compound subjects *(Cats and dogs)*, compound verbs *(run and chase)* compound objects *(mice and squirrels)*. Two sentences joined with one of the coordinate conjunctions form a *compound sentence: The sun appeared, **and** the flowers opened.*

compound-complex See 6b.

concrete noun See 4a.

conjunction See 4f.

conjunctive adverb A conjunctive adverb is similar to a coordinate conjunction: both connect full sentences. The conjunctive adverb requires a semicolon: *The radiation was not lethal; **however** it was very dangerous.*

Conjunctive adverbs include *also, anyway, besides, consequently, finally, furthermore, hence, however, incidentally, indeed, in fact, instead, likewise, meanwhile, moreover, nevertheless, next, otherwise, still, then, therefore, thus.*

coordinate The term *coordinate* means equal in order; it constrasts with *subordinate*, lower in order. For example, here is a sentence with two coordinate clauses: ***The engine started, and the train lurched forward.*** Note the same sentence with one of the clauses reduced to a subordinate status: ***When the engine started,*** *the train lurched forward.* The subordinate clause is no longer a complete sentence.

coordinate conjunction See 4f.

correlative conjunction See 4f.

dangling modifier See 18a.

declarative sentence See 6a.

demonstrative adjective See 4d.

demonstrative pronoun See 4b.

dependent clause A group of words containing a subject and a verb but not a complete thought: *Your monkeywrench is **where you left it.*** Dependent clauses begin with relative pronouns or subordinate conjunctions. The three kinds of dependent clauses are adjective clauses, adverb clauses, noun clauses. See 5i.

direct object See 5d.

elliptical construction A deliberate omission of part of a sentence: *The order arrived ten days late.* [Such a delay is] *Amazing! Your generation is the past, mine* [my generation is] *the future.*

expletive The word *there* or the word *it* in an *anticipatory construction:* ***There*** *were limpets and periwinkles strewn along the shore.* ***It*** *is rainy at the higher elevations.* (*Expletive* can also mean an obscenity or profanity: *They edited all his expletives out of the transcript.*)

finite verb A verb that is limited with reference to person, number, and tense. Gerunds, infinitives, and participles are nonfinite.

fragment Words that do not make up a complete sentence: *We knew that the party had finally ended.* ***When the lights went out.*** Often the fragment is part of the preceding idea and merely needs to be connected to it. Accidental fragments can confuse readers and may give them the impression that the writer is careless. Avoid fragments. See 7.

gender A designation of sex: *feminine, masculine,* or *neuter.* In English grammar, gender is a characteristic of nouns and pronouns.

gerund A noun derived from the present participle (-*ing* form) of a verb. *Swimming is one of the best exercises. They said their hobby was cross-country **hiking.***

gerund phrase A phrase containing a gerund plus many modifiers or objects: ***Shooting the rapids** was the most hair-raising part of the trip.* Formal writing requires possessive nouns or pronouns with gerunds: *We knew **the girl's playing** was of professional quality. **My dancing a waltz** is something you'll never see. **Their saying they are innocent** doesn't make it so.*

helping verb See 4c.

imperative The mood of a verb expressing an order or request: ***Stop** making so much noise. Please **open** the door.* The subject (an understood *you*) is often not expressed with imperative verbs. See *Mood.*

indefinite articles *a, an.* See 4d.

indefinite pronouns See 4b.

independent clause The main clause in a sentence. The independent clause is the part of a sentence that could stand alone: *Because the trees provided enemy cover, **our planes sprayed a powerful defoliant on the forest.*** See 5i.

indicative Mood of a verb stating a fact or asking a question. *Water always **seeks** its own level. When **will** this class **end?***

indirect object See 5e.

infinitive The word *to* plus a verb *(to talk, to think, to write).* See 5h.

inflection Differences in meaning indicated by word endings: for example, plurals, *(word, words);* possessives, *(word's, words');* subjective and objective case, *(who, whom);* verb tenses, *(pay, paid);* degrees of modifiers *(blue, bluer, bluest).*

389

intensive pronouns See 4b.

interjection See 4h.

interrogative pronoun See 4b.

intransitive verb See 4c.

inverted order Any arrangement of the words in a sentence other than subject—verb—object: *This victory we will never have* [object—subject—verb].

irregular verb A verb that forms its past or past participle without the suffix *-d* or *-ed:* for example, *drive (drove, driven); lie (lay, lain).*

linking verbs See 4c.

main clause See *independent clause,* 5i.

main verb The simple predicate; the verb that specifies what the subject of a sentence is doing. See 4c.

misplaced modifier A word or word group apparently modifying something the writer does not intend: *Fluids dripped through a tube into a bottle **in her nose.***

modal auxiliary The helping verbs *may, might, must; can, could; do, did, does; shall, should, will, would.*

modifier That which describes or limits. Modifiers may be single words, phrases, or clauses used like adjectives and adverbs. *We loved **the old** house. We loved the old house **on the hill.** **When everyone left,** the old house looked lonely.*

mood The mood of a verb indicates how the action or state is viewed by the speaker. Statements and questions are in the indicative mood; requests and commands in the imperative; and wishes, conditions, qualified statements, requests and recommendations with *that* are often in the subjunctive. See *imperative, indicative, subjunctive.*

nominal Like a noun. *Nominal* is sometimes used to describe gerunds and noun clauses.

nonrestrictive A phrase or clause that is not needed to tell *how many* individuals are meant or *which ones. My motorcycle, **parked***

near the overpass, has run out of gas. The youngest doctors, who were unfamiliar with plague, *were unable to explain the symptoms.* See *restrictive.*

noun See 4a.

noun clause A clause used like a noun: *That anyone could be so cruel was unbelievable.* See 5i.

number The form of nouns, pronouns, and verbs indicating whether they are singular or plural.

object Objects receive action or complete a meaning. There are several kinds: *direct object, indirect object, object of a preposition, object of an infinitive, object of a participle, object of a gerund. Get Saul* [indirect object] *a message* [direct object] *by telephone or cable* [objects of preposition *by*].

object complement A verb complement after a direct object: *They elected her president.* In this example, *her* is the direct object, and *president* is the objective complement.

objective case See *Case*

participle A verb form used like an adjective (*chirping* bird, *driven* snow, *buried* treasure).

passive voice A construction in which the subject is acted upon, instead of being the actor. *The bill was passed by congress* is a passive sentence: the subject *(bill)* is acted upon. *Congress passed the bill* is an active sentence (has an active verb): the subject *(Congress)* is doing the acting. See 14.

past participle The form of a verb used with auxiliary verbs *have,* or *be* (have *spoken,* is *frozen,* has *drawn,* was *known,* had *sunk*). The past participle is used in the perfect tenses (present perfect, past perfect, future perfect). The past participle can be used as an adjective: *broken* clock, *worn* tires. See 11.

perfect tense Verb forms using the helping verbs *have, has, had.* The perfect tenses indicate relationships in time:

PRESENT PERFECT
I *have spoken,* indicates action completed prior to present time. (I have spoken here before.)

391

PAST PERFECT

I *had spoken,* indicates an action completed prior to another event in the past. (I had spoken for about a minute before the bell rang.)

FUTURE PERFECT

I *will have spoken,* indicates action to be completed after another event in the future. (By the time the bell rings, I will have spoken for an hour.)

person Relationship between speaker, subject, and audience of nouns and pronouns: the speaker (I), *first person;* the audience (you), *second person;* and the subject (he, she, it), *third person.* Third-person singular pronouns and all singular nouns require *s*-form verbs: *she works, he writes, it squeaks, Alice works, the poet writes, the door squeaks.*

personal pronoun See 4b.

phrase See 5h.

plural More than one. Most nouns indicate *plural* by adding *-s* or *-es: tacks, bushes* (see section 39 for exceptions). In contrast, verbs add *-s* only with third-person *singular* nouns and pronouns.

positive degree See *comparison.*

possessive Possessive nouns and pronouns indicate ownership: *Sissy's orangutan; our computer.* Note that gerunds are preceded by possessive, not objective, pronouns: *his swimming.* See *gerund.*

possessive pronoun See 4b.

predicate See 5b.

predicate adjective See 5g.

predicate nominative See 5e.

predicate noun See 5e.

preposition See 4g.

prepositional phrase See 5h.

present participle The *-ing* form of a verb *(seeing, wishing, voting).*

progressive tense The progressive tenses—past, present, and future progressive—are written with the *-ing* form of a verb *(are working, was cooking, will be thinking)*. See *gerund, participle*.

pronoun See 4b.

proper adjective See 4d.

proper noun See 4a.

reflexive pronouns See 4b.

regular verb A verb that forms its past and perfect by adding *-d* or *-ed (dated, opened)*. See *irregular verb*.

relative clause A clause beginning with a relative pronoun: *They sent us the book **that you mentioned**.* In this example, the relative clause is used like an adjective to modify *book*. The relative pronoun is not always expressed: *Here is the candidate* [whom] ***our school needs!***

relative pronouns See 4b.

restrictive A phrase or clause that limits, or restricts, the word or words it modifies. *The man **running down the street** has just robbed the bank. The flowers **that are growing near the sidewalk** are a rare form of tulip.* See *nonrestrictive*.

run-on See *sentence*.

sentence A group of words expressing a complete thought; a completed relationship between a subject and its predicate. Contrast with *fragment, **an incomplete sentence, an incomplete thought**.* See 5.

simple predicate See 5b.

simple sentence See 6b.

simple subject See 5a.

split infinitive Placing a word between *to* and its verb creates a split infinitive *(to quickly leave, to really work)*. Avoid split infinitives in formal writing.

squinting modifier A modifier that seems to modify two words ambiguously: *The funeral directors bought **frequently** used coffins.*

subject See 5a.

subjective complement See *predicate adjective, predicate noun.*

subjective case See *Case.*

subjunctive Mood of a verb expressing doubts, wishes, probabilities, and conditions contrary to fact. *If he were alive, Daniel would be pleased. I wish I were in Tahiti.* See *mood.*

subordinate clause See *dependent clause.*

subordinate conjunction One of the conjunctions that start an adverb clause. See 4f.

superlative degree Of an adjective or adverb, the highest degree: *strong, stronger, **strongest**; quietly, more quietly, **most quietly**.* See *comparison.*

syntax The order of words in a sentence and their grammatical relationships to each other. See sections 4–6.

tense That part of the verb that identifies it as *past, present,* or *future. He jumped the fence. He jumps the fence. He **will** jump the fence.*

transitive verb See 4c.

verb See 4c.

verbal A verb form used for other than a verb function. Verbals include *gerunds, infinitives,* and *participles.* See 5h.

voice The classification of transitive verbs into active and passive forms. The subject of an active verb is the actor: *I* [subject] *swam* [active-voice verb] *the river* [object]. The subject of a passive construction is acted upon: *The river* [subject] *was swum* [passive-voice verb] *by me* [object].

GLOSSARY OF FORMAL USAGE

Formal writing requires conventional language, and therefore, language choices that might be acceptable elsewhere are discouraged in this glossary. For example, some of the expressions discouraged here may be used in writing at the level of formality of some newspapers, magazines, and books aimed at popular audiences. Such expressions are not "bad" or "incorrect"; they are simply not found very often in formal writing. The same is true of many expressions here marked *nonstandard,* meaning only that they are acceptable in oral English in some situations but are not generally used in formal written English.

a, an Use *a* before words beginning with a consonant sound: *a web, a unit, a history of China.* Use *an* before words beginning with a vowel sound or silent *h: an elephant, an ox, an hour.*

accept, except *Accept,* a verb, means "to receive, or to take": *I accept your apology. Except,* a preposition, means "but": *Everything worked except the altimeter.*

ad Informal for *advertisement.* Avoid clipped forms in formal writing *(auto, exam, photo, plane).*

A.D. *Anno Domini,* "in the year of the Lord." It is redundant to write "in the year A.D. 1985." Note that A.D. precedes the number, and should be handwritten or typed in capital letters with no space between them and without underlining: A.D. See B.C.

adapt, adopt *Adapt* means to "change; alter to fit." *Adopt* means to "take, acquire." *They have adapted the old terminals to the new circuitry. We have adopted a uniform system of documentation.*

advice, advise *Advice* is a noun and means "a recommendation, or suggestion": *Our advice is to buy the cheaper model. Advise* is a verb and means "to give a recommendation or suggestion.": *They advise us to buy the cheaper model.*

affect, effect *Affect* means "to influence." *The temperature affects the chemicals. Affect* also means "to pretend or take on airs." *She affects a wealthy lifestyle.* As a noun, *an affect (af'fect)* is an emotional response. *Effect* means "to bring about directly, make happen." *We will **effect** the repairs on your motorcycle immediately.* To *put into effect* is to make happen: *Your orders will be **put into effect** without delay.* As a noun *an effect* is a result or outcome: *The **effect** of nitrous oxide on the metal was corrosive.*

aggravate Informal for *tease* or *annoy*. In its formal sense *aggravate* means "to make worse, to intensify negative conditions."

agree to, agree with *Agree to* means "to consent," and *Agree with* means "to concur." *They **agree to** the test, and we **agree with** the need for the test.*

allude, refer *Refer* means "to mention or point out specifically"; *allude* means "to make indirect reference." *The report **alluded** to Iran as "a disruptive influence in the Middle East," but did not **refer** to Iran by name.*

allusion, illusion An *allusion* is an indirect reference (see *allude*): *Reagan's **allusion** to Carter was sarcastic. Illusion* means "ghost, imaginary vision, false appearance." *The magician created the **illusion** of a woman floating in air.*

alot Misspelling of *a lot.*

already, all ready *Already* means "before, previously." *We had **already** mailed the check when their bill arrived. All ready* means "everything is ready": *The police are **all ready** for the riots this summer.*

alright Misspelling of *all right.*

altogether, all together *Altogether* means "completely, entirely." *All together* means "everyone is here, everything is assembled." *The scientists worked **all together** on the project until the work was **altogether** finished.*

among, between *Between* suggests two, *among* suggests more than two: *The argument was **between** the dean and the provost. The money was divided **among** the members of the team. The choice was **between** England **and** [not *or*] Germany.*

amoral, immoral *Amoral* means "neither good nor bad, without moral judgment or values." *Arithmetic is an **amoral** means of determining facts*. To say that someone is *amoral* means he or she is innocent, without moral values; animals are *amoral*. *Immoral* means "bad, that which is prohibited by moral law."

amount, number Use *amount* for measurement of volume: *amount* of wheat, *amount* of snow. *Number* is used for things that can be counted: *number* of people, *number* of tires. In general, use *amount* of money and *number* of dollars.

and which, and who Requires a preceding *who* or *which* clause. *He has written a book **which** explains the causes of revolutions **and which** I would like to read* [not *He has written a book explaining the causes of revolution, **and which** I would like to read*].

anymore Misspelling of *any more*. In the sense of "today" or "now," *anymore* is nonstandard. ***Today*** [not *Anymore*] *students don't learn penmanship*.

anyplace *Anyplace* is an adverb: *Put the books **anyplace.*** After a preposition, *place* is a noun: *You can live **in any place** you like*.

anyway Informal for *despite*, or *nevertheless*. Avoid using it as an all-purpose transition [not ***Anyway,** I can't think of anything else to say.*].

anyways, anywheres Nonstandard.

around Informal for *about* or *approximately*: *There are **approximately*** [not *around*] *one thousand affected cells nearby*.

as, for, since None of these is a good substitute when your meaning is "because." *We ordered new rheostats **because*** [not *as, for, since*] *the old ones burned out*.

as far as Not a substitute for *concerning*: ***Concerning*** [not *As far as*] *new work, we seem to have enough*. But note: ***As far as** new work **is concerned**, we seem to have enough*.

as good as, as much as Informal for *almost, nearly*: *We were **nearly*** [not *as good as*] *caught when the door first opened*.

as if, as though Formal writing requires *were* as the verb with either of these, but *was* is accepted in less formal writing: *The substance behaved as if it **were** [not *was*] alive.*

assure, ensure, insure All three of these words share the same root, *-sure*, "to give guarantees." But traditionally, *assure* is limited to *oral promises: We **assure** you that the material will be ready. You have our **assurance**.* Some writers use *insure* only when talking about insurance and reserve *ensure* for all other instances of making certain. *We will **insure** our equipment for $50,000. We are making further tests to **ensure** that our conclusions are valid.*

at, to Avoid adding redundant *at* or *to* to questions and statements about place. *Where is my pencil [not *at*]? I don't know where my pencil **is** [not *is at*]. Where are you **going** [not *going to*]?"*

at this point in time Either *now* or *at this time* is less wordy and less pretentious.

awful Avoid using as an adverb (*awful* hard, *awful* expensive, *awful* bad).

a while, awhile Following a preposition, *while* is a noun. *We let the hotdogs cook for **a while** so that we could have time to talk. Awhile* is an adverb. *We talked **awhile** and then ate the hotdogs.*

bad, badly Use *bad* to describe emotions, state of health, or negative or unpleasant conditions, actions, and so on: *He felt **bad** all day. The beach looked **bad** after the storm.* Use *badly* as an adverb to describe actions. *They spoke English **badly**.*

B.C. *Before Christ*. Avoid adding redundant *in the year* or *in the year of* with B.C. dates. *Confucius died in 479 **B.C.*** Note that B.C. (unlike A.D.) follows the date. It is handwritten or typed without space between the letters and without underlining: B.C.

being, being as, being that Nonstandard substitutes for *since* or *because*. ***Because** [not *Being that*] we lived in New Jersey, we visited New York often.*

beside, besides *Beside* means "next to"; *besides* means "in addition to." *The tanks were lined up **beside** the trucks. Many laboratories can do this kind of work **besides** ours.*

better, best Use the comparative *(better)* to express comparison between only two items. *He is the **better** [not best] of the two players.* Avoid oral constructions like the double comparative *more better, more slowlier)* and the faulty comparative *(more good, more soft).*

blame for, blame on Both are used in formal writing. *Don't be too quick to **blame** an employee **for** this; it's too easy to **blame** mistakes **on** workers.*

bring, take Use *take* when you mean to "carry from a near place to a far one": ***Take** [not bring] these reports to Jackson when you go to see her.*

bursted Not accepted in formal writing as the past or past perfect form of *burst*. *By the time we got there, all the pipes had **burst** [not bursted].*

bust, busted Slang for *arrest* or *burst*

but, hardly, scarcely Avoid constructions with other negatives *(didn't have no tools but wrenches; couldn't hardly see the work; hadn't scarcely begun).*

can, may Distinctions between *can* and *may* are now ignored by many writers; both are acceptable.

cause is due to Redundant. *The **cause** of the revolution **was** [not was due to] poverty.*

censor, censure To *censor* is to deny permission to publish broadcast, write, or say something, usually because the censored material is offensive in some way. To *censure* is to express disapproval of an action.

childish, childlike *Childish* is usually negative, a term of disapproval: *We need to put a stop to his **childish** outbursts. Childlike* is often positive: *She has a charming **childlike** innocence.*

cite, site *Cite* means "to refer to": *The footnote **cited** Shakespeare. Site* means "place": *The hill overlooking the town will become the **site** of a new factory.*

climactic, climatic *Climatic* means "of the climate"; *Climactic* means "of the climax": *Our instruments measure any **climatic** changes. We waited for the **climactic** moment in the play.*

compare, contrast *Compare* means "to show similarities and differeces." It is not necessary to say "compare *and* contrast," since *contrast* is already implied in *compare*. *Contrast* means "to show differences only." *After we had **compared** the two models, their advantages and disadvantages were clear to us. The **comparison** revealed that their **contrasts** were only minor.*

complected Nonstandard for *complexioned The light-**complexioned** [not complected] soldiers were not suited for desert warfare.*

compliment, complement To *compliment* is to comment favorably upon: ***Compliment** them on their new schnauzer.* To *complement* is to balance or complete: *They played soothing music to **complement** the muted colors of the walls.*

consensus of opinion Redundant. *The **consensus** is that smoking is bad for you.*

contemptible, contemptuous *Contemptible* means "that which deserves contempt"; *contemptuous* means "feeling contempt for": *They were **contemptuous** of his **contemptible** maneuvers.*

continuous, continual *Continuous* means "without interruption": *The earth's rotation is **continuous**. Continual* means "happening frequently, but not without interruption": *No one can work with these **continual** annoyances.*

contrast from, contrast to Informal for *contrast with: The male cardinal has brilliant red feathers, in **contrast with** [not to] the female's gray-brown with a reddish cast.*

could of Nonstandard for *could have.*

credible, credulous *Credible* means "believable," such as a witness or testimony. *His manner was so sincere that the jury found him a highly **credible** witness. Credulous* means "believing too easily, gullible": *The child was **credulous** enough to believe that Santa would come down the chimney.*

data, media, criteria These plural words are sometimes used as singular words. In formal writing they are treated as plurals: *These data are insufficient. The media have been notified. The criteria were selected.* The singular form of *media* is *medium* (television, a communication medium . . .), and the singular of *criteria* is *criterion* (one *criterion* of success . . .).

different than Formal writing requires *differ from* and *different from: The Eastern dialect differs from the Western. Southern speech is different from Northern.* But *than* is widely used in less formal writing.

disinterested, uninterested *Disinterested* means "impartial, unbiased": *The duty of the judge is to serve as a disinterested observer. Uninterested* means "having no interest": *They were uninterested in old horror films.*

due to the fact that Wordy for *since* or *because.*

each and every Redundant.

egoist, egotist An *egotist* is a conceited person. An *egoist* is someone who believes in the theory of *egoism*—that human behavior is governed by self-interest.

emigrate, immigrate To *emigrate* is to leave one's native country to live elsewhere. To *immigrate* is to enter a country other than one's native country to live.

eminent, imminent *Eminent* means "well-known, outstanding": *eminent* physician. *Imminent* means "approaching": *imminent* danger.

enthuse, enthused, enthusing Informal derivatives from *enthusiasm,* these words are not recognized in formal writing.

equally as Nonstandard for *as: We were as* [not *equally as*] *surprised as they were.*

expect Informal for *suppose* or *believe: I suppose* [not *expect*] *you will need new filters for that pump.*

farther, further In formal writing, *farther* suggests physical distance: *We had walked farther than anyone else. Further* suggests degree or progress in time: *The further I read, the angrier I got.*

Less formally, the words are interchangeable, except when you mean "additional": *It was clear that **further** surprises were in store.*

few, less *Few* suggests countable items: *few* trees. *Less* suggests items measured by volume or degree: *less* water, *less* heat.

for free Redundant.

for the simple reason that Wordy for *because*.

former, latter When there are only two items, formal writing prefers *former* and *latter* instead of *first* and *last*: *We elected Benson and Cheney, the **former** a biologist, and the **latter** a chemist.*

frightened of, scared of Informal for *frightened by, afraid of*.

fun Nonstandard adjective for *enjoyable, pleasant*.

general public Redundant; use *public* alone.

go and, take and, try and Informal. *Go* [not *go and*] *see what is in the box. **Try to** [not *try and*] lift the crates.*

good, well Use *good* to mean "attractive, promising": *This looks **good** to me.* Use *well* to describe actions: *The motor runs **well**. She writes **well**.* To describe state of health or general condition, use *well: You seem to feel **well**.*

had ought, hadn't ought Nonstandard for *ought, should not*. *You **ought** [not had ought] to have that lanced. They **should not** [not hadn't ought to] light matches near the oil vats.*

hanged, hung *Hanged* means "executed by hanging": *The stranger was **hanged** for horse stealing. Hung means "suspended": She **hung** the crossbow in her locker.*

he or she Write *he or she* when referring to a generic or hypothetical individual who could be either male or female. *The researcher should work until **he or she** begins to see a pattern in the data.* A better alternative is to write in the plural. ***Researchers** should work until they begin to see a pattern in the data.*

himself, herself, myself Not acceptable as substitutes for *him, her, me: The class couldn't decide between Alice and **me** [not myself].* However, *-self* words are correct when used to refer to a preceding pronoun or to add emphasis: *She gave **herself** a shock. Alice **herself** did the work.*

how Nonstandard for *that: We were annoyed **that** [not *by how*] the computer kept saying "error."*

if, whether Use *whether* to express doubt: *They asked **whether** [not *if*] the prices were higher in the country. Whether or not* is redundant: *I don't know **whether** [not *whether or not*] I should go.*

incidence, incidents An *incident* is an event: *There was an unfortunate **incident** when the two gangs collided. Incidence* means "rate of occurrence": *They have reported a high **incidence** of cancer of the lungs in cigarette smokers.*

ingenious, ingenuous *Ingenious* means "clever"; *ingenuous* means "naive, innocent": *You are an **ingenuous** child. You will never be able to resist their **ingenious** maneuvers.*

in, into *Into* suggests from one place to another: *He walked **into** the room* [*from outside it*] *as if he owned it. In* suggests action at one place only: *He walked **in** the room* [*once he got inside it*] *as if he owned it.*

in the affirmative, in the negative Pretentious for *yes* and *no.*

in the neighborhood of Informal for *approximately. There were **approximately** [not *in the neighborhood of*] 10,000 subjects with the symptom.*

in this day and age Wordy for *now* or *today.*

infer, imply *Imply* means "to suggest": *He claims to be innocent, but the facts **imply** otherwise. Infer* means "to deduce": *From this evidence we **infer** that someone else was in the room.*

in regards to Not a substitute for *in regard to* or *as regards.*

inside of Redundant; *inside* is less wordy. *She is **inside** [not *inside of*] the house.*

in view of the fact that Wordy for *considering that, since,* or *because.*

irregardless Nonstandard. *They continued to work on the bomb **regardless** [not *irregardless*] of the danger to themselves.*

403

its, it's *It's* means "it is" or "it has": *It's now twelve o'clock. Its* is the possessive form of *it: The surface of the table has lost its shine.*

-ize Many *-ize* words are rejected by serious writers as pretentious invented terms (neologisms): *prioritize* (to set priorities), *finalize* (to make final). However, the linguistic principle is well established: *alphabetize, authorize, systematize, theorize.* Avoid inventing words in formal writing.

kind of, sort of In formal writing, *kind* and *sort* are singular and are followed by singular phrases: *kind of book, sort of plant.* The plurals for the examples are *kinds of books* and *sorts of plants.*

learn, teach *Learn* means "to take in knowledge"; *teach* means "to give knowledge": *In theory, students learn and teachers teach. She taught* [not *learned*] *us the alphabet.*

leave Nonstandard for *permit* or *let: Will you let* [not *leave*] *me do it?*

lie, lay The past tense of *lie* is *lay: Today I lie in bed; yesterday I lay* [not *laid*] *in bed all day.* See 11d.

like, as Formal usage avoids using *like* in place of *as. Like* is a preposition or verb: *Your son looks like you. They like ice cream. As* is a conjunction: *They persuaded her to sing again as* [not *like*] *she had in the old days.*

literally Very informal for *nearly.* In formal writing, *literal* means "actual, in the dictionary sense of the word." Thus *literally bankrupt* means "truly bankrupt, absolutely bankrupt." The word should not be used figuratively, as in *She literally exploded with anger. We literally died with fright.*

loose, lose *Loose* means "free, unrestrained"; *lose* means "misplace" (an object) or "have taken from you" (property, rights, life): *Our ship broke loose in the storm; we can't afford to lose it.*

-ly Use *-ly* modifiers to describe actions: *work carefully, speak slowly.*

might of Nonstandard for *might have.*

404   **mighty** Informal for *very. It soom became very* [not *mighty*] *hot.*

most Nonstandard for *almost* or *nearly:* **Nearly** *everyone* [not *most everyone*] *approves of charity. He hits the ball* **almost** [not *most*] *every time.*

must of Nonstandard for *must have.*

nice Avoid using *nice* as a vague word of approval. *Nice and* is informal: *The engine started* **easily** [not *nice and easy*].

not too distant future Wordy for *soon.*

no way Slang for *under no condition:* **Under no condition** [not *No way*] *would I do it.*

nowheres Nonstandard for *nowhere.*

off of, off from Redundant: *Take everything* **off** [not *off of*] the floor before you leave.

OK, O.K., okay Informal for *acceptable* or *yes.* All three spellings are used.

ourself Nonstandard: *She said we had to do the work* **ourselves** [not *ourself*].

outside of Nonstandard for *except: There was nothing to do* **except** [not *outside of*] clean up the place and leave. Informal for *outside: We went* **outside** [not *outside of*] the house.

particular Redundant with *this, that, these,* or *those:* **This type** [not *this particular type*] *of nuclear waste is highly toxic.*

past history Redundant.

plan on Informal for *plan to: We* **plan to** *open* [not *plan on opening*] *a new branch office soon.*

plenty Informal for *very: The patients were* **very** [not *plenty*] *disturbed.*

phenomenon *Phenomenon* is singular; its plural is *phenomena: Many new* **phenomena** [not *phenomenon* or *phenomenons*] *were discovered with the new telescopes. Phenomenon* is oral English for *success, outstanding person or event: She is a* **success** [not *phenomenon*] *in the industry.*

405

poorly Informal for *poor health* or *ill: I've been feeling* **ill** [not *poorly*] *for several days.*

prejudice Nonstandard for *prejudiced: He soon discovered that they were* **prejudiced** [not *prejudice*] *against his ideas.*

pretty Informal for *very, somewhat, rather: We thought the work was* **very** [not *pretty*] *hard.*

principal, principle *Principal* means "the chief or main thing," as the *principal* of a school, the *principal* battle in a war, the *principal* sum of money (on which interest is earned). *Principle* refers to "ethics, theories, guidelines, or moral qualities": *The* **principle** *of nonviolence is alien to most Americans.*

proceed *Proceed* means "to continue, to resume; or to march or move in procession." It is pretentious when the context requires *go: She said we should* **go** [not *proceed*] *to the movie after dinner.*

prophecy, prophesy *Prophecy,* a noun, means "a prediction"; to *prophesy,* a verb, means "to make a prediction."

rarely ever Redundant: *Intructors* **rarely** [not *rarely ever*] *give surprise quizzes in math.*

real Nonstandard for *very: Their data looked* **very** [not *real*] *interesting.*

reason is because Redundant: *Later it was determined that the* **reason** *the bridge collapsed* **was that** [not *was because*] *unreinforced concrete had been used.*

reason why Redundant: *The report said the* **reason** [not *reason why*] *the engines stalled was worn oil seals.*

refer back Redundant.

repeat again Redundant.

right Informal for *very: They do a* **very** [not *right*] *good analysis of materials sent to them.*

said In phrases like *the* **said** *property, the* **said** *individual,* a legalism to be avoided in all but legal documents.

406 **should of** Nonstandard for *should have.*

sit, set *Sit* means "to take a seat"; it is usually followed by a place expression and does not take an object: *Sit down; sit in the chair*. *Set* means "to put or place" and always takes an object. *Set the books on the table*. See 11d.

so Overused conjunction between sentences. Formal writing requires precise connectives: *We were tired from long hours of observation; **therefore** [not so] we postponed any additional sessions for one week. So* is informal in the sense of "very": *She thinks she is **very** [not so] smart.* But note that *so* can be used in the formula *so . . . that: He is **so** strong **that** he can do the work of two men.*

somewheres Nonstandard for *somewhere.*

such a Informal for *very: We had a **very** good [not such a good] time at the party. He is a **very** poor [not such a poor] sport.* But note *such . . . that: He is **such** a poor sport **that** we don't want him on our team.*

suppose Nonstandard for *supposed: We were **supposed** [not suppose] to receive new supplies in a week.*

sure Informal for *very* or *certainly: It was **very** [not sure] hot.*

teached Nonstandard for *taught.*

that Informal for *very, so,* or *too: I never liked algebra **very** [not that] much.*

theirself, theirselves, themself Nonstandard for *themselves.*

this here, that there Nonstandard for *this, that.*

today's modern world, today's modern society, the modern world of today Wordy and redundant for *now* or *today.*

try and Informal for *try to: you must **try to** [not try and] brush your teeth regularly.*

use to Nonstandard for *used to: We **used to** [not use to] live on Maple Street.*

was, were Formal writing requires *were* to express wishes, doubts, probability, conditions contrary to fact: ***Were** it not for her intervention, her employees would have lost their jobs. We wish it **were** [not was] true.*

ways Informal for *way: They drove a long **way** [not *ways] into the country looking for strawberries.*

when Informal for *in which: An assault is any attack **in which** [not *when] the threat of violence exists.* But note: *An assault **occurs when** violence is merely threatened.*

where Informal for *in which: They were revolted by the scene **in which** [not *where] the snake ate the rabbit.* Also informal for *whereas: Today calculators are relatively cheap, **whereas** [not *where] before they were very expensive.*

who, whom *Who* is used as a subject; *whom* is used as an object. See 10e.

who, which, that In general, *who* refers to people, *which* refers to other living things and to objects, and *that* refers to inanimate objects. *That* frequently replaces *which* for restrictive clauses: *The letter **that** [or *which] they sent last week has not yet arrived. The dog **that** bit the mailman has been quarantined. That* is also often used in place of *who: the man **that** [or *who] gave the order should be prosecuted.* Avoid using *who* to refer to something other than a person: *General Motors is a company **that** [not *who] knows what it wants. I have a dog **that** [not *who] can count to twelve.* Avoid using *which* to refer to people: *A person **who** [not *which] has a cold should be avoided. She is a woman **who** [not *which] knows her own mind.*

-wise Avoid using *-wise* as an all purpose suffix meaning *concerned with* or *pertaining to* (transportation-*wise,* usage-*wise).*

would of Nonstandard for *would have.*

would . . . would avoid redundant conditionals: *We knew that **if** we **did** [not *would do] it, they **would** be surprised.*

Index

409

Solidus, 207
Somewheres, 406
Sources:
 of evidence, 292–293
 of subject matter, 4–5
Spatial order, 282
Specific language, 250–253
Specific to general order, 283
Spelling, 236–242
Split infinitive, 138, 393
Squinting modifier, 138, 393
Stance, shifting, 142
Standard English, grammar, 35,
  41–42, 245–246
Statistical data, 293
Straw man, 298
Structure:
 in literature, 356–358
 in reports, 371–377
Style:
 effect on reader, 128
 good, 35
 immature, 170
 in reports, 370–371
 pretentious, 34–35, 261
 readable, 35
 revising, 27, 34–40
Subject Guide (card catalog),
  308–309
Subject of composition, 3–14
Subject of sentence, 61–63
 pronoun case of, 95
Subjective case, 95, 96
Subjective complement, 67
Subject matter
 attitude toward, 21
 sources, 4–5
Subject-verb agreement, 88–94
Subjunctive mood, 113–115, 394
Subordinate clause, 69–71,
  128–129
 for emphasis, 147–148
 for variety, 160
Subordinate conjunction, 59,
  147–148, 394
 begin adverb, noun clause, 70,
  154–155
 begin dependent clause, 160
 shifting, 144
Subordinate paragraph, 275
Subordination
 excessive, 130
 for emphasis, 147–149

 faulty, 130, 148
Such a, 407
Suffix, 119
Summary, 367–369
 as conclusion, 288
 in notetaking, 313–314
 revising, 368
Superlative degree, 118–119
Suppose, 407
Sure, 407
Syllogism, 291
Symbol in literature, 359
Synonyms, 244–245, 248
Syntax, 394

Teached, 407
Tense of verb, 107–108, 111–113
 inappropriate past, 113
 unjustified shifts in, 112–113
Than, inexact use of, 132
That:
 in subjunctive, 114–115
 informal for *very, so, too,* 407
 reference to animals, 105
 relative pronoun, 51
Theirself, theirselves, themself,
  407
Theme in literature, 357
The said, 406
Thesaurus, 34, 245, 248
 and inflated diction, 261
Thesis question, 6, 316
Thesis statement, 2, 3, 4, 10–14
 avoiding problems in, 11–12
 appropriate for reader, subject,
  writer, 12, 13
 controlling first draft with, 6–7
 defined, 10
 evaluation of, 13–14
 relation to changes in
  organization, 31
 relation to title, 24
 revised for new focus, 28–31
 writing situation and, 12
Third draft, 41–43
This here, that there, 407
Timely data, 293
Time order, 282
Titles:
 agreement with, 92
 of composition, 24
 of long works, 224–255

419

Correction Symbols

ab	abbreviation problem	38
adj	adjective problem	4d, 15
adv	adverb problem	4e, 15
agr	agreement problem	9
awk	awkward	
cap	use capital letter	37
case	case problem	10
coord	coordination problem	16a-b, 20b
cs	comma splice	8
dm	dangling modifier	18
doc	documentation problem	46j-k
frag	unintentional sentence fragment	7a
fs	fused sentence	8
gr	grammar	5-6
gr gloss	see grammatical glossary	
hyph	hyphen problem	35
ital	italics (underlining) problem	36
lang	language-use problem	41, 42
lc	use lowercase letter	37
log	faulty logic, invalid argument	45
mm	misplaced modifier	18b-d
ms	manuscript format problem	3e
nos	number/numeral problem	38
pn ref	pronoun reference problem	10
punct	punctuation problem	21–33
ro	run-on sentence	8
sp	spelling problem	39
shift	sentence consistency problem	19
sub	subordination problem	16c-d
t	tense problem	12
u gloss	see usage glossary	
vb form	verb-form problem	11
wordy	make more concise	20a
ww	wrong word	40, 41

Correction Symbols

Symbol	Description	Reference
¶/no ¶	use new paragraph/no new paragraph	43a-c
¶ coh	paragraph coherence problem	43b
¶ dev	paragraph development problem	43c
//	use parallel construction	20d
[ ]/no [ ]	use brackets/delete brackets	32
:/no :	use colon/delete colon	24
⌄/no⌄	use comma/delete comma	21, 22
( )/no ( )	use parentheses/delete parentheses	33
./no .	use period/delete period	26
?/no ?	use question mark/delete question mark	28
" "/no " "	use quotation marks/delete quotation marks	29
;/no ;	use semicolon/delete semicolon	23
ℒ	delete	
^	insert	
⑦	unclear	
#/no #	space/no space	

A REVISION CHECKSHEET

Use this checksheet to evaluate writing drafts. Revise, edit, and proofread scrupulously to make sure your writing represents your best work. Be sure to let a draft "cool off" before you start to revise. (3a)

Assignment: Does your composition fulfill the assignment? (1a) Is your writing purpose clear? Will readers understand your point of view? (1b) Can your aim be made clearer for your readers? (2a, 3a) Have you followed the special requirements of assignments that call for research (46), writing about literature (47), summaries and reports (48)?

Title: Does your composition have a descriptive title suited in tone to the rest of your composition? (2f)

Introduction: Does your composition have an effective introductory strategy? Have you avoided weak introductions? (43d)

Thesis: Does your composition have a clear thesis statement? Is it specific, limited, worthwhile? Have you avoided overly general, broad, intangible, trivial or overworked subjects? (1e) Does your draft fail to support the thesis anywhere? Is the digression justified? Do you need to change your thesis to make it match your draft? (2b, 3a)

Ideas and Reasoning: Have you thoroughly explored sources of subject matter? (1c) Have you found a new and worthwhile idea to write about? (1d) Check your use of evidence. (44) Are your data good and sufficient? (44a) Do you understand the differences between and merits of primary and secondary evidence? (44b) Are your arguments valid? Have you avoided fallacies of reasoning? (45a-d)

Organization: Mark your draft anywhere its developmental strategy can be made clearer to readers. Does your outline match your draft? Could a reader outline your draft? (2c, 3a) Does your outline reveal the logic of your organization? Are there any weak spots? (2e, 43)

Point of View: Does your language reflect your point of view? How does the draft show your concern for voice, tone, and attitude? (2d, 3a)